Ian McShane:

All his film, theatre & tele
plus a whole lo

Gary Wharton

Photo: Author's Collection

lushington **PUBLISHING**

lushington **PUBLISHING**

ISBN: 978-1-9999083-3-1

design: gary wharton vetchbook@yahoo.co.uk

Printed by Beacon Printers Ltd,
Leyshons Buildings, Cornerswell Road,
Penarth, Vale of Glamorgan CF64 2XS
Tel: 029 2070 8415

1. Treading the Boards and into film

Realising that a career as a professional footballer like his Scottish father before him, a young Ian McShane found that acting was something that came naturally to him. Geography teacher and mentor at Stretford Grammar, Leslie Ryder cast him in a couple of school productions as well as getting him to read aloud in class when required. It was Mr Ryder who spoke with Ian's parents to suggest that he might consider a career as an actor. Performing made him "uncomfortable but comfortable," as he later told the Nerdist podcast. He would act in Sartre's satire Nekrassov and Rostand's Cyrano De Bergerac before becoming the first non-London member of the National Youth Theatre.

Aka the 'NYT', they presented Julius Caesar at the Queen's Theatre (now the Sondheim theatre) in London in August 1960 with Michael Croft, its founder in 1956 taking on directing duties. Controlling an enormous cast of talented young amateur actors including Martin Jarvis, Hywel Bennett and Ian, as Strato, the seventeen-year-old joined a production seeing the group wearing modern-day dress. Commemorating Shakespeare's 400th birthday in 1964, the new channel BBC 2 presented the first of five NYT productions during the 1960s to be televised. Shown at 7.30 pm on Thursday 23 April 1964, many of those from the 1960 production repeated their roles but the author is uncertain as to whether or not Ian was involved: I suspect not.

Attending an audition at the prestigious Royal Academy of Dramatic Art in London with his mother, Irene, in tow, young Ian still had little interest in becoming an actor. However, after being accepted, plans to become an accountant would soon be shelved. He began his course in October 1960 aged 18 and it would run through to March 1962.

Before working as a professional actor, Ian gained experience in several productions subsequently including, whilst a student at

R.A.D.A. in summer 1961, when Shakespeare's The Tempest was presented at the Vanbrugh Theatre with a role amongst its cast for Ian and David Warner. Fellow players included the 2 Michaels: Jones & Jackson and Judi Bloomand. According to brittanica.com, "The school's Vanbrugh theatre replaced an earlier structure that was destroyed during WWII. In the late 1990s, the theatre was razed…"

Shown on a Sunday night on the ITV network, on 1 November 1962, Thank You and Goodnight was the first of 2 episodes of Armchair Theatre directed by the brilliant Philip Saville. Written by Robert Muller, also his initial involvement; the story opens with flailing pop singer Roddy Cain (Ian) crooning a ditty called Honey Baby at a gig down in Brighton, or "London by the Sea" as it has long since been known. Getting the late train back to London, it is here that he meets 22-year-old Veronica (Sarah Badel, whose father was also an actor). She is a classical music student a couple of years older than Cain returning to the capital after a disastrous weekend planned with married lover John Stratton (the acting profession is an incestuous one; with one of his last acting roles being a 1991 episode of Lovejoy).

Roddy is equally despondent after seeing his girlfriend Eleanor (Hazel Wright) going off with his manager, played by Peter Bowles.

Ian had been uncertain whether or not he could sing on camera but had gained great confidence after singing in his film debut The Wild & Willing (also 1962). In the TV play, he also wore a gold and black squared jacket once worn by teen fav Cliff Richard. He sang a couple of songs and was asked to record them but he never did. Since then, he has warbled on film and television and by 2000 was starring in the musical comedy The Witches of Eastwick at the prestigious Theatre Royal Drury Lane.

The Wild and the Willing aka Young and Willing, found Ian at acting school and taking a bus to attend an audition where he acted out a scene alongside the charming but ill-fated Virginia Maskell. He had told his tutors that he had a dental appointment and after winning the part of Harry Brown, they were not best pleased with his deceit! Close pal Johnnie Hurt, who had won a scholarship at the academy shared a flat with McShane before appearing in the film together and Miss Maskell was also cast. Hurt was due to leave that year whilst Ian had a term remaining.

Depending upon whose memory you trust, John recommended Ian for the role, selecting for himself the less-prominent part of Phillip instead. However, author David Nathan interviewed many involved with the film for his biography of John Hurt (see bibliography) and all contradict this. Director Ralph Thomas said that he visited R.A.D.A. and was duly impressed with Ian, John and Samantha Eggar and subsequently auditioned the two men before Hurt preferring to play the troubled Phillip. Agent Julian Belfrage recalls McShane being cast and then getting his pal involved.

After watching the film, it would be hard to see different castings. Paid a healthy £2,500 for their involvement, both were amazed to be housed at the plush White Horse Hotel, in Lincoln, whilst working on the film and hammering the drink! John had lived in Lincoln, previously and some filming would also occur back at Pinewood Studios. Equally well-known as exciting talents, they were soon to forge long careers.

On-screen, Ian and his university chums look like they are having a splendid time when we first meet them, with Harry (Ian) enjoying his involvement in the rugger team and marvelling in the camaraderie with pals Johnnie Briggs, Hurt and others. He also has a girlfriend, Samantha Eggar, to romance but despite all the merriment and good times, beneath the surface, most of the youngsters are unhappy and worrying about their futures. A second-year student at the fictitious Kilminster University (with Lincoln being the actual location utilised by the film-makers) he has an accent with a Northern twang. It is fun to see Mr McShane as a fresh-faced 20-year-old in a film shot in black and white by Ernest Steward, under the direction of Ralph Thomas.

Sharing a room in halls with Phillip (a ridiculously youthful and often grimacing Mr Hurt), the two are very close; whilst Harry often battles with old schoolmate Sarah (Katherine Woodville) and her boyfriend John (David Sumner) about politics and various other scintillating pretentions.

Invited to a house party thrown by Professor Chown (Paul Rogers), the gauche Harry fails to ingratiate himself but the older scholar sees the obvious potential in Brown, earlier acknowledging him as, "a most obliging young man," to his dissatisfied wife Virginia (the excellent, BAFTA-nominated Miss Maskell). She is hugely sensitive, longs for affection and has vacuous affairs with students, the latest about to be with the bolshie Brown (McShane).

Photo: Cherry Red Records

Back with his mates, Harry often enjoys a raucous sing-song with them, and fellow cast member Johnny Sekka warbles the moody song Harry Brown, which was recorded by Ian and released as a single on the Columbia label in 1962. Ian's lovely, rich baritone, reminiscent of Marty Robbins, is included on And This Is Me: Britain's Finest Thespians Sing Various Artists (Cherry Red Records, 2016). Its B-side, The Tinker, also happens to be the name of the play co-written by Laurence Dobie and Robert Sloman that the film was based upon. Their third work, in 1960 Ian's role had been played by Edward Judd.

Following the latest squabble with Josie (Ms Eggar), Harry overindulges in the drink and ends up at his professor's home with Virginia, whose husband is away, and you can probably imagine the results. It is an uncomfortable scene, as she is quite pathetic, asking him not to pity her but to "Love me! Love me!" It is she that gives Harry the idea to climb the tower in aid of the upcoming rag week (raising funds for charity) as it can be seen from the house.

An affair commences between them until the passionate young man pleads with his older partner to build a new life away together. We know that she can never leave Geoffrey and his unexpected return sees Harry voice his love for Mrs Chown. It fails to sway her and the professor is all matter-of-fact with him whilst Virginia aches for him to articulate his love for her. He does but it is so stifled that she remains unfulfilled whilst Harry is devastated. Oddly, her husband talks of Brown's possible academic brilliance after reading his latest essay but what his wife needs is for him to express himself to her.

Philip returns after a long absence from the film, joining Harry and the others at a bowling alley where the latter tries to get someone involved in his stunt. In love with but rejected by Sarah, Phil pleads with his roommate to join him on his early morning climb: reluctantly he agrees.

At 1 am the two sneak out and begin their precarious descent up the outside of the turret walls and up towards the tower, as a crowd starts to gather below. In actuality, it is the Observatory Tower of Lincoln Castle that was used and on the highest turret, the filmmakers built a wooden top that was added specifically for the film. It is where Harry (Ian) shimmies up its flag pole to place the student's rag flag. Josie and Sarah had both tried to dissuade them to perform the stunt earlier but Harry had fobbed them off. In the windy conditions, Phil struggles on a few occasions until his pal helps him along. Tragedy strikes though on their descent, the trickiest part of the proceedings according to the police gathered below, and Phil falls 80 feet down to his death after Harry fails to hold on to him.

In a touching moment earlier, Phil had expressed his gratitude to his friend for supporting him whilst at University.

At the subsequent Coroner's Court hearing attended by Harry, Philip's parents, and others, the judge presiding is sympathetic to the events of the tragedy. However, the young man has to live with the knowledge that he directly contributed to his friend's death. Phil's parents tell him not to blame himself and they thank him for being possibly their son's only true friend.

Pushing his way through the small, packed streets where crowds are enjoying the rag parade, Harry makes a final call at the oddly-named Chowns. After being told to leave the University, only George (Rogers) has spoken up for his shining academic potential. He says goodbye to Virginia and pals Dai (Briggs), Gilby (Jeremy Brett) and Reggie (Sekka) before telling Josie that he will see her at the coach station. Another touching moment occurs with Reggie, with the latter breaking into song in a peculiar moment where he sings of the character as we watch Harry skulking off.

At the station, the now-gone St Mark's utilised, the couple say farewell after Josie pleads with him to allow her to leave with him. Looking on from the bus, Harry (Ian) glances towards the tower as the bus moves away and the film ends.

As well as much of the castle area being seen in Willing, Bishop Grosseteste University was also used. Miss Maskell and Mr Rogers were billed above the title with a playful introduction to Ian and the cast seen on screen as they walk along.

A premiere at the Odeon cinema, Leicester Square, London, saw Ian accompanied by his parents, Irene & Harry. He still has a photograph of the three of them on the wall of his L.A. home. The film also proved significant in that Ian met his future wife Suzan Farmer, whilst shooting the film. They married in 1965.

Ian and best pal John Hurt rejoined forces after working on Willing for Infanticide in the House of Fred Ginger a controversial Fred Watson play saddled with an unsavoury theme that will not be detailed here. McShane was cast as Charley before John came aboard as the wonderfully-titled Knocker White which, director William Gaskell told biographer David Nathan, "Hurt and McShane came together in those days, like a package deal." The cheeky duo performed in a production for the Royal Shakespeare Company which played the intimate New Arts Theatre Club in London. Its press night was Wednesday 29 August but the length of its run is unknown at a venue that was converted to live theatre use in 1927 with a small auditorium accommodating 300.

Mr Nathan remembers that the playwright told him that the piece required lots of work to knock it into shape and even then it was not to his satisfaction. He also commented that the play was a brutal work with an abrupt use of coarse language and a hard watch. The dialogue, agreed as its strongest element, remained intact but the main plot was problematic in its subject matter. Hurt thought

it a decent piece, not without humour and some menace.

Some years later a film was considered of the play but it never materialised. He later worked as a G.P. and died in 2008.

A play for adults in 3 Acts, How are you, Johnnie? ran at the Vaudeville Theatre on the Strand in London where patrons could purchase a souvenir programme for the price of shilling.

Ian was 20 when appearing there after recently acting in the aforementioned Infanticide. He joined Nigel Stock, fellow N.Y.T. member Derek Fowlds, Hilda Fenemore, Lucinda Curtis & Mr Philip Newman in the cast.

Directed by Guy Vaesen, it had premiered at the Connaught Theatre, Worthing on Monday 26 November and the youngster gained terrific notices in The Stage & Television Today (29 November), "Whatever degree of success the 'unknown' Ian McShane has enjoyed in recent film and television appearances, his casting as Johnnie is indisputably well justified." Mr Vaesen had by then established a long association with the venue whilst the writer already had several works produced. Plotwise, Johnnie Leigh (Ian, pictured below with Ms. Fenemore and NIgel Stock) played a hard-nosed lorry driver alongside sensitive gay mate (Fowlds) still living at home with his mother and oafish stepfather.The latter he does not get on with and discovering his infidelity, Johnnie confronts him.

A scuffle ensues seeing the older man killed. An investigation follows concluding with the 2 men being taken off for questioning in a play "which starts out one way and ends in another," as remembered by critic Pat Wallace (Tatler magazine, 20 March) "Mr Ian McShane in the title role, which is a long and exacting one, expresses his emotions sympathetically enoughthough his perpetual slouch gives him the appearance of a beefy question mark."

The 1963 York Festival presented its epic York Cycle of Mystery Plays this year (pictures on opposite page).

Bill Gaskill provided direction for this medieval drama by JC Purvis which presented a young Ian McShane in the role of Lucifer, amongst a massive cast with some now-recognizable names but the author is uncertain if they are the same actors we would come to know. Detailing the bible from the Creation to the Last Judgement, the work was performed in the ruins of St Mary's Abbey.

Gareth Lloyd Evans of the Observer commented, "The largely amateur company at first gets no nearer conviction than slightly folksy medievalism slouching...This is intensified by the battering of their teeth against the alliteration. But later, emboldened by the excellent playing and speaking of Alan Dobie (God and Jesus) and Ian McShane (as Lucifer) they accept the craggy poetry and act. Suddenly the bunched-up drama in the lines explodes."

Back on television, Alan Sharp's First Night: Funny Noises with Their Mouths aired on BBC1, Sunday 20 October 1963 in the 9 pm slot. Following an episode of Perry Mason, Ian acted in episode 5 as Max, in a show that featured a great many soon-to-be huge actors including Michael Caine & John Hurt.

ITV Play of the Week presented an acting job for the young McShane with a role in The Truth about Alan. He was cast in the title role of this 90 minutes story which aired on Tuesday 4 June 1963. It was the first of his 4 appearances in the highly-regarded series which began in 1955 and ran through to 1974 with others.

By now into series 3 of the popular police drama, Z Cars was a hugely-popular police series when Ian featured in A Stroll along the Sands. Broadcast on BBC 1 on Wednesday 29 January 1964 at 9.45 pm this particular story was written by Joan Clark.

Arriving on British television back in January 1962, Ian portrayed Barry Hepworth. Recorded live, a repeat followed at end of March that same year.

Ian's second and third appearances on Play of the Week both came in 1964; A Question of Happiness/ Watch Me I'm a Bird. Broadcast on Monday 11 May, he portrayed Arthur in a drama that also featured the aforementioned Hurt and was directed by future Disraeli helmer Claude Whatham.

Sandwiched in-between, Love Story was an ITV drama series in which Ian worked on episode eight of its second series: A Girl Like Me. Made between 1963-1974, his particular involvement was presented on Tuesday 26 May.

Ian played Ralph in The Easter Man amongst a cast that included Robin Hawdon, Derek Smith, Angela Pleasance & Karin Fernald. Cast changes were made by the time it played the Globe theatre (now the Gielgud) on Shaftesbury Avenue, London, with Suzan Farmer, Roy Patrick & Lucy Young joining. John Harrison directed this comedy in two acts which are set in a New York apartment with the final act Sunday before Easter.

Before the West End, from Tuesday 2 June the Birmingham rep theatre offered a world premiere of the play with a 4-week run which birmingham-rep.co.uk remembers as being a part of "a series of more daring contemporary plays is presented. Evan Hunter's The Easter Man, Anne Jellicoe's The Knack & Bill Naughton's All in Good Time are not well received by some of the more conservative audience members." Hunter, who died in 2005, was a prolific writer and is better known as crime fiction author "Ed McBain".

By Monday 29 June he could be seen on the telly as Frank Barnes in A Spanner in the Grass Roots alongside the lovely Jane Asher and future Sky West & Crooked cast member Pauline Jameson. There was also a role for Richard Vernon, an actor that would work on a 1994 episode of Lovejoy.

The Beatles headlined a special midnight revue at the London Palladium, entitled Night of a Hundred Stars, in aid of the Combined Theatrical Charities Appeals Council. Staged on Thursday 23 July, a photo shows Ian and others wearing Victorian bathing suits. These were writer Lionel Bart and actors Charles Hawtrey, Gary Raymond, Keith Baxter (who would later act in Will Shakespeare with him) and Gary Miller.

On a personal note, Monday 5 October saw Ian marry Hammer horror icon Miss Suzan Farmer but work would keep them apart for long periods. She passed in September 2019.

The Sullavan Brothers was another popular ATV drama that allowed Mr McShane to add to his CV in a busy year for the young actor. Set in the legal world in London, he was cast as David Hemming in episode 4, in a story titled A Face in the Doorway. Viewers could see him on Saturday 24 October.

With a film and several TV appearances notched up, Mr McShane made an appearance next on Redcap, a superlative ABC TV drama that presented roles for many talented actors across its 2 series and 26 episodes. John Thaw is Sgt. Mann, a trouble-shooter for the army sent worldwide to investigate crimes and misdemeanours involving military personnel. One such case takes him to British-occupied Aden. Here he is to seek out the truth about an incident involving Sgt. Rolfe (Leonard Rossiter) and a local man, landing the latter in a coma before dying.

A youthful Ian is Sapper Russell, a miserable soldier billeted alongside others which include the bullying Baker (an effective Kenneth Farrington). Constantly goading the "pretty boy" into retaliating, Russell seldom gets any peace in an environment coupling searing heat and overbearing personalities.

Some 18 months in, Russell had worked in a factory previously and wanted to keep his trade. Keen to travel, he joined the army but soon regretted it. Mike Pratt, soon later to play a corrupt prison officer in Sitting Target co-stars as a sergeant friend of Rolfe's who allowed his colleague to abuse the Arab man. Sgt. Rolfe is devoted to army life and is unquestioning about his role. For him, his job is to train the raw recruits and keep them alive in hostile environs. However, this means that his rigid working methods make him disliked by many; including both Baker and Russell.

Heading a small team sent out to repair a sabotaged bridge, Rolfe orders that during the night each soldier will complete a 2-hour watch, with Russell (Ian) filling the 2-4 am shift before him. But during this time Sgt. Rolfe falls to his death. In the morning in the communal tent news comes the men are told the news and watch Ian sprawled on a cot clutching his rifle with anxiety across his face.

Back on camp, the men wait. Happy to have gotten rid of Rolfe, Baker is the only one to admit this. Taking charge, he offers Mann a signed group statement of the events but when some details are omitted he decides to interview each man individually. Unable to control himself, Russell snaps and thumps Baker.

A skilled investigator, Sgt. Mann next quizzes the young recruit before telling him that Baker has fled and has a gun with him. Or at least that is what he suggests. He had attended an autopsy and discovered that Rolfe had been struck before falling and that the likely culprit might be Sapper Baker. Highly agitated, Russell reveals the truth: the actor adopts an accent that sounds a bit London-like and says to protect himself he retaliated when Rolfe throttled him after he was discovered asleep whilst on watch. It was then that he struck the blow that saw him lose his footing. Concerned that Baker might be held accountable, Russell asks; Mann replies, "He's already given himself up." Redcap was shown on Saturday 31 October 1964 at 9.10 pm, following the ITV news, and before an episode of The Sullavan Brothers (but not one featuring Ian). Epitaph for a Sweat was written by the talented Richard Harris and directed by film and TV man Peter Graham Scott.

If you are wondering about the title, this is due to the red hat worn by the Special Investigation Branch of the Royal Military Police (of which Mann is a representative) although the series was shot in black & white!

Unfortunately, accepting a role in Joe Orton's latest theatre piece did not turn out to be a happy experience for anyone connected with the project. The play, in which Kenneth Williams co-starred with Geraldine McEwan, Duncan Macrae and Ian, toured the UK in early 1965 but was not a success and closed after 56 performances. Most of the middle-class audiences either didn't understand it or quite simply were shocked by it and walked out. These days are recorded in Williams' diaries and he was undoubtedly miserable. Later retitled "Loot" by Kenneth Halliwell, Orton's partner, Peter Wood directed and made lots of script alterations that unsettled many cast members.

Ian played Hal, the son, whilst a droll David Battley was the off-beat undertaker; this terrific actor would much later appear in Lovejoy. Williams wrote in his diary "Ian McShane made a wayward son alarmingly acceptable..."

Opening on 1 February in Cambridge, by its third night structural changes were made and the play rejigged into 2 acts.

By the sea, in Brighton, at the Theatre Royal, local paper The Argus loved it: 'brilliant farce…first-class writing' whilst the Gazette declared: 'I think it is stupendous.'

On to the Golders Green Hippodrome, then booed at the Bournemouth Pavilion and Opera House, Manchester and by the time it reached Wimbledon on 15 March there was no saving it. The show closed on Saturday 20.

In the following year after Orton heavily reworked the script it subsequently won the prestigious Evening Standard Award.

According to cast member Annette Wills, the finished version of The Pleasure Girls (1965) film was somewhat different from what she and others had signed up to.

Following the lives of those living at the madhouse known as "Flat 48 Lexham Walk, Abingdon, Kensington, London W8", newbie Sally (Francesca Annis) arrives in London joining friends there. We find Ms Wills (Angela), Rosemary Nicols (Marion), Colleen Fitzpatrick (Cobber), Suzanna Lee (Dee) all cared for by queer mother hen Paddy (Tony Tanner).

The whole story takes place across a few days before Sally is due to start at modelling college on Monday. Occurring in the jam-packed weekend are relationships woes, an unwanted pregnancy, violence and youngsters socialising and having fun in-between it all.

Ian & Francesca are the leads and a rousing theme song by girl group The Three Quarters (a single in May '65) gets things moving with a young cast sounding plummy-mouthed.

At a firework's house-party we find Keith (Ian) and others including Prinny, the ponce (Mark Eden) enjoying the evening and it is here that Sally catches the attention of cheeky photographer Keith (a 23-year old Ian McShane). Someone who normally looks for a good time and nothing more, popular with the ladies, things will change when he falls for the country lass and a courtship swiftly develops between them.

Enjoying a dance, they have terrific chemistry although Mr McShane's moves are limited.

After having a groovy time, come the early morning and Keith walks Sally back home through the deserted London streets. Having made an instantaneous connection, he jokes that he doesn't want to sleep with her and they laugh before smooching in a telephone box (long since removed from the locality which is identifiable today: the flats even have the same "48" numbering).

Shot in black and white, films like this and Saturday Night Out are visual and historical delights, shot on real streets where the public are going about their business only to be startled by a crew and actors goofing about.

The music soundtrack is loud at times but The Pleasure Girls has a lot of energy albeit looking a bit dated. Written & directed by Gerry O'Hara, his original screenplay was titled A Time and a Place before director Clive Donner took on the project. Mr Donner directed What's New Pussycat? & Ian would star in its forgotten sequel Pussycat, Pussy Cat, I Love You.

After shooting for almost a month, the producers were disappointed with the rushes and demanded more adult content. Donner departed and O'Hara added bedroom scenes and lingering shots of some of the female cast which led the film to be given an 'X' certificate. This meant it had a limited theatrical release and proved to be fodder for the sleaze sex cinema clubs. Oddly though, it could have been an entirely different film. At least the catchy theme tune proved a memorable late addition. Alternate scenes are included on the joint Blu-ray/ DVD release by the BFI in 2010.

Back to the story and stepping out together the same evening, Sally & Keith are seen passing the Royal Court theatre in SW1 and later enjoying a meal and a dance. His sexual frustrations increase as elsewhere dodge pot businessman Nikko (a skeletal Klaus Kinski who voices his lines as if he has no idea of what he is saying) continues his dealings with people that should most definitely be avoided. Wonderfully, decades later Ian would work with his daughter, Nastassja, on the feature film Exposed.

Come Sunday morning and the gang at the flat are planning a roast lunch. However, the unexpected arrival of Keith (Ian) in a Mini complete with his family dog sees her whisked away for a day in the chilly country. Snapping her, he makes it clear that he wants them to be intimate.

In the evening, they rendezvous with other pals and the fledgling couple enjoy another dance together (Ian repeating his chicken-like moves; head forward and shoulders back ala Max Wall). The pressure to sleep with her new beau increases but Sally tells him that she has ambitions and marriage might not suit her (we have to remember that back in the day, marriage equated to a sexual relationship and many youngsters tied the knot). She asks Keith to be patient and discloses that she is a virgin, "It's not as easy as that," begins the charmer, "Sex is like a drug and I can't kick it that easy." Resulting in a stalemate, she storms off back into the flat.

Monday morning sees all the inhabitants of Flat 48 about to leave and who do we see outside but Keith. Wanting to give her a lift into college, their romance continues.

The title is a bit of a misnomer as the film is a simple snapshot into the lives of youngsters across a brief period.

Next, Gwen Ffrangcon-Davies, Anna Massey, George Baker and Ian were the above title cast members in the classic Tennessee Williams play The Glass Menagerie. Directed by Vivian Matalon, he was a Manchester-born creative talent who started as an actor before turning to directing. He died in 2018 and in his New York Times obit, a photo showed him at home in 1980 with framed posters of his past work on the walls behind him; one of them was for Menagerie.

Ian played Tom, son of Ms Ffrangcon-Davies' Amanda, Ms Massey as Laura, her daughter, and George Baker as The Gentleman Caller. Playing at the Theatre Royal, Haymarket in the West End from Wednesday 15 December, the cost of a programme was a shilling. It ran through to 8 January 1966. Coincidentally, Ms Massey was then married to actor Jeremy Brett, whom Ian worked with previously.

Glass had previously toured the provinces, commencing with the Yvonne Arnaud Theatre, Guildford; Alexandra Theatre, Birmingham; Theatre Royal, Brighton; Golders Green Hippodrome and the Bournemouth Pavilion Theatre and somewhere in between, the Arts Theatre, Cambridge.

After Hayley Mills' writer mother Mary Hayley Bell had fashioned a story called Bats with Baby Faces both she and her actor husband John thought it would make a good film. He took the project to Rank and they agreed to make it, with him directing but alas, not involved as an actor, and with his daughter starring. Renamed Sky West & Crooked (1966), John sought old work colleagues Waterhouse & Hall to write a screenplay but unfortunately, they were unavailable and after several others, John Prebble co-scripted a screenplay with Miss Bell.

They employed an unusual technique of framing their film's story by showing a brief establishing scene, pivotal to many characters involved, before the screen freezes and is stamped with the unusual title. It is immediately after that we have our first glimpse of Ian seen at a sprawling gipsy camp, smoke billowing around and 2 specks seen running across the fields. A young man in black is pursuing a speedy young girl in a yellow dress (Hayley Mills) rushing towards a village church graveyard.

However, from the off, Mr Mills felt that the script wasn't quite right but studio space had been booked and a location in Little Badminton, in the county of Gloucester was found for it to be set. All of the cast and crew were given a script to be familiar with the story and to feel a part of the proceedings.

Providing a lovely look to the film, cinematographer Albert Ibbetson's images mesh perfectly with a music score by Malcolm Arnold which was released under its bland alternate Gypsy Girl monocle on the Mainstream label. Its cover featured the image of the screen couple gazing longingly at each other whilst the song of the same name by Milton & Anne Delugg saw Miss Mills providing vocals. A single was put out with her singing on both tracks and The Wayfarers recorded a 1966 version of the main Arnold-composed theme.

Story-wise, in Sky West, Brydie (Miss Mills) is a naïve youngster in the aforementioned worn, pale yellow cotton dress who spends all day outside avoiding returning home to her fragile mother; the excellent Annette Crosbie. She is reliant upon alcohol and is barely able to care for her as she is burdened by Brydie's involvement in the tragic death of an 8-year-old boy several years previously something that they never discuss. Seemingly unaware, the young woman often spends time in the churchyard putting flowers in front of a plot belonging to 'Julian' but seems incognizant of the significance. Physically grown-up and aged 17 onscreen, in actuality, when the film was made in 1965, Hayley was 19 whilst Ian, 24.

Brydie is an unusual girl, whose personality and nature proves either intoxicating or exasperating to whomever she comes across. A young Romany called Roibin, (Ian) is interested in her but quite selfish in his desire. He watches her from a distance as she tends to the grave of the little lad. But when her trusted dog seems like he is going to wee on the gravestone, he is shooed away by the furious Sexton (Hamilton Dyce). A scuffle ensues between them until Roibin intervenes and pushes him over. He calls him a "gypo" and Brydie a "half-witted girl" and orders them to keep away from the grave as the boy's grief-stricken father has ordered it (Laurence Naismith). A few years older than her, the two exchange names and we notice Ian's lovely red neckerchief.

As a director, Mills uses the camera to show Hayley's natural beauty and the viewer notices how lovely her face is. "Hayley was superb and a joy to direct," offered her father in his autobiography (see references).

A person with a curious sensibility, Brydie enjoys the rural life and is often shoeless; she has been left a permanent reminder: a scar on her right temple, marking a past tragedy that she has blocked from her memory. Again observing her with a pal in the graveyard, from the road, Roibin jumps off a passing hay bailer to spy on them. Walking up to her once she is alone, we notice how young she looks.

They have another chat and joke about him being a "gypo" before he asks her how she got the scar. She declines to answer. Having a similar twangy Welsh accent to hers, he seems to be thinking through his eyes.

Brydie and the other children she spends time with, all a fair bit younger than her, care about animals and begin burying them in the church graveyard. Geoffrey Bayldon as Philip, the put-upon vicar of the parish, with a thoughtful wife, Pauline Jameson, has to placate everyone affected by this. St Michaels & All Angels was utilised and is still there today, with parts of the building dating back to the 13th Century. Amusingly, she can see the extraordinariness of the young girl and even mentions to her sherry-drinking friends that she had to give her their family dog as the canine liked her so much more! This comes when they are outside the vicarage and the mischievous Brydie shoots her catapult at the ample posterior of Judith Furse.

A film with a clear distinction between adults and children, Philip is perturbed by the girl. Her logic is a cerebral delight and is hard to disagree with especially when she decrees that people have animals in life and so why shouldn't they, the "deaders" have them when they have passed away? But concerns from some but not all of the dismissive adults within the village are raised, with some using Brydie as a scapegoat for the unusual occurrences. Sky West sees the actress in another role speaking candidly in that provocative way children do: challenging and without the weight of adult-soaked boundaries. If you would like to read more about her interesting career my book Hayley Mills IN PROFILE can be ordered direct: see references for details.

The vicar visits Dacres to ask if the children might use his dormant meadow for their burials. He is still affected by the loss of his son in a fatal accident involving Miss White (Hayley Mills) and his shotgun. The two will come together in a violent scene later which sees the man confront Brydie but whose actions lead her into trauma.

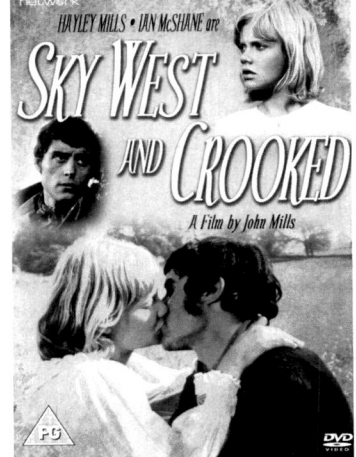

Photo: Author's Collection

Moments after, running and screaming, the distressed young woman flings herself into the fast-flowing river as images of Dacres, Roibin and her mother flash across the screen in the semi-darkness as Brydie fights for life. Out in the woods, Roibin hears her cries and dives into the water and manages to pull her out. Exhausted and barely conscious, a couple of boys approach and they tell him that everybody is looking for her, including the police. In a way, this is when her troubles are exacerbated; Roibin takes her back to the camp and much to the alarm of the others there, is cared for by grandma Rachel Thomas.

Despite their denials after the police ask if she has been there, Brydie is tended to by the woman and Roibin and when she does recuperate enough, she asks to return home. He guilt's her into remaining by making her feel obligated. Interestingly, the viewer may or may not have empathy for him initially but not always. The actor was in his early-20s at the time and his character does seem more worldly-wise than she; whilst Brydie is mid-teens but has the mental capacity of one much younger.

Introducing McShane as a leading man in the cinema, here his character pleads with her to stay with him; to start a life together but she wants to see her mother, unaware of her fate.

In their strongest scene together, the youngsters are chatting in a meadow and he prompts her to remember the incident with Julian. Traumatized, she tells him that she remembers it as being "... like a dream, really..." He reminds her that she puts flowers on the dead boy's grave and in a deeply moving response, Brydie expresses her despair at nobody explaining to her why her friend never played with her anymore. They hug and she confesses that she doesn't want him to leave the area when the group moves on. She kisses him passionately and we wonder what their fate is going to be. Brydie is overwhelmed by the way her suitor speaks to her and experiences love for the first time, for her a dreamlike state, she reassures him that she feels the same way, with a "thumping" in her stomach telling her to hold on to his affections.

The two are discovered by the other children and they inform her that her mother has died. A distraught Brydie White rushes back whilst the pleading gipsy voices his fear that they will not see each other again.

He tells her that he will wait for her after enlightening her about the "speaking sticks that tell the way"; a secret form of relaying information to those that can decipher it.

Brydie is seen in a state of distress at the graveside (in a dodgy bit of overacting from Hayley Mills) whilst her friends call for the help of the vicar. He comforts her and guides her back to the vicarage where wife Gertrude cares for her. But Brydie makes it clear that she needs to see Roibin and asks if he will marry them.

The vicar consoles her, wondering about his absence but reassures her that he will leave him a message to come to the house in the morning. Unfortunately, he asks Bill Slim (Dyce) to relay the request. So when he visits them, Slim orders them to move on from the village and makes no mention of the intended message. The others are furious with Roibin for bringing further harassment to the group and set on him.

Come the morning, the local bobby visits the vicarage and seems satisfied with seeing Brydie returned. The vicar and his wife think that she will need to go into care until she shows him the intertwined hairband which Roibin gave to her as a reminder of the bond between them. The kindly clergyman recognises and recites some text relating to its meaning/ significance which resonates with him. He tells her to get a coat as he is going to attempt to reunite them.

Unfortunately, when they reach the encampment it is empty but Brydie reads the sticks left as markers for her to follow (another will be a piece of cloth draped prominently etc). She dashes on without the vicar who returns to get his bicycle and catch up with her. Brydie ambles casually along but misses one of the twigs meant for her due to 'dog', her trusty cocker spaniel, grabbing it before she notices. Hearing a fellow hound barking, he jumps over a wall and into the neighbouring field. Brydie stands and looks and voices her love. In a long shot, we see the lovers reunited alongside a solitary 'wagon' (wooden caravan) in the distance. This is observed by the delighted cleric, Yes. That's it!"

A late-January premiere in a cold Leicester Square, London, occurred with Ian accompanied by wife Suzan and the Mills family rubbing shoulders with various celebrity guests in advance of the film being released generally on Sunday 6 February 1966 as an 'A' certificate. In a double feature with Mission for a Killer, Sky West and Crooked was not a box office success and Mr Mills never directed again. In 2009 the film got a rare public screening at the Wotton Electric Picture House in Gloucestershire. Four days earlier, Ian had been a guest on A Whole Scene Going, a teatime BBC TV programme for youngsters.

Back to Sky West, if you are wondering where the peculiar title comes from it is an unsympathetic description of Brydie made by Slim (the versatile Mr Dyce).

More telly work followed with Ian featuring in all 7 episodes of ITV drama You Can't Win from Thursday 7 July 1966. Adapted from autobiographical novels by William Cooper set in 1939 and a decade later, McShane is Joe Lunn; a character that appears in two books. A production still exists of the actor with his screen love, Myrtle (R.A.D.A. alumni Patricia Garwood, who sadly passed away in 2019). His hair greyed to show the passing of the years, the two made the cover of TV Times listings magazine also.

His second appearance on ITV's Armchair Theatre, following his television debut back in 1962 on another episode, was in The Signal Box of Grandpa Hudson. Broadcast on Saturday 27 August 1966, Wendy Barrow (Suzan Farmer) is reluctant to take her new boyfriend Geoffrey (Ian) to meet her family as she is embarrassed about some of the things that they do. John Woodvine was Fred, Margery Withers, Mildred and Billy Russell played Grandpa.

Remaining on the box in 1966, The Caretaker was Ian's final performance on ITV's Play of the Week. Aired on Tuesday 25 October, this adaptation of the Harold Pinter play saw Ian cast as Mick, alongside John Rees and Roy Dotrice in this black and white presentation. McShane would later act in another Pinter piece, The Homecoming.

By the close of the year, the latest offering of the BBC's The Wednesday Play came on 23 November at 9.40 pm, the week following the broadcast of Cathy Come Home. Directed by Alan Gibson and written by Christopher Williams, The Private Tutor was a softer comedy-drama than the ground-breaking Cathy. Detailing the introduction of a lodger to a family, Ian played Frank, in amongst a solid cast.

Written by Aleksei Arbuzov, translated by Ariadne Nicolaeff, The Promise was directed by the Cardiff-born Frank Hauser with Ian playing Leonidik, joining Judi Dench & Ian McKellen in the three-hander. Stationed at the New Theatre, Cardiff, from 21 November, for one week, then from Tuesday 29 November at the Oxford Playhouse, then onto the intimate Fortune Theatre in London's Covent Garden and into the New Year. Then it was off to the States and a successful stint at Henry Miller's Theatre, New York from Friday 3 November 1967 to Saturday 2 December.

Mr McKellen remembers the play proved a hit in Oxford and that Sir Noël Coward saw it and commented in his diary entry for 19 March 1967, "…a nearly good play perfectly acted by Judi Dench, Ian McShane, and Ian McKellen. It really is fascinating to see the young do it as well as that. I came away from the theatre bubbling with pleasure." A canny Miss Dench had declined the opportunity to join the 2 Ians on Broadway and after a mere 27 performances, including previews, it closed. Perhaps a Russian play was not the most sanguine choice for the tumultuous times in America at that period. Reviewers also mentioned the fact that American actors had picketed the opening night, "The reviews all referred to the demonstrations," recounts the actor via the excellent mckellen.com, "further diluting the impact of a play which they didn't much enjoy anyway." Remarkably, on Thursday, 25 November, Thanksgiving Day in the States, "….our audience was under 20 people," concludes the stellar actor.

Ian found the repetitive nature of performing the same play night after night trying. Not for him the often traditional way of an actor cutting his chops in rep theatre. In the play, all the characters age and the necessary make-up alterations took some time.

On into the New Year and Ian was back at the Beeb via Wuthering Heights as Heathcliff to Angela Scoular's Cathy, also a graduate of R.A.D.A. like Ian, co-starring as doomed lovers in the Emily Bronte classic novel. Filmed many times both before and since, Laurence Olivier, Timothy Dalton, Tom Hardy & Ken Hutchinson have all taken a stab at the role. A couple of DVDs have been released, one showing Ian looking like he has just stepped away from The Beatles and another saw it included on a pricey BBC DVD under the collective monocle of "The Bronte Collection".

Running across 4 episodes, this version commenced on Saturday 28 October 1967, on BBC 2, at 7.55 pm. On after the rugby, The Val Doonican Show was on BBC1 at the same time. A little piece of trivia: Ian sprained his wrist whilst shooting the serial.

Following the failure of his first marriage, Mr McShane tried again this year, marrying model Ruth Post at Kensington registry office, London, on Saturday 8 June 1968. The two had originally met in Manchester and the union would last into the 1970s producing 2 children: Kate & Morgan.

Shown on Monday 26 August 1968 as part of the ITV Playhouse series, the blackest of comedies Funeral Games was a Joe Orton script filling the one hour slot. After his theatre role in another play by him, here Ian was Caulfield and is seen with a severed head and holding a meat cleaver before delivering the line, "I couldn't get her head off. It must be glued on." To which, McCorquodale (Bill Fraser) replies, "She was always a head-strong woman."

Goodreads.com termed it "a lightweight, very funny noir comedy about the usual Orton subjects: murder, extramarital sex and body parts." It had been written swiftly between July and mid-November in 1966 by the former drinking partner of Ian's who was murdered in August of the following year. Now deemed lost, a clip featuring Mr McShane has survived. Also in the cast were Vivien Merchant and Michael Denison.

A return to film acting came in 1969 from If It's Tuesday, This Must Be Belgium. With the usual adage of a sailor having a girl in every port is replaced here by the international tour guide and specifically, Charlie Cartwright (Ian). Based in London and within spitting distance of Big Ben, he resembles Tony Curtis from Spartacus, with his curly hair brushed tightly forward. The seasoned chaperon of some 6 years works for World Wind Tours, a company offering American travellers a breakneck tour across Europe: 9 countries in 18 days for a ticket price of $448.50 (this being 1969 and all). Made up of older married couples, bachelors, a younger family with a pubescent daughter, solo male and female travellers, Tour No.225 is to be memorable for Charlie.

"These stops are officially called a layover, you know," quips the libidinous guide to Samantha (Suzanne Pleshette). Ms Perkins resists his charms and sees him for what he is, thus making her all the more attractive to the sly host.

After London, Holland, where the various ladies on his tour bus constantly interrupt his intimate liaisons before Belgium gives way to Luxembourg and then Germany.

Switzerland sees the group having bonded and despite seeing a different side of Sam (a slightly older Ms Pleshette) when drunk, his scheming to get her into bed is again thwarted.

Italy proves appealing, with Charlie (McShane) and his gang seen on gondolas in Venice and as Lovejoy, you might recall an episode took him them some decades later.

With Charlie and Sam getting closer, he tells her that his parents were buskers before going into a little song and dance routine for her in a charming distraction.

Necking on the gondola returning them to the hotel, the unexpected arrival of her estranged partner puts an end to their shenanigans; but all she can think about is Charlie. Coincidentally, the actress would work with her friend Peter Falk on a television episode of Columbo in 1971, beating Ian by a few years (he would make an appearance in the final series broadcast in 1990).

On to Rome and the quirky group visit the Spanish Steps, as the tour and film come to an entertaining if slight, close.

Come the morning and we see Sam taking in the sumptuous rooftop view from an apartment before returning to the bedroom where a grinning Charlie awaits. He wants her to stay.

Bidding adieu to his guests at the airport, Charlie takes Sam aside and asks her to marry him. Is this simply an unanticipated holiday romance or something more? Is the previously non-committal Mr Cartwright ready to settle down with the feisty American? Curiously, the screenplay written by David Shaw, itself nominated for a Golden Globe & by the Writers Guild of America in 1970, leaves us wondering.

Back in the UK and once again Charlie repeats his usual spiel to a new group of tourists on his bus. But this time, he adds that perhaps some of them will find romance, after all, it has happened before. The camera cuts to a container with some flowers in it, the same as those picked by Sam that night she spent with him at the Viale delle Ceno Fontane (the Hundred Fountains) in Rome. Others have read the ending as signifying that the young womaniser has been played.

Particularly memorable amongst Tour no.225 are Norman Fell and Aubrey Morris. The latter proves most amusing as a kleptomaniac solo traveller and the former a married man whose wife inadvertently joins a different travel group and has a great time! Morris would work with Ian again in the mini-series Disraeli; portraying his father and some years later in 2 episodes of Lovejoy & appearing in Deadwood.

A soundtrack LP was released and the film is available on both DVD & Blu-ray.

One of six episodes written by David Wildeblood, Rogue's Gallery was unusually set in Newgate Gaol in the 1750s, with each self-contained story told to its main character. Playing David Garrick in episode 2 of series 2, his tale was titled The Wicked Stage and was broadcast on Saturday 17 May. His character ran an acting group at Drury Lane in London.

Released in cinemas this year, Battle of Britain presented McShane with his final film appearance this decade. With France invaded, defeated and abandoned by the Allies, the next conflict would be the Battle for Britain. Utilising locations in England, France & Spain, the film is a tribute to the R.A.F. and the part it played in defending Great Britain from what seemed an inevitable invasion by Nazi Germany during WWII. In 1940, Britain was ill-prepared for such a confrontation but what a defence it put up.

Adapted from the book The Narrow Margin co-authored by Derek Wood & Derek Dempster, James Kennaway & Wilfred Greatorex fashioned a screenplay. With a tremendous cast including Michael Caine, Trevor Howard, Laurence Olivier and many others utilised to tell the story from both perspectives, The Battle of Britain is a classic in its genre.

With 3 stripes on his arm, Sgt. Pilot Andy (Mr McShane) is seen early on in the film as one of the returning Spitfire and Hurricane pilots back after one of their numerous sorties. A close pal of fellow flyer Archie (Edward Fox) we see the men in that iconic blue uniform later seen worn by Ian's character in The Great Escape: Part II. A youthful James Cosmo, later reuniting with Ian in children's fantasy The Seeker, is here seen as a fellow pilot when we are introduced to Ian, Edward & others at their base.

Duxford Airfield and its hangars were put to use extensively for location filming (the sites being used during the war and now an Imperial War Museum property).

The often-exhausted crews were scrambled into action during the period with the German invaders initially gaining the upper hand. Ian and the others are seen dashing out to take to the skies, putting on his goggles and protective equipment once inside the cockpit we see the devastation wrought by the enemy.

Andy (Ian) is one of the lucky ones to make it back but only after parachuting out and into the cold Channel (not seen onscreen). Squadron Leader Robert Shaw is delighted to see a chilly McShane upon his delayed return to base and offers him a lift to visit his wife and children.

History has informed us that if the Nazis had continued to strike London instead of the ports, then the war might have had a different outcome. Places like the East End were heavily bombed by the Luftwaffe and it is here that he locates his wife and 2 young sons in a church hall. There locals had taken refuge during the night-time raids with fires, debris and people seen rushing away as he makes his way to find his family.

Presenting the boys with toy planes, he snaps at his wife for returning after he had gotten them a move to safety elsewhere. Once volunteers are called to assist nearby bombing victims, Andy goes off to help after which time his life will never be the same.

In the night-time light, on his way back, we see him walking alongside a cheeky young boy who doubts that he is a pilot, and a devastating sight greets them: the church halls is a bombed ruin and alight.

With the conflict unrelenting, come the following morning Andy is seen getting a lift with neighbour Mr Shaw and they drive off silently, with not a word said about the tragedy.

As the air battle rages, we watch as many planes zigzag each other at high speed with dogfights a plenty. Ian, Edward and others return, tired and seated outside the comms. room, waiting for another call to scramble. A false alarm sees them stand down but one less experienced pilot amongst the group who have a great sense of camaraderie, steps outside and vomits. Such was the life of these brave people that they never knew if they would return from a mission. Many did not.

Snoozing outside, we see Andy next to Archie and others but they do not receive a call. The plan to invade having been abandoned after believing the blitzkrieg would be completed in 48 hours.

Narrating the 2013 documentary How We Used to Live, whose score was by Saint Etienne, Ian mentions working with Battle's First A.D. Derek Cracknell: father of the group's terrific singer, Sarah.

29

2. Lots of films, cult TV & a football has-been makes good: The 1970s

With the Sixties over, 1970 saw indubitably the worst film that he has appeared in: Pussycat, Pussycat, I Love You.

Playing Fred C.Dobbs, a randy playwright unable to resist the ladies despite being married to Millie (Anna Calder-Marshall who astonishingly was nominated for a Golden Globe for this rubbish). He also has a mistress, his wife's sister, Ornela (Beba Lončar). As dreadful as it sounds, the film was written and directed by the vastly experienced Rod Amateau and supposed sequel to the 1965 hit What's new Pussycat? This even has a Tom Jones sound-a-like crooning its theme song!

Before the opening credits roll, we see Fred at it with a busty lass in a car which reminds Lovejoy fans of the little Morris minor "Miriam" and the standard is set: low. As the delectably attired Mr Dobbs, Fred has a penchant for calling people "pussycat" and the costumes worn by the actor received their own credit (they are from "Nikki's of Just Men, London", in case you wondered).

Shot at Cinecittà Studios in Rome, Ian was back in Italy after making If it's Tuesday, It Must Be Belgium. Early on he does speak a few Italian phrases but the location proves superfluous.

He looks immaculate in a burgundy suit when socialising with a young lady at a restaurant and accidentally setting alight a curtain in an amusing moment in a screenplay otherwise bereft of humour. Pussycat's problem is that its attempts to be funny are so clumsy that it simply proves tiresome. Mr McShane offers lots of incredulous looks, much like the viewer, but this is a film that proves a struggle to watch all the way through. It is hindered by a Vincent Price-intoned narrator commenting on scenes and characters and hampered by cartoonesque visual gags and sound effects which leave the audience fatigued.

Fred visits the bizarre and sex-obsessed Dr Fahrquardt (Severn Darden), more a quack than the scalp specialist that he purports to be when the young man seeks to address his follicle-loss worries.

Elsewhere, Fred visits the 'Battle of the Bulge' spa and accidentally loses his towel at a ladies-only whilst in pursuit of the scrumptious Liz (Veronica Carlson, who died in 2022) in a scene that has comic potential but remains untapped. He also has a recurring dream involving a "big, hairy, horny gorilla" called Milton and we enter Carry On Up the Jungle territory.

By the time the couple's maid Flavia (Gaby André) gets Fred to hire her nubile niece Angelica (Katia Christine) as his secretary, to whom he immediately takes a fancy, the viewer no longer cares.

Offering an enormous contrast to Pussycat this year, The Ballad of Tam Lin can only be filed under the 'curios' section of Ian McShane's acting CV. The only directorial effort from actor Roddy McDowall, he clearly poured all his efforts into this. A willowy soundtrack with music from Stanley Myers and The Pentangle, the former would furnish the same duties on 3 other Ian films, enhances a beautifully photographed film from D.P. Billy Williams.

31

Shot in the UK and at Pinewood Studios in 1969, the Scottish Borders provided much of the backdrop for the final screenplay from writer William Spier, he in turn had taken his inspiration from the Robbie Burns poem of Tam Lin. Ian is Tam, Hollywood veteran Ava Gardner Queen of the fairies and cult favourite Stephanie Beacham, the comely Janet.

As Micky, the sensuous Miss Gardner plays an older rich woman collecting various waifs and strays including Joanna Lumley, Madeline Smith and Sinéad Cusack who had worked with Ian on an ITV Playhouse story shown this same year. Joanna would reconvene with Ian for three episodes of Lovejoy in 1992 but here they only share group scenes. But here, Micky's current partner is Tom (a beautiful Ian McShane, then in his late-20s whilst Ms Gardner was by then in her late-40s), whom we see with her in bed at the start of the story. The couple love each other but behind her strong exterior, Micky is insecure about their relationship whilst Mr Lynn wants to escape from it. Her spy, accountant and PA, Elroy (an oddly specs-free Richard Wattis) later informs Tom that he is merely her latest young lover, some of whom died terrible deaths afterwards.

Possessing an insatiable sexual appetite and a strong sense of mischief, we catch a revealing glimpse of Ian's lily-white bottom in a moment of fun between the couple. Micky might seem glamorous and attractive but beneath her polished veneer she is insecure.

Her latest gaggle jumps into one of her many expensive sports cars and drive at great speed to her country pile in Scotland at the sumptuous Traquair House but it is Mr McShane who leads the pack by driving her luxurious Rolls Royce.

Georgia (Ms Lumley) falls victim to having to deliver one of the occasional banal lines of dialogue and it is whilst the young people are enjoying themselves in the grounds that Tom first sees Janet (Ms Beacham). Incidentally, the property today functions as a visitor's centre with accommodation.

Tom and Janet share an instantaneous attraction and out on a walk on the lush hills to ease another almost daily hangover, he sees her again. And in a delightfully understated scene, they kiss, with McDowall curiously using snapshot photography to express the moment. Although not explicitly shown, it is clear that sexual contact has occurred and later Janet falls pregnant.

A distraught but knowing Miss Cazaret (Ms Gardner) is made aware of the liaison by the trusted Elroy whose job it is to know of such occurrences.

Another snapper, the fashion for young men in the mid-1960s, as Tam (or Tom in modern parlance) he obsesses with a picture that he took of Janet; he has developed feelings towards her. Desperate to get away from Micky's control, he pleads with her to allow him some time away which she acquiesces. However, she also threatens him by saying that he has a week, time proving important to her in the film, after which he will be killed. The young man is afraid of her and knows that she is not somebody to be trifled with.

As the male lead, Ian looks terrific in tailored suits provided by his alluring screen lover, including a smart burgundy number. Indeed, the actor always looks good in a suit, doesn't he? With their unexpected love for each other blossoming, Janet (Miss Beacham in a demure and understated performance) wants Tom to leave Micky but it proves hard for him to make her understand his predicament. He is fretful and as the story moves to its somewhat ludicrous end, here the author found it hard to take seriously. But remembering its source material, things enter the super camp realm, with some laughable but effective close-ups of an evil Ms Gardner belonging to a different movie. McDowall adored the actress and Miss Beacham has since mentioned that she mentored her through her early career. There are some onset location stills featuring Ian and the cast with their director and attending a birthday party for Ava on Christmas Eve 1969.

A visual treat, Tam Lin was largely forgotten after its clumsy 1970 theatrical release in the UK it was repackaged as the Devil's Widow for its American audience and presented there in 1972. Forgotten until a late VHS offering with an introduction from its director, a 2013 Bluray presentation helped make it available to curious viewers.

Returning to the story, after reuniting the lovers escape to a caravan being rented by Tom with the stunning Forth Bridge as its backdrop. Deciding to flee, their whereabouts have been discovered by Elroy and his heavies who beat Tom up before bundling him away in a car and back to the Evil Queen.

Back at the Scots lair, the spurned Micky forces her estranged love to drink from a goblet and we suspect that its contents will not be conducive to his health, as is soon proven.

Surrounded and bullied by a new crop of youngsters, a terrified Tom can barely focus or move as a studious young man takes charge of a game wherein Tom is obliged to play the victim. Given an opportunity to flee via one of her expensive vehicles, the impaired Tom stumbles out and away, barely able to stay on the roadside as a terrified Janet, who recently found him, pleads with him to stop. But he only has three minutes before the cackling pack, led by Micky, is set upon him. Poor Tom is feeling the effects of the hallucinogenic forced upon him but still, his response to flee remains strong.

Eventually stopping in what looks like marshland but most probably was Pinewood, at one point he imagines that his arms are on fire and that a giant serpent is enwrapping him. It is all very distressing for the exhausted and bare-chested young man as Micky, Elroy and others arrive. The latter acknowledges to his new partner that the plan has failed but wisely denies that it is his responsibility.

The hunters arrive but they all subsequently leave the pitiful Tom who is sprawled on the ground and being held by Janet. Touchingly, despite his duress, he reaches out his hand to hers.

Several photographs were taken of Ian on location for the ITV Playhouse comedy/ drama offering A Sound from the Sea broadcast on Monday 17 August at 8.30 pm. Shown on the ITV network in the UK, it was episode 38 in series 3 of the long-running show and co-starred Ian as Tom with Bryan Murray (as Charlie), hitchhikers finding themselves trapped in an Inn run by John Collin and Mary Merrall and Sinéad Cusack, I believe. Written by Alan Sharp, it was directed by John Jacobs, the same man who would go on to direct Ian in the ABC Playhouse TV offering Rocket to the Moon in 1986.

Along with Get Carter, released in 1971, British films in the ilk of Villain are not made anymore. A memorable, gritty feature, this and the sadly-neglected Freelance, Ian's other film appearance this year, both merit repeat viewing or rooting out if they are unfamiliar.

Richard Burton is Vic Dakin, head of a gang ably assisted by hard nuts Duncan (Tony Selby), Terry (John Hallam, later to co-star in Sexy Beast) & Webb (Del Henney). Running protection rackets and more across his London manor, Dakin is somewhat of a contradiction, as he lives at home with his elderly mother but anyone who crosses him is either cut or killed: simple as.

Elsewhere, the strangely-named Wolfe Lissner (Ian) and his attractive girlfriend Venetia (the excellent Fiona Lewis) are in the bedroom at his Battersea flat. Planning to meet up with her later, Wolfe is smart, dressed in a black leather jacket set off by a favoured polo neck sweater. But the man is a wretch, pimping her out to M.P. Donald Sinden (playing against type brilliantly) at a country home where all kinds of sleazy parties or "kinky weekends" occur. Wolfe procurers girls and sometimes boys, whilst also hustling in other ways such as selling drugs.

Returning to his flat in York Mansions, after driving home in his Ford Capri, "Wolfeyboy" is met by 2 of Vic's heavies with a request from their boss for him to get in contact.

The local police want to arrest Vic but need evidence so Matthews (a dogged Nigel Davenport) sets out to get it, assisted by the cheery Binney (Colin Welland).

Danny, as played by Anthony Sagar, proves a pivotal character in the story, which was scripted by Dick Clement & Ian La Frenais from an adaptation by actor Al Lettieri. That in turn came from a 1968 novel written by James Barlow. A police grass (informer), he astutely terms Vic a "nutter" whilst Matthews labels him a "psychopath". Delusions of grandeur should also be added. It is Danny who gives the gangster information appertaining to the delivery and transportation of money from a local bank to a plastics factory on the outskirts of the city.

Vic meets up with old friend and fellow "King of the castle" Frank (T.P. McKenna) and his ailing brother-in-law, Edgar Lowis (the ill-fated Joss Ackland). Villains like these like to use the local knowledge of fellow low-lives and bent employees to gain valuable insight into areas of prospective criminal opportunities. Here, Frank wants in on the deal. The two have a long-established criminal past together and Vic begrudgingly agrees to have some of his old mate's lads in on the job.

A half-hour into the film, at a popular casino haunt patronised by Wolf and Gerald Draycott (Sinden) and losing heavily at the gaming table, the latter thanks him for introducing him to the carnal delights offered by Venetia but is abruptly stopped before going into graphic detail. Wolfe gets the point. Also, present nearby, is Vic, who notices him there.

Later that same night, on a drug run to a local club, Wolfey is obliged to go off with 2 heavies to be taken to see Vic whether he likes it or not.

The older man is unhappy at learning of Wolfey's return to his old hustling ways and mentions having given him £100 a week and the use of a car as sweeteners to keep him as his boyfriend. Begrudgingly going upstairs into a bedroom with him, Vic punches him in the stomach in some kind of grotesque foreplay. It seems so, but the villain repeats the cruelty later on when unable to contain his jealousy and anger.

Meanwhile, Detectives Matthews & Binney know all about Ian's character and give him a pull outside a local betting shop and advise him to change his ways.

After surveying all the issues and details involved, the robbery is unexpectedly brought forward. Vic gets directly involved and dishes out the violence when called upon to do so.

The heist is completed but messily so, with the crooks escaping with the money and needing to establish alibis for when the police inevitably call.

Back at the flat, Wolf and Venetia are about to be intimate when the doorbell rings and Vic and Terry arrive. Mr Dakin is furious to discover her there and can barely hide his contempt. He is there to get Wolfey to arrange a viable alibi.

After Edgar (Ackland) is brought in by Matthews, Lissner is ordered to telephone him and ask why he is late for their meeting. Confused, he tells Vic an unfamiliar voice answered.

Out in the London W11 streets and large flats seen in The Pleasure Girls, Ian and Duncan (Selby) call on Patti (Elizabeth Knight) a casino worker and girlfriend of Benny (Stephen Sheppard) a man assaulted by Vic and his boys at the start of the film. Forever the opportunist, he forces the frightened young woman to attend one of the sordid house parties.

Elsewhere, a worried Vic Dakin checks that others are not going to implicate him in the robbery. This he does by using violence against disillusioned bank clerk Brown.

Vic takes his mother there for a day trip to Brighton and a trek onto the now-lost West Pier. Followed by the police, he is outraged to be arrested and obliged to return to London to face questioning. But he is a man with connections and soon Draycott (Sinden) is singing his praises and providing a false alibi, despite the two despising each other. The politician is persuaded to do so after being shown incriminating photos of him by Wolfe, where he is engaged in sexual shenanigans with Patti. An infuriated Matthews vows to reveal his deceit.

Discovering his dear mother dead in bed, Vic immediately calls Wolfe and demands he be with him. At her subsequent funeral, we see both men in attendance and Matthews and co there in the background.

Venetia calls at her boyfriend's flat only to discover him acting sheepishly: does he have another woman? No, stepping out from behind the bedroom louvre doors is Vic wearing a dressing gown. Seeing her leave, Wolfey attempts to reassure Vic that she meant nothing to him but gets another punch. Despite this, the insecure villain orders him never to leave him.

With Lowis (Ackland) in police custody, the head villain wonders where the stolen lolly is, also fearful that he might confess all about the robbery. Learning that he is being moved to a hospital, Vic plans for his boys to remove the man and thus the threat.

Proving themselves hugely efficient and confronted by little opposition, Eddie is taken away but Wolfey fears that it was too easy and that this could be a trap. A paranoid but still confident Vic assures him that it was merely a job well done but the audience knows that Matthews allowed it to be so, as part of his plan to safely procure his capture.

Vic takes Wolfe along with him to see nervy Edgar at a disused industrial estate and then onto arches somewhere in Battersea. Dragged out to gather the stashed cash, Vic is furious with him when he tells him that he cannot locate it. The whole thing was a set-up and with the police approaching, Dakin shoots Edgar.

Rushing off with Wolfey in tow, the latter stops and it is only then that Gangster no 1 realises that the game is up. A startled Dakin thinks that they can still get away but for his lover, it is over. We watch as uniformed officers take Wolfey away and a bewildered Vic finally understands that his reign is over. He is not untouchable after all.

Villain is a terrific film and assuredly directed by feature film debutante, the Berlin-born Michael Tuchner.

Speaking about the film retrospectively, Ian recounts drinking heavily alongside Burton whom he would join in the star's trailer for a breakfast consisting of kippers, grapefruit and vodka added to by many a lunchtime pint!

"But can you see a chap killed and say nothing about it?"

Also known as The Conman (and The Freelance) for its American audience, Ian was top-billed next to co-star Gayle Hunnicutt in Freelance (also 1971); a bleak and rather neglected crime thriller set in London. As Mitch, McShane is a chancer; a sharply-dressed character always working on deals and scams to make a few quid, no matter how legit. Indeed, we are introduced to him as a facilitator for a select group viewing of a silent, super8mm sex film to put a few notes into his pocket.

Set in the late sixties/ early seventies, Freelance finds Ian being directed by Francis Megahy, who also co-wrote the screenplay with Bernie Cooper. The former would subsequently direct the actor in Sewers of Gold aka Dirty Money and in several episodes of Lovejoy; some of which he also scripted.

Back to the story, leaving the makeshift screening Mitch is walking home towards the flat that he shares with Chris (Miss

Hunnicutt whose last acting role seems to have been in the 1990s) when he witnesses a street mugging. Little realising that the attack was pre-arranged; he purses the aggressor along the streets and finally corners him. The thug, Alan Lake, in suitably snarling mode, draws a cosh and so Mitch backs down. Dean (Lake, recently out of prison for real) works for gallery owner/ villain Peter Gilmore; slightly miscast here, who later demands that the witness, vaguely known to the protagonist, be permanently silenced. The attack proves to be fatal and it seems that it was a planned underworld job. And so follows an elongated pursuit of the "little berk" by the heavy.

Meantime, the canny Mitch realises the precariousness of his situation and confides to fellow chancer Gary, the equally well-spoken Keith Barron, of not wanting to be called as a court witness. Initially, the viewer perceives Gary as being a police officer but he supports his friend, a fellow philanderer, throughout the film as the net tightens. A similarly like-minded individual, Gary & Mitch are pursued by other heavies looking for the latter by the cuckold husband of Luan Peters, whom as Rosemary, Mitch met earlier. This is the cue for Ian to do his comedy shuffle running, something he would later hone to perfection via the Lovejoy series. A bit of a ladies' man, the effete Mitch is known well by girlfriend Chris but her patience is going to be pushed to the limit.

With the reluctant gun-toting Dean on the hunt, Mitch remains one step ahead; something that he manages to do throughout Freelance. Still working and organising schemes, he continues developing a property investment deal with the visiting McNair (Charles Hyatt) whilst Chris voices her distrust of Gary. She wants Mitch to take on a legitimate job from a friend and so is surprised when he accepts. With the proviso of a vacant flat being thrown in, Mitch fails to disclose being pursued by Dean and so relocating suits as it will put a distance between them.

Snuggling together at the new place, their contentment is shattered by the bumbling attempts at breaking and entering by super thug Dean (Mr Lake who would also be cast in Yesterday's Hero later). They manage to flee but this proves enough for Chris, who leaves Mitch. But such is the depth of their relationship that it will not be the last time they see one another.

Moving again, Mitch takes a room in a dingy boarding house whilst Gary helps him raise some much-needed funds. Can he be trusted? Dean consequently appears just a step behind on several occasions and normally when the pals meet up at their usual rendezvous, a public house. A coincidence or is their shared manor rather small?

Accompanied by a jazz soundtrack, Mitch jumps onto a bus and is pursued by Dean in his car as the former takes a long trip out of the city and into the countryside.

Alighting from the bus, Mitch is followed in a scene shot in the winter. Taking pot-shots at him, Dean is led into a trap and spoiler alert, killed. Mitch is one bright cookie and we see him riding away from the location on a vintage motorcycle. As an aside, Ian would later narrate a clip show released on the Mansquest VHS video label titled For the Ultimate Sports Motor Cycle Collector.

Freelance concludes with Mitch seen behind the wheel of a fashionable foreign car and pulling into a posh hotel back in the city to conclude the deal with McNair. However, two heavies sent by the impressed Gilmore bring him to him and the film ends with Mitch seemingly forced to work for the former from this point forth.

Never receiving an official DVD release, the film did make it to VHS where it had an illustrated likeness of Ian and his fellow cast members accompanied by the strapline "When he turned – the hunters became the hunted!" Freelance does exist on the internet but it is a cut version with a tasty scene featuring Miss Peters cavorting with McShane & Baron having been removed.

Advertised on television, 1971's The Hellstrom Chronicle won an Academy Award (and BAFTA) in 1972 as Best Documentary. An 'A' certificate, it features clips showing Ian in scenes from If It's Tuesday, It Must Be Belgium. Why? Because the Executive producer was David L. Wolper who had performed the same duties on that film comedy. Detailing the intimate lives of insects, Hellstrom was a hit with audiences but not so much with critics at the time.

Part of ITV's Sunday Night Theatre, Whose Life is it Anyway? was made by Granada TV, who broadcast it on Sunday 12 March 1972. Directed by Richard Everitt, its cast featured Ian as Ken Harrison, The Forsyte Saga's Suzanne Neve as Dr Scott and fellow R.A.D.A. graduate Philip Latham as Dr Emerson. More well-known as a play subsequently and filmed in 1981 and starring Richard Dreyfuss in the role of Ken.

To close the year, Ian could be seen in 2 feature films: Sitting Target and The Left Hand of Gemini.

SITTING TARGET x ＿STARRING OLIVER REED · JILL ST. JOHN · IAN McSHANE

EDWARD WOODWARD · FRANK FINLAY · Screenplay by ALEXANDER JACOBS · Produced by BARRY KULICK · Directed by DOUGLAS HICKOX

METROCOLOR   Released by MGM ⊕ EMI

SITTING TARGET

Sitting Target, an 'X' certificate in UK cinemas, with 'AA' feature The Gang That Couldn't Shoot Straight as its support, there is something quite awesome about 1970s British films featuring actors with such real screen presence as those found here. Ian was third-billed after Oliver Reed & Jill St John in another gritty British crime thriller here directed by Douglas Hickox from the Laurence Henderson novel.

Harry (Reed) and pal Birdy (Ian) conspire to break out of their high-security prison after the former has been incarcerated for a 15-year stretch following a manslaughter charge; we don't know what Ian's character is in for but the two have a criminal past together. As Lomart, Reed is on the edge of collapse when he is visited by his wife Pat (the oddly-cast American actor Ms St. John) who tells him she is pregnant by another man and wants a divorce as she can't wait for his release. This sends him apoplectic and he almost succeeds in strangling her before the guards and Birdy stop him.

A prison break is excellently filmed, with screws like Mike Pratt bribed to allow their access away but the duo have fellow con MacNeil (Freddie Jones) with them and getting out proves quite a task in the night-time scenes. Following an athletic climb over barb wire walls, Lomart is attacked by a guard dog before his mate Birdy batters it to death with a brick! The scramble up some scaffolding sees the trio high above the prison and a shimmy along a rope connecting it to the exterior wall proves exhausting but successful.

Met by accomplices in an army wagon outside, they flee and MacNeil partakes in a bit of sex with a woman supplied by his cohorts with Williams (Mr McShane) looking on keenly. He also indulges whilst the cuckold Harry remains resolute upon focussing on murdering his wife.

Ian has since said that after filming the scenes he came away feeling he would not wish to experience being locked up for real!

On their return to London, Harry & Birdy stop off for the less-stable married man to pick up a gun from a contact. Birdy intervenes when the deal looks to be going bad and as the more steadying influence in the friendship, he tries to persuade Harry not to use a "shooter" aka a gun. But he is determined to use it to kill Pat as well as protect himself against other villains unhappy at his return.

They have a 200k stash from a recent robbery but the time is not right for them to utilise it and despite his fury, Harry considers his friend throughout, here saying that once he has done his wife in that they would need to separate.

Elsewhere, Inspector Milton (Edward Woodward) calls in on Mrs Lomart at her hi-rise flat which turns out to have been turned over by Harry. It was the copper who was responsible for sending her husband down previously and he is keen to offer her full police protection against the unstable Harry. Unfortunately, this has not been the case for her thus far.

After having to bide his time, Harry visits the flat again and surprises his wife but is interrupted by Milton and the two struggle on the narrow balcony with its long drop down.

Forced to flee after shooting 2 motorcycle police officers and causing mayhem below, Harry is luckily collected and driven away by Birdy in a transit van. Williams is an opportunist thief and nothing is secure against his sticky fingers.

Marty (Frank Finlay) is their only contact outside and slyly, the two escapees manage to get inside the love nest shared by the married Mr Gold and his other woman, Maureen, as played by Jill Townsend. She and Lomart (Reed) make quite a connection, as observed by Birdy, but it is he that sleeps with her. An agitated Marty arrives and telephones his police connection to say that Harry has been in contact and that he is worried. He has their money stashed but he fails to realise that both men are in the mews flat waiting for him. Calling for Maureen, he is shocked to see them there and makes to escape by smashing a glass at Birdy before he is accidentally killed by Lomart. If not earlier, by now the audience starts to distrust Birdy Williams but would he double-cross his old pal?

Fortuitously able to collect the bag of cash from an abandoned theatre, Harry rejoins his mate in a film delivered by a stupendous screenplay from Alexander Jacobs.

In an attempt to create a diversion to help flush out Pat in the high-rise, Birdy sets fire to a trackside building. The explosion brings residents to the window, far off in the distance but not an issue for Lomart to view via the small telescopic lens of his German-made Mauser gun (but would the weapon have been able to hit such a distant target?). Ollie trains the sights on her and fires.

Distraught at what he has done, in a moment of despair; Birdy (Ian) kicks him in the face rendering him temporarily unconscious, in a sickening moment of betrayal.

Pinching the cash and running off, Birdy joins up with Pat (Ms Ireland) in a waiting car. It transpires that it was a policewoman decoy at the flat and not her. We also learn that she wrecked the place to make it look like poor Harry had broken in. And as if this was not enough, she faked the pregnancy and concocted the whole thing with Birdy. Harry might be a psychopath but you have to feel for him after all this.

The deceitful duo drives away, thinking that Ollie has been dealt with but as in all films, the end has not quite been reached. Suddenly behind them is a maddened Lomart in a stolen jeep-type vehicle.

An exhilarating car chase follows; there was always one in these films, concludes with Ollie bashing into the old Anglia repeatedly until disabling it completely. Inadvertently killing his wife in the process, Williams survives and runs off on foot.

Shot at repeatedly, with banknotes flying all around him, Birdy dies, with the rail tracks behind him once more in a superb finale. The actor was annoyed to discover that his death scene had been cut by the censors after being told by a journalist. He had not seen the finished film in the cinema.

However, Sitting Target is not over yet. As Harry, Mr Reed climbs into the vacant driver seat next to Pat, kisses her and sits back prior to the vehicle exploding.

The police arrive, including a startled Milton (Woodward) as the film ends. Stanley Myers provided the soundtrack and he would repeat similar duties on Yesterday's Hero and Ian features prominently in the rare CD booklet, see below.

Not a film that can easily be viewed, The Left Hand of Gemini (also 1972) finds your author only able to mention it in passing, alas. A sci-fi pilot for a proposed series that never got made co-stars included Patricia Blair, Richard Egan and Ursula Thiess.

The Last of Sheila saw Ian in the big time when co-starring in this Hollywood film in one of the 1973's biggest theatrical releases. Well-promoted and with various media tie-ins; there was also a novelisation of the screenplay which had been co-written by Psycho man Anthony Perkins and composer/ game addict Stephen Sondheim, who sadly died in late 2021. Despite having people in the calibre of James Coburn and James Mason in its cast, the story proves initially unengaging.

A group of six friends joins producer Clinton Green (the toothy Coburn) aboard his large luxury yacht 'Sheila' for a supposed fun week away in the South of France. However, the recently-widowed film man has plans to tease the group into revealing embarrassing aspects from their past via a game of deduction. Each is given a card which we later learn reveals S-H-E-I-L-A.

43

Ian is Anthony Wood, bland manager and partner to actress Alice (a breathy but wooden Raquel Welch of whom many in the production did not work well with), alongside feisty agent sexy Dyan Cannon who's anyone's, whilst the only happy couple seems to be screenwriter Tom Parkman (Richard Benjamin) and Lee (Joan Hackett). These people live glamorous lives consumed by the machinations of the film business but all struggle within it to varying extents.

Indulging Coburn with his game, things start to turn nasty when Christine (a voluptuous and funny Ms Canon who steals the film) is almost killed in a propeller incident.

The Last of Sheila looks great and is ably directed by the esteemed Herbert Ross but surely for a movie to work the audience has to be interested in the characters? The author found this aspect a test but the longer the film goes on, it's almost 2 hours, the more engrossing it becomes.

As the long-haired Anthony, Mr McShane doesn't do an awful lot apart from goofing around with glove puppets and looking well-dressed. His past is revealed seeing him imprisoned on two occasions whilst more recently, his partner has been having an affair with Tom. As a couple, The Woods display little affection towards each other.

Lee's inheritance is worth a cool $4m but tragedy strikes when she commits suicide after accidentally believing that she has killed the irritating Clinton. He had exposed her as the driver responsible for the death of his wife, Sheila, seen at the start of the movie, in an alcohol-fuelled hit and run tragedy.

But this being a murder mystery, the screenplay provides many twists, "Whose fault is all this? asks Parkman and we do wonder. But all will be revealed.

It is left to the wonderful James Mason to fill the Marple-type role, unravelling the clues left by Clinton and the guilty party. Studying it all, director Philip dissects the evidence alongside Tom but puts himself in harm's way upon revealing the latter as being responsible for faking the suicide of his wife to reap her inheritance. In an inadvertently hilarious moment, the 'tache-tastic Tom attempts to strangle Mr Dexter (Mason, who along with Ian, was later in episodes of mini-series A.D. He could also be seen in Jesus of Nazareth) with Anthony's creepy puppets only to be fortuitously interrupted by the libidinous Christine who had remained aboard for a liaison with a crew hand. She had heard the conversation and confession and alongside Philip, the duo blackmail double-murdering Tom to turn the nonsense into a film screenplay.

Black humour runs through the script enhanced amusingly via the closing song Friends performed by Bette Midler.

Shot on location on the gorgeous French Riviera, La Victorine studios in Nice were also utilized after filming onboard the boat proved problematic. This had been further complicated at the start of the production when the vessel to be used was destroyed by fire.

A one-off project, friends Sondheim and Perkins won the Edgar Allan Poe award for their shared screenplay. Mr Perkins had a further McShane link: see Chillers.

January 2020 saw a 45th anniversary screening of the film attended by Benjamin & Ms Canon but the author is uncertain as to whether Mr McShane attended.

What was certain was that he and charismatic co-star James Coburn were reunited at a pre-Golden Globes party in 1989.

Running from the mid-1960s well into the early-1980s, ITV Playhouse gave Ian several acting jobs including in episode 3 of series 7 in a story called What Would You Do? A comedy-drama, it was shown on Tuesday 19 February 1974 with Ian cast as Derek.

Ransom was a star vehicle for Sean Connery who found the actor as "...the agent who takes on The Terrorists," in a film thriller shot on location in Oslo, Norway, back when Ian was still a heavy drinker (he awoke one morning after a heavy night, with a chipped tooth and a broken arm!) Shepperton Studios in the UK were also utilised. Aka The Terrorists, the former 007 man was presented with the AFI Life Achievement Award in 2006, with Ian there talking about working on location with him, struggling with the cold and compensating by excessive drinking. It seems that they had known each other for a long time.

Written by Paul Wheeler and the final film to be directed by Casper Wrede, its soundtrack was furnished by the prolific Jerry Goldsmith, with Ian joining Sean above the title.

Oddly set in a snowbound, generic "Scandinavia", I love how big Tam never bothered with an accent as Colonel Tahlvik, the prickly Head of Security.

Second-billed, Ian McShane is introduced some 13 minutes in, as a pistol-toting plane hijacker Ray Petrie taking control of a flight from London which has now parked up on the snowy runway. Besuited, he leads a team of 4, part of a group with its other cell led by Barnes (Jeffrey Wickham) holding the British Ambassador and his colleagues hostage elsewhere. As an aside, Ian would narrate a 2003 documentary called Terror in Moscow.

As Petrie, his demands are heard by Tahlvik (Connery). A serious and reticent man, he contacts Scotland Yard for a background check and he most definitely is not quite what he seems. He has been helped by those in authority; his true identity is revealed in an exciting finale.

The countdown begins after an early attempt to get onboard by a commando is thwarted and subsequently, all the demands are met. With the order for the return of their colleagues met, this gives Petrie and his team an intended false sense of security.

A vehicle with hostages is cleverly switched by Connery and his team but the scheme is discovered when Tahlvik goes aboard the plane afterward as "Barnes"; one of the terrorists. Sheppard (John Quentin), one of those responsible for kidnapping the Ambassador earlier, discovers the rouse before Petrie, who had never met his colleague so was unaware of what he looked like. The quick-thinking Connery creates chaos by telling him that Ray is a British police officer. Shepherd is shot dead by him after he reaches for his gun in the confusion. Ian and Sean's characters scuffle and others do likewise as the plane is amidst taking off. The powerful Tahlvik (Connery) knocks his opponent to the ground and goes off to help elsewhere. Groggy, Petrie aims at the unsuspecting Head of Security before a female colleague kills him stone dead by a single shot to the left temple. Connery pistol whips the other gang members and the siege ends with the death of 2 men and the Ambassador saved.

A slow-burner of a film, Ransom might not be the most exciting of films but Connery is fine and McShane acts everybody off the screen with both stars eminently watchable.

A British Lion presentation
A Peter Rawley Production

SEAN CONNERY
RANSOM A
IAN McSHANE

Director:
CASPER WREDE
Producer:
PETER RAWLEY

Written by:
PAUL WHEELER
Music by:
JERRY GOLDSMITH

FROM THURSDAY FEBRUARY 27th
ODEON MARBLE ARCH TELEPHONE: 723 2011

"The AUTHOR who wrote "A Night to Remember"....Eric Ambler...The DIRECTOR who gave you "Butterfield 8"...Daniel Mann...THE CAST, which reads like a "Who's Who" in films...."

1975 was a curious year in which Ian's acting roles saw him feature in the motion picture Journey into Fear, followed by a trio of television guest roles and concluded by an appearance in The Lives of Jenny Dolan, a feature-length telly film. It was also significant for him on a personal level as he relocated to live in the States this year.

Charismatic leading man Sam Wanamaker heads a star-studded cast as Howard Graham; referred to as "Mr Graham" throughout the film, an American engineer/ geologist who spends the movie avoiding being killed by various people. Before the opening credits, he survives two attempts until the noisy Alex North-composed soundtrack announces the film. Writer-producer Trevor Wallace fashioned a screenplay from the original 1940 Ambler novel which had been filmed in 1943 and which featured Orson Welles and saw Jack Moss in the role that Ian took on.

Met in Istanbul by Turkish agent Kopelkin (Zero Mostel), Graham is a fish-out-of-water representing a U.S. oil company keen to develop its interest in the region. Taken to a club by his host, it is here that a rather grubby-looking man in an ill-fitting suit is seen taking a keen interest in the new arrival: that man is Ian McShane. Mr Graham has a comprehensive knowledge of his industry and this makes him a valuable commodity, after all, as Vincent Price later states, "oil is money."

Not once does Ian speak in the film; we learn that he is a disliked Romanian assassin working for Muller (Price on excellent, quietly-menacing form). With his swarthy, unshaven look, the naturally curly-haired actor is equally threatening. Unconcerned with his appearance in unkempt, creased suits that look too small, for some reason Norman Wisdom's gump character sprang to mind upon viewing the film.

Seeking to fly out of Turkey and onto Paris, Graham sees his plans thwarted by the carnage at the airport wreaked by Banak (McShane) whose attempt to kill him results in many deaths.

An entertaining film that moves along at a pace as Wanamaker's anxiety grows; he is advised to travel to France via Italy, in a slower manner: boat.

And it is here that a number of characters are introduced: Yvette (Mimieux Josette); Kuvetli (Donald Pleasance); the Mathews (Shelly Winters & Stanley Holloway) and Dervos (an incognito Mr Price). Graham and Yvette had met in Istanbul with the latter a singer who shares a mutual attraction that is developed whilst onboard. Ian is also on the ship, disguised as a Greek businessman with a glandular problem; something of a running joke in the film. He has the cabin opposite.

Many of the travellers prove not quite what they seem and following a port call in Athens and another murder attempt upon him, Mr Graham (Wanamaker) panics. This is compounded by seeing a grinning Mr McShane back on deck. In a terrible state, he fears for his safety following a major stare-out with Banak before rushing away and like the former, perspiring profusely.

Remembering that Kopelkin had given him a pistol, which he hid under his mattress, upon searching for it again, he discovers that it has been removed. And knowing Banak's true identity, he concedes to Yvette that he is "no man of action". She is equally concerned for him and suggests he break into his room and purloins his gun whilst the assassin is observed playing cards elsewhere. Sneaking into his cabin, he is unable to locate the weapon and returns to his room only to find the formerly convivial Mr Price pointing it at him! Terming him a "man with the proverbial nine lives," Price reveals his true identity and offers the American a deal that he cannot refuse.

Docking in Italy, former ally Kuvetli (Pleasance on great form; he and Ian would reconvene in 1992 for an episode of Lovejoy and both would feature in Jesus of Nazareth) is found dead by the oilman and so it looks as if he will have to go along with the villainous Muller, Banak and other heavies waiting at the quayside.

Led to the waiting vehicle, Graham is not going along passively or not just yet; sandwiched between Mr Price & Mr McShane in the back seat, he manages to create a diversion that allows him to flee. Pursued by little Ian through the backstreets of Genoa, a protracted and taught foot chase ensues.

It concludes with a fatal scuffle in a derelict building with Banak falling through a broken staircase railing and hanging over the edge, with a considerable dropdown. Grappling to get a hold of the gun held by Graham above him, the latter lets him drop and he falls to his death.

A similar fate was later experienced onscreen by Ian in The Pillars of the Earth.

A moment later and Mr Price appears in front of the exhausted American who declares that it is all over. But as Muller, he still wants something more. Graham then shoots him with a flare gun taken from the ship and his other tormentor falls down in agony and drops dead next to Banak. As Graham, Wanamaker casts down his weapon, turns and walks back out of the building.

Journey into Fear is the type of film perfectly suited to watching on the big screen but even at home, it proves a treat.

Possessing one of the best television themes, Ian ventured into a perceived future via a Space: 1999 teleplay from Johnny Byrne; his third for the show, and one he has acknowledged as being pleased with. Shot between May-June 1974 here in the UK at Pinewood studios, his appearance in the Force of Life episode would be one of a handful of small-screen appearances this year, all others via American-made shows.

Here, U.S. stars, then-married couple Martin Landau & Barbara Bain, headlined a sci-fi show where beige outfits with a dash of colour on the arm and a zip-up sleeve were the favoured attire. With a brown sleeve signifying his role as a specialist technician, Anton Zoref (McShane) deals with the after-effects of a nuclear reactor emergency on Moonbase Alpha, a scientific research centre situated on the moon, which results in a profound change in him and danger for others. This includes his partner, Eva, Gay Hamilton, who keen-eyed Lovejoy fans might remember from a 1991 episode.

The first of two series (or seasons as the Americans like to term them but not Ian whenever he has given an interview) had the habit of offering brief highlights of what each episode had on offer during the opening credits and Mr McShane features prominently as a guest star.

Zoref is deeply affected by the event and soon starts to change; at first feeling cold, short-tempered and rather peculiar but then much worse. Life on the sanitised, "quasi-military base", as scriptwriter Christopher Penfold termed it, runs smoothly until an aggressive alien force enters and begins to absorb power via Zoref and we ponder: just what is the new energy source doing to him?

When he is inadvertently responsible for the death of a colleague, who freezes to death, he has become possessed by an alien force and this is a cue for the actor to do lots of Munch's The Scream poses in a show primarily aimed at younger audiences. Annuals, paperbacks, toys and more were produced whilst today the show has attained understandable cult status.

A failed attempt to explain how he feels sees him become a security risk to all on Alpha. A worried Commander Koenig seeks to contain the danger posed to anyone that comes into contact with Zoref (McShane) after fatalities occur. He roams the anonymous corridors whilst crew members run away and it proves amusing to see how he simply walks on, perspiring heavily and having coloured lights shone across his face.

Escaping from the shackles of the lovely Dr Russell's monitoring, he throttles a co-worker before Eva (Miss Hamilton) finds him. In a show which is beautifully lit, Eva naturally wants to help him but as Zoref motions toward her, he is pulled away and during the melee, he simply walks off.

About to reach out to the Commander, he is fatally zapped by a colleague and completely, shockingly fried. Possibly not now played by the actor, a blackened corpse returns to the Anti-Radiation room, opens a huge vault-like chamber which causes a major explosion. Fortunately for those on Alpha, it is contained and the crew watch as a little blue light is seen moving off into the sky, whilst Doc Russell ponders why they had been chosen to be visited.

Look out for another future Lovejoy actor, the late Zienia Merton, a Space cast member seen in the control room as the crew begin tracing the whereabouts of the perilous Anton.

Co-created by Gerry & Sylvia Anderson, Space: 1999 had commenced production back in November 1973 this cult classic, sci-fi gem ran for a gargantuan 48 episodes. Ian's episode originally aired on Thursday 11 September 1975.

Matt Helm was a U.S. television adaptation of a character once played by Dean Martin on the cinema screen in a succession of 1960s films. Coincidentally, McShane would later lend his velvet tones to a BBC Omnibus tribute to him in 1999.

The small screen version premiered in the 8:30 pm slot with Tony Franciosa in the lead as the agent at work eliminating spies, enemy ops and more.

Helm had been a popular character in numerous books written by Donald Hamilton, previously.

Running for the solitary season, Ian guest-starred as Paul in episode 2; Now I Lay Me Down to Die, which aired on Saturday 27 September this year. Earl Bellamy directed the story. Another 11 episodes followed, like Most Wanted, Matt Helm was another zippy show with appealing opening credits and a theme by Morten Stevens (who also composed the Police Woman theme).

Matt is a slightly-older investigator assisted by lover and colleague Kronski (Laraine Stephens) and aided by useful police connection Hanrahan (Gene Evans). Asked by his philanthropist friend Chris (Shelley Fabares) to investigate the murder of a close associate, with no leads and a loud, funky soundtrack, husband Paul (Ian McShane) seems contemptible towards his wife, waiting for her inheritance to mature so that he can plough cash into a business and wipe out his already-heavy debt. Cohort, Frank (Burr DeBenning) attempts to run Helm's car off the road and this leads the investigator to suspect Paul's involvement; after all, who else knew about it? What peculiar minds the writers Gerry Day and Bethel Lessie had in creating this storyline which requires that the viewer suspends their disbelief long enough to accept that friends and colleagues of Chris fail to recognise her in only a Harpo Marx-styled curly wig as shapely alter ego 'Tina'. And also, if the murder victim slept with 'Tina' wouldn't he recognise his dear daughter-figure?

Even the seasoned detective is confused after discovering Chris as 'Tina' after her attempt to bludgeon him to death is thwarted by the unexpected arrival of Frank. He knocks Helm unconscious and by the time he awakens, both have fled. It seems that Chris has more than a migraine to cope with.

Returning with her, Paul sees that his wife is hysterical and that she is going to spend some time recuperating in a sanatorium. She then re-emerges as 'Tina'; feisty and controlling and ordering them to eliminate Matt Helm permanently, as he is a threat to her receiving her inheritance windfall. In the dual role, singer/actor Miss Fabares proves convincing as McShane is a crook, conning others and with a dubious moral compass.

After surviving Frank's botched attempt to shoot him, Mr Helm arrives at the charity fundraiser at Chris & Paul's luxury home. He and Kronski mingle, observed by Frank & Paul, resplendent in their cowboy shirt attire at the Western-themed event (Ian being a big cowboy and western fan). The henchman is ordered to be certain to kill Helm the next time.

Snooping around for evidence or clues appertaining to Tina, Helm moves into a nearby stable. Here he is confronted by the conniving, pistol-totting duo but in the semi-darkness, Frank accidentally shoots his buddy in the leg. Meanwhile outside Tina stacks hay around the exit and ignites it.

After Paul (McShane) is disabled by the gunshot, Helm and Frank engage in a shoot-out. The latter is finally subdued and Helm draws his gun on Paul after he has narrowly been missed by a pitchfork! Paul stops after spotting the fire from outside. Fortunately for all concerned, Miss Stephens, as Kronski, rescues them whilst Matt pulls out 'Tina' after she is struck by one of her horses corralled there.

They say that a police officer is never off duty and that is the case for the attractive Suzanne 'Pepper' Anderson (the delightful Angie Dickinson) in Police Woman. About to set off on a much-needed vacation, she intervenes in a bag snatch and ends up in hospital after being hit by a truck as a result.

Here, the so-called, good Samaritan Helen (Hollywood veteran Ida Lupino in one of her final acting roles) manipulates her into making a bogus insurance claim and is oblivious to her law enforcement status. Miss Anderson plays along and informs her colleagues including Bill Crowley (Earl Holliman) who begin an investigation.

Acknowledged by a "Special Guest Star" title, Ian is Dan Markson, terming himself an "engineer" rather than Attorney who works alongside Helen and permanently-sloshed Lawyer Calhoun (Edwards Andrews). They are money-grabbing fraudsters or "Ambulance Chasers"; a practice of faking a car crash or personal injury case to extort money. Pepper visits Markson and convinces him to take her on as a new employee, exploiting his obvious attraction to her. He engages her and alongside Helen (Ms Lupino) shows her how they do things and concedes that their approach is far from legitimate.

A slightly different-looking McShane is on view here, wearing his hair styled a little away from usual and not complemented by bad 1970s tailoring. We see him in the pre-opening credits montage which reveals all the best bits from the coming storyline. Episode 5 of the second season, The Chasers was written by Irvine Turnick and was one of 13 directed by Barry Shear. Miss Dickinson acted in a total of 90 storylines and proved so popular that there was even a Barbie doll-type figure of her to collect! Morton Stevens provided the now-classic 70s theme to add to his collection (Hawaii Five-O was another from the man who later composed the music to Ian's Code Name: Diamond Head TV pilot).

Employing crooked garage man Hawkins (John Smith in one of his final acting roles) to fake crashes, outside a hospital that Pepper had been recuperating in, a security guard recognises her. However, he innocently reveals knowing her from police training to a startled Helen. With her identity blown, Helen & Markson and his gang decided not to reveal this and along with Hawkins, they overload a decoy car to be used in a fake collision with 'gas' and plan to get rid of both her and a troublesome colleague.

Snooping in the office filing cabinet, Pepper is interrupted by a still stoned Calhoun who casually advises her to leave after also telling her that they know she is a cop. Ian arrives and forces her into the car.

Pepper demands Hamilton (Paul Benjamin) to pull over but he is having none of it and is subsequently killed in an explosion alongside 2 drunkens to have been used in the crash. With the police closing in, a dejected Calhoun kills himself at the office before Officer Anderson is rescued from a burning apartment ignited by a callous Hawkins. Following Helen's arrest and confession, a disbelieving Markson is arrested whilst at a restaurant with a powerful Senator and that marks the end of his involvement.

The year proved to be an active one for the actor, with 4 appearances and a film role secured.The Lives of Jenny Dolan was an American TV pilot that failed to be picked up by NBC. A vehicle for the rather attractive Shirley Jones (the mom from The Partridge Family), who stars as a recently-married newspaper reporter returning to work after her old boss Joe (Stephen Boyd) persuades her to investigate a complex conspiracy story. When a politician is murdered at a sporting event, she will later discover that this is no crackpot lone killer but part of something larger created by an organisation called The Group; a power centre of men who want a new world order and will kill to establish it.

A young-looking Ian is the mysterious 'Fourth Man' seemingly culpable for several associated deaths (including the trio seen with him when planning the murder). It will later be revealed that he sent the paper a graphic clue showing a link between several men which leads to Ms. Dolan delving into things whilst putting her and others at risk by doing so.

After raising more questions than answers following an initial investigation, Jenny's husband is killed and she is convinced that the shadowy organisation is responsible. Her fear heightens but she continues to seek out the truth despite others disinclined to believe what she subsequently digs up.

An audio recording of the gathering of 4 men who persuaded another to kill the politician is replayed in a flashback sequence, with a youthful-looking Ian McShane only shown in silhouette at this stage (but we recognise that voice). When he does reveal himself in one of his few scenes, wearing a suit with a white shirt and thick glasses that he constantly takes off and puts on again, as Saunders he presents a quiet, brooding malevolence.

Pumping up the hysteria, Dolan (Ms Jones) realizes that nowhere is safe including a local police station.

Returning to the plush apartment block she had earlier visited,

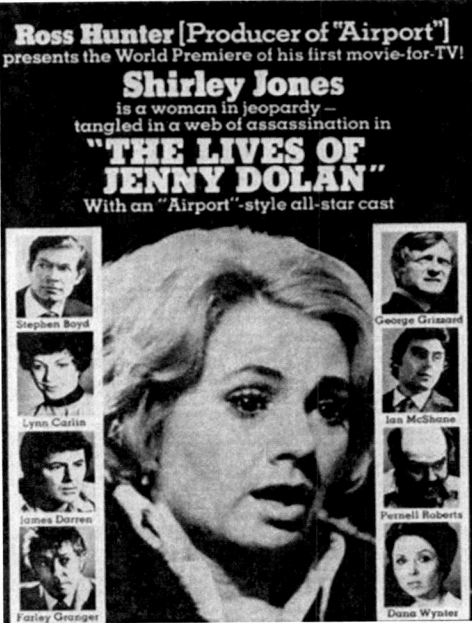

Jenny is accompanied by a gun-wielding Professor Saunders (Ian McShane) anticipating the return of another man who will eliminate him (no one is indispensable in the organization, it seems). Taking her to the home of a woman recently widowed, she is shocked to return to discover him dead on the floor below the high-level apartment. A pursuit ensues.

Miss Jones looks terrific in various outfits and conveys fear well as those around her start to drop and the ending proves quite dramatic too. A curious piece, dimly lit at times, its soundtrack from Pat Williams (who provided the same on Most Wanted; another series within which Ian appeared) is memorable in enhancing the intricate storyline created by Richard Alan Simmons and dramatised by Roots writer James Lee. Filmed in just 16 days, it aired on Monday 27 October, at 9 pm.

It seems that As you Like It was performed for one night only on Sunday 1 August 1976, at the not-for-profit community arts venue Center Theatre, Long Island, Los Angeles. One of the final productions directed by Tony Richardson, beloved for his kitchen sink classics such as A Taste of Honey, to read more about the star of that film, Rita Tushingham, see the reference section of this book. It featured cast members, Stockard Channing and Bruce Davison, with Ian in the role of "the melancholy Jacques".

Most Wanted was Ian's only premiered television work shown this year. A "Quinn Martin Production", it starred a pistol-wielding Robert Stack and featured great, dynamic opening credits. Mr McShane was in a story called The Slaver which aired on ABC for an hour on Saturday 23 October 1976. This particular episode was directed by Virgil W. Vogel who also steered most of the others and already had a long association with the Quinn Martin brand on American television. In total, 23 episodes were made, with Ian's appearance in episode three as Colin Wyatt.

A huge publishing event and creating the same amount of interest when it was made into a 1977 television series, Roots was adapted from the Alex Haley novel telling his family story through American slavery and beyond. Its 21 hours running time meant that it was divided up into 2-hour chunks and Ian's appearance differs depending upon whether you watched it in America or the UK. David L. Wolper was the Executive Producer.

McShane joined a stellar cast alongside George Hamilton and Chuck Connors as the wretched Tom, all involved in the horrid, so-called sport of cockfighting. After jumping through to 1841, Ian makes a spectacular entrance as a fellow "game cocker" and gentleman, Sir Eric Russell. An Englishman dressed as garishly as anything that the actor would wear in Disraeli, he is outfitted in a long pink suit with tails, all set off by a large felt top hat. Finding mixing with the rough male crowd at the fight most unappetising, the men there find his refined ways hilarious. John Dennis Johnston, who seems to have acted in every 1970s TV series, laughs, "Let him speak. I love the way he talks!"

In a thankfully brief but still unpleasant scene, Sir Eric's bird is pitted against Moore's "A speck of red", trained by his devoted slave Chicken George (Ben Vereen who can also be seen in A.D.). Offered his freedom if Red wins, Moore accepts a huge wager with the visiting "Britisher" but his bird is killed.

A curly-haired Ian is seen in one more scene; speaking with Tom about repaying the debt. Unable to pay, he begrudgingly accepts allowing Sir Eric to have George and the latter is obliged to leave his family and travel to England with his new master.

What a gorgeously diverse year '77 proved itself to be for Mr McShane. If American TV required an actor to play a Brit abroad then it seemed that Ian was the go-to man.

Work-wise, an episode of the aforementioned classic Roots gave way for a peculiar role in The Fantastic Journey. Another project lasting for only a solitary season, he pops up in the pilot episode as a "rough-and-ready" Englishman some 300 years out of time and stuck on an island near the Bermuda Triangle. Written by a trio of writers with a lot of TV work on their CVs & directed by the vastly experienced Andrew V. McLaglen, Ian acted in the opening entry "Vortex" and the episode aired on Thursday 3 February.

A team of marine biologists led by Professor Jordan (Scott Thomas) with his son Scott (popular 1970s child actor Ike Eisenmann), Jill (Karen Somerville), Eve (Susan Howard), Carl Franklin and two other men intend to spend the summer on one of the Bermudan islands until a peculiar blue sphere in the ocean maroons them on an island where the past, present and future co-exists, as do several groups. Varian (Jared Martin) is keen to avoid tangling with the "Privateers"; an earthy bunch of Brits led by the handsome Sir James Camden (Ian).

However, Jill and a couple of the others are captured by Paget (Don Knight, an actor soon to be seen again with Ian in Codename: Diamond Head), a face amongst the dastardly blaggards and after more than a decade of not seeing a "fair-skinned woman", they are not keen to share their spoils with Sir James. Looking stylish in knee-length boots, brown suede sleeveless jacket, lemon yellow shirt and a thick belt with the requisite dagger, he and Paget will fight for her.

Swords drawn, as Camden, Ian strikes the fatal blow and re-establishes his control. He also takes an immediate shine to Jill, understandably so, as she is rather shapely. Camden still believes that his beloved Elizabeth is on the throne and that England is at war with Spain. A cave full of purloined treasure fails to satisfy his craving to escape the "cursed island". He cannot grasp the fact that Jill and the others did not arrive by ship and so the distressed young woman blurts out that it is 1976. "I have been patient. I have shown you hospitality. I have shown you courtesy and you repay me with lies and trickery," gasps the disbelieving Englishman.

Varian and the others instigate their rescue plan whilst Jill is put in front of a fire, to be burnt at the stake at the bequest of Sir James! And that is the last we see of Ian in the episode.

The premise of The Fantastic Journey was an intriguing one, with a total of 10 episodes made of this interesting show which is still remembered fondly.

Running for a little over 6 hours and shown in 4 parts via NBC in America and ITV in the UK, the epic mini-series Jesus of Nazareth from Franco Zeffirelli caused controversy before its screening to those that had not even viewed it. With an unforgettable Robert Powell, mesmerising as Jesus, his seminal role began on UK television on Sunday 3 April 1977 and ran for consecutive weekends in 2 x 2-hour slots. A huge TV event in its day, Jesus of Nazareth was in development for 3 years before making it to the small screen and it is peopled with a Who's Who of acting talents including James Mason, Laurence Olivier, Michael York, Rod Steiger, Peter Ustinov and many others. A bearded Ian portrayed Judas Iscariot, a scholar acknowledged as one of the 12 disciples who comes into the story on the hour following the killing of John the Baptist (York). Whilst others around him seek revenge by marching on Jerusalem and overthrowing King Herod, both he and another reject force in favour of peaceful methods to allow Jesus to speak his truth.

Violence does follow whilst Judas joins Jesus and speaks with Zerah (Ian Holm) who is a part of Sanhedrin; the supreme council of the Jews. Earnestly proclaiming him King of the Jews, the latter is sceptical. Regarding Judas, we all have our opinions; accurate or not but the moment that Jesus is arrested by Sanhedrin guards, is ambiguous, "This is your hour, Judas," begins a tearful Jesus, "The hour of shadows."

As Judas, Ian kisses him, "Oh master."

"You betray your master with a kiss." He concludes as Judas gives a shake of the head.

Distraught by the resulting confusion and cries of betrayal, Iscariot rushes to the temple and demands that he is there to hear Jesus speak. A confused Zerah informs him that his master is on trial for blasphemy and not to preach his gospel. And in his last moment on screen, Judas is given a pouch of money with the indication that he has performed well.

In a 1992 documentary Jesus Christ, Movie Star, narrated by Ian and shown in the UK on Channel 4, it was revealed that Mr Powell auditioned for Judas before being cast in the lead.

A Month in the Country was a BBC TV movie helmed by experienced director Quentin Lawrence and with a screenplay by Derek Marlowe, which was an adaptation of an Ivan Turgenev play and produced by Journey into Fear man Trevor Wallace. Country was a project originally devised in 5 acts and published in 1850. Considered one of the major works in Russian literature, it is not to be confused with the JL Carr book of the same name. Susannah York led the cast as Natalia, with Ian as Alexey Beliayev, tutor to young Kolya, son of Islayev & Natalya.

Lots of people had acted in versions of the play including Ian McKellen in the same role as Ian but back in 1959 and Martin Jarvis followed in 1965. Here, the cast also included Linda Thorson and Brian Wilde.

"One man stands between the release of a deadly gas….and the fate of the world."

That was the tantalising by-line for the latest Quinn Martin production; Code Name: Diamond Head. Also an Executive Producer, Martin's unsold pilot never made it into a series. Known for his small-screen successes including The Fugitive, The Untouchables & The Streets of San Francisco, Code did receive a VHS release on the Good Times Home Video label and features illustrated likeness of its cast, including Ian, on its box. Directed by Jeannot Szwarc, an experienced TV director at the time, it starred the charisma-free Roy Thinnes as Johnny Paul, a reluctant spy in a story written by past Academy Award nominee Paul King.

Arriving in Honolulu disguised as a vicar with a cigarette holder ala Audrey Hepburn, there is a quite nasty start with a bespectacled Ian and his men capturing the officer tailing them and seeing Ian push him to his death down a bell tower.

The aggressive delivery of dialogue by Ward Costello as Johnny's boss "Aunt Mary" sees him show him a photograph of Sean Donovan (Ian), "A British agent. One of the best," he begins, "Until he went freelance. And sold out his whole network: 28 agents...he has a new identity with Codename "Tree" and has re-emerged. He likes ladies and he likes gambling..." Diamond Head aka Johnny, is tasked with finding out why he is around, assisted or hindered by singing partner Zulu. Impersonating a Navy Colonel, ala Too Scared to Scream later; we see him applying make-up, a grey wig and fake 'tache in a naval uniform and hefty peaked cap. Substituted for the real one, also Ian, he visits a waterside base where the military has an experimental lab below sea level, where boffins are developing a deadly gas that could prove lethal in hands of wrongdoers.

It is always fun to see what fashions Ian is dressed in and Code proves itself to be an especially rich source. Back in town, Donovan is seen playing cards at an establishment run by Tso-Tsing (France Nuyen), lover of Paul (Thinnes) who has her own secret past. He looks smartly casual in an open shirt with long collars and an oversized cravat. As Donovan, Ian's screen persona is an expert and knows that he is being followed and it is whilst he is incognito that he comes across Diamond Head at the gaming table.

Making a return visit to the base as the Colonel, he subdues the military people in the lab and pinches the precious formula before fleeing and meeting up again with his cohorts.

Later calling unannounced at Tso-Tsing's home, he forces her away by drawing a pistol on her. The villain compels her to her large trimaran boat and is ordered to take him and his colleagues away. Having been captured, Donovan casually gives orders to kill Jonny's side-kick Zulu and thus hide any evidence. Fortunately for the former, Diamond rescues him and they set out to halt the escape. After watching the episode it is easy to see why the format failed to be picked up as a series; Ian puts in his usual convincing performance but it all seems a bit formulaic.

Mr McShane's next two television roles this year were based upon actual people: Shakespeare and Disraeli.

Just who was William Shakespeare? Some believe that he never existed or that the plays were created by a stream of people. Who knows? John Mortimer expands upon his early life in the London of 1590 onwards via this six-part ITV series which was made by ATV and RAI. They had recently collaborated on Jesus of Nazareth in the previous year.

Filling the 9 pm slot, Will Shakespeare or Life of Shakespeare or William Shakespeare: His Life & Times commenced its run on Tuesday 13 June. Second billed as playwright Christopher Marlowe; our Mr McShane features in its opening episode only: Dead Shepherd. The dialogue is overwrought and it takes time to acclimate but is exuberantly delivered by the cast in a modestly-budgeted production.

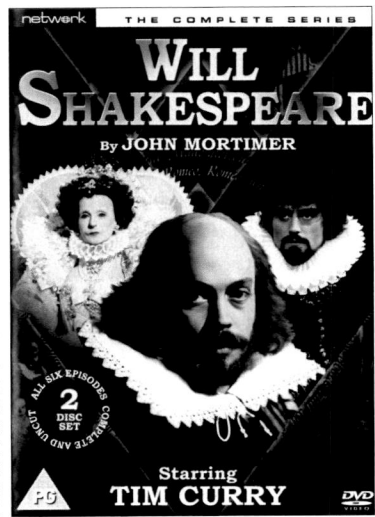

Marlowe is presenting a play at the Rose theatre in the round when cheery, aspiring actor/ author Will Shakespeare (Tim Curry) arrives. Keen to make a success of himself and confident in his ability to be able to provide something more challenging than the norm, he irks the established Kit (Ian) with his "blow-up bladder of conceit". Seen enjoying a bit of horseplay with swords, Marlowe is portrayed by a bearded Ian McShane, elegantly dressed in the high fashions of the day, the Elizabethan era of shirts set off by ruffs: a pronounced frill around the neck of the shirt which could also be worn around the wrists.

He imbibes many a tankard of "firewater" and regularly enjoys the company of friends and those of the Establishment. But as Will discovers, he is a man unhappy with the restrictions prevalent in modern theatre. Backstage a drunken Marlowe is astonished to hear Will proclaim that he could offer much better work than the play being performed. The latter is ignorant of the fact that it is Marlowe's piece!

Despite this rather clumsy introduction, he calls upon young Shakespeare, an ebullient Mr Curry, to help him complete another work. The results prove startling and Marlowe is impressed with the newcomer and the work proves a success in front of an audience.

Religion rears its ugly head via the battle betwixt the Catholic church and Privy Council, with Marlowe somewhere in the middle and being asked to spy for the latter.

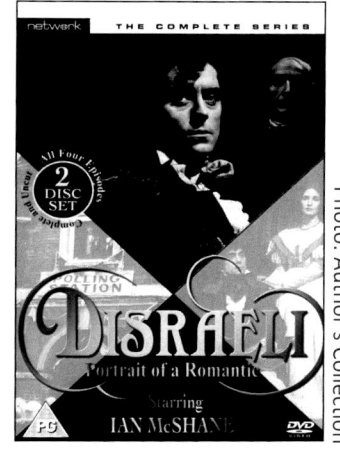

A great scene, which must have proven tricky to shoot, sees maestro theatre director Peter Wood cleverly use mirrors whilst the actors speak the dialogue. As Marlowe, Ian holds court and he and Will speak of religion and theatre whilst the devoted Ingram Frizer, the Earl of Southampton, tends to his bathing lover. Preparing for his fluffy, curled hair look, Marlowe readies himself for dressing; all the while Shakespeare speaks up, growing in confidence at the power of his plays.

Out dining with Privy Council associates, Marlowe is unable to pay the bill before Frizer humbly offers to do it on his behalf. He will have none of it, cruelly saying, "The world is divided into the payers and the paid for. Step not out of the role written for you. When lambs eat with wolves; that is when Ingram Frizer shall buy my supper!" A scuffle ensues with the actor/ writer holding onto a food knife before falling dead from a balcony onto the ground below. The real Marlowe died under similar circumstances.

"I felt overtaken...in a way, it was a very concentrated job and I was totally involved in doing it. It was challenging and enjoyable and I found myself looking forward to every day on set." That was Ian discussing his role as the dignified and determined British politician Benjamin Disraeli in the four-part TV series Disraeli: Portrait of a Romantic. Broadcast in the UK commencing Tuesday 5 September when TV Times magazine cost 13p. Ian proved most adept at portraying a multi-talented individual, who possessed a dogged desire to serve the people "Dizzy" as friends knew him, became one of the country's most respected politicians.

However, he was not the first to play him, as George Arliss had won an Academy Award back in 1930 for his portrayal.

"A genius, part dandy and part actor," observes his new friend Count D'Orsay, as played by Leigh Lawson, who had a child with Ian's Sky West & Crooked co-star Hayley Mills. Scholar David Butler's script is full of elongated sentences which help demonstrate Disraeli's mastering of the English language. He was a clever man, able to use his connections well and advance up the greasy pole of politics, as he once termed it.

We watch as Ben networks amongst influential people in society but was looked down upon by some for his Jewish heritage. He also freely flatters fawning female fans who adored his romantic novels (although he aspired for more and was forever in debt).

Disraeli follows the man over many years and the actor wore several hairpieces to reflect this. However, his initial appearance sees Mr McShane sporting a hefty mop of hair, displaying a killer curl ala Bill Hayley! Whilst in later times he resembles one of The Lollipop Kids from The Wizard of Oz.

Infamous for his outrageous outfits, the author had to stifle a few giggles upon seeing our Mr McShane extraordinarily dressed in velvet outfits of suits of yellow and greens and other times with a hefty, felt top hat that has to be seen to be enjoyed (think Brunel or Peel & you will have the classic Victorian look but minus Disraeli's abundance of colour).

He falls for Henrietta (Madlena Nedeva) an unhappily married woman whose husband is having an affair with his former lover (Rachel Bell) but when the relationship becomes public, the couple is castigated for it. Forever in debt and suffering with a sense of 'vaulting ambition' simmering barely beneath the surface, he is keen to step into politics but it takes five attempts to win a seat, thanks partly to Wyndham (Will Russell) & Mary Anne (Mary Peach).

Many political and private trials and tribulations follow, with Disraeli stepping into Chancellor of the Exchequer and the Prime Ministerial shoes on 2 occasions, after being advised to tone down his "fancy way of dressing" by ally and friend, Lord Bentinck (Anton Rodgers). A number of his touching relationships are covered, including with his father, portrayed by Aubrey Morris and with Queen Victoria (a fittingly regal Rosemary Leach). Particularly meaningful in his life was Mary Anne, whom Disraeli spent many years married to following the death of her husband. Her support of him proved unwavering.

After a stodgy start, the series proves a captivating watch and is well-worth seeking out. An ATV Network production shot at Elstree Studios and on location, a couple of Futura tie-in paperbacks were released, authored by David Butler, and each showing Ian on its cover in the role of Mr Disraeli. In North America, PBS screened the series commencing in August 1980, with Mr McShane there to promote the work. Incidentally, all episodes were directed by Claude Whatham, Ian had worked with him back in 1962 on an ITV Play of the Week.

Remaining in 1978 CBS America presented their 4 hour TV adaptation of the Harold Robbins novel The Pirate with future John Wick 2 cast member Franco Nero as Nadyr, the man in question. "In a world of money, beautiful women and power....Nero rules an Arab empire...." proclaimed the TV spot, promoting it across Tuesday & Wednesday 21-22 November.

Adapted by Julius J. Epstein one of the writers that created Casablanca, it was directed by Kenneth Anakin. He soon worked with Ian again on big screen outings The Fifth Musketeer & Cheaper to Keep Her.

As Rashid, McShane has his name included on the opening credits. He can be seen in scenes with Mr Nero, Michael Constantine (who died in 2021 and appears in If It's Tuesday, It Must Be Belgium) and Anne Archer, who would later act alongside him in the 1984 silliness Too Scared to Scream. Armand Assante from 1985's Evergreen series also appears.

Looking very 1970s in a suit jacket with shirt, no tie, and wide collar, back in the office he adds a tie. Working for Baydr (Nero) he is seen aboard his private jet arriving in Nice and the first thing we are struck by is his heavy mop of hair.

Adopting a foreign accent, his eyelids are darkened to give a more exotic look whilst his hair is definitely a precursor to Lovejoy's!

Naturally in a Harold Robbins piece, there is lots of sex. A blockbuster author with his trashy books translated into many languages, he was also a master at selling himself and his work. A few years before the small screen transfer, in a UK TV interview, he defined The Pirate as "...a story of a modern-day Arab: the Arab emerging into our society..." He died in 1997.

"For a cool $15 million, they tunnelled in the Sewers of Gold".

Alternate opening titles were filmed for this big-screen outing for Ian who had his name above the title despite acting alongside a pedigree cast that included Warren Clarke as the leader of a right-wing group seeking to combat the rise of the "Reds" across Europe. The political aspects of the film are barely mentionable apart from a subtle glimpse of a swastika flag and Hitler portrait seen in Bert's hillside hideaway.

Not to be confused with the 1979 French-language film Les égouts du Paradis, both films took Albert Spaggiari's book as their source. He claimed to be Bert 'The Brain', the part Ian took on, and the main figure behind what was then the biggest robbery in the world. McShane was in his late-30s when Sewers was released (it is also known as Dirty Money & The Great Riviera Bank Robbery. Reuniting with screenwriters Francis Megahy & Bernie Cooper, whom he worked with back at the start of the decade on Freelance, many of the same crew members also contributed. Megahy also directed and would later collaborate with the actor on a handful of Lovejoy episodes. Francis died in 2020 and Mr Cooper in the following year.

Rewatching, the author assumes that Sexy Beast writers Louis Mellis and David Scinto would likely have seen the film.

Arriving at a civic building via the backseat of an unmarked police vehicle, we see Bert (McShane) smoking a stogy before revealing that he is handcuffed to an officer to see his brief. A photographer and former soldier, once inside the building he manages to flee and get speeded away on the back of an awaiting motorcycle. This is when Ian's voice over tells the story of originally joining Jean (Clarke) after saving him from a major kicking from two men, and mentioning that he lost his liberty for being involved with the group.

In the Dick Francis trilogy of TV films broadcast in 1989, we find Ian sporting a pleated cloth cap and here wears a suede one.

Bert mentions the idea of robbing a safe deposit room to Jean but the leader isn't initially keen as it will mean working with a criminal team.

Both actors are well-dressed and equally well-spoken men and as actors, they would reconvene for a memorable 1991 episode of the delightful Lovejoy.

Joined by Serge (Christopher Malcolm), the break-in is to be meticulously planned and involve lots of logistics, uniquely, they will enter the building via the sewerage system running around Nice (where the film is set and the actual events occurred). Career crims Stephen Grief (Rocco), Eric Mason and others join them in an uneasy alliance for an arduous job involving working in sweaty confined places across the next 2 months. "Better get used to it, John," offers Brain (Ian), "from the shit to the stars!"

A well-orchestrated heist movie with a good soundtrack, some of the fashions look dated, particularly Ian when we see him wearing a suit with an open shirt ala Pacino in Scarface.

One Friday night, after chiselling away, they eventually reach their point of entry: to their collective relief. Once inside they begin prising open as many of the 4000 boxes as is possible within the weekend. After discovering compromising photos, money, jewellery and gold bars, Bert issues a stern order to leave with only 317 boxes opened. There is a great shot of the actor seen through the burnt-out middle of a safe. Exhausted, the small team begin to leave but not before Bert daubs onto a cabinet "Without Violence. Without Arms. Without Hatred." This puzzles Serge who had heard him talk about "smashing" opponents!

The robbery may have been a success but the hard work continues for the shattered team, being obliged to count all the banknotes and divide them between the activists and the other for the criminal team. This takes almost 3 days and Ian's voice-over mentions that the bank finally realised that the vault door had been welded shut from inside, on the following Monday.

And now to dispose of gold bars. This proves to be the downfall for Bert after the extensive media coverage sees one criminal interviewed by police and disclose that he had met The Brain in Marseilles, where he had been keen to dispose of the bullion to any interested party.

The police start to investigate and swiftly arrest Rocco and his boys whilst elsewhere; the determined Bert shows his stash of automatic weapons, grenades and more to Jean (Clark).

Subsequently nabbed by the police, Bert tells the detectives what he wants from discussing the case and his involvement. It is whilst doing this that the film returns to the start where we see him jump from the high window before climbing onto a motorcycle and speeding off.

Amusingly we see shots of Ian clinging on to the visored Serge driving at high speeds along the streets and coast roads. A similar hair-raising experience would also come for the actor in Cheaper to Keep Her.

Sewers closes with the caption: "'The Brain' is believed to be alive and well and living among friends in South America."

The Fifth Musketeer aka Behind the Iron Mask was another of those atypical 1970s films combing established names with emerging stars, the screenplay from the talented Daniel Ambrose (after an early start by George Bruce) was photographed by esteemed cinematographer Jack Cardiff. Directed by Ken Annakin, in quite a gear change, he worked with Ian again immediately after. Annakin enjoyed a long and eclectic career and died in 2009. Originating from an Alexandre Dumas novel, its soundtrack by Riz Ortolani was to be released to accompany the film but somehow failed to be and only surfaced in recent years.

"Pure adventure is back...for the fun of it!" shrieked the tag line on its cinema poster and the film also got a subsequent VHS release on several different labels including Guild Home Video. Containing some gratuitous nudity from its principal female stars Ursula Andress and Sylvia Kristel, an uncut version of the movie is also available but at a high selling price.

Miss Kristel was already on her way to cementing her name in the film business with the saucy Emmanuelle franchise and she and Ian began a relationship whilst on location.

Perhaps she was swayed by the sight of him in a heavy wig and knee-length boots; along with most of the cast, he looks dashing when handsomely outfitted in dandy fashions.

Early on, we see him in what can only be described as a frilly neck carpet-styled jacket! The Dutch actress died in 2012.

The familiar story takes place in a dangerous time with conspiracy, double-crossing and power struggles ongoing. As the petulant King Louis XIV, unpopular King of France, this offered the first of two roles for Beau Bridges. The lesser-talented of the Bridges boys, his father, Lloyd, plays one of the infamous Musketeers, now long-in-the-tooth, with some relaxed acting from screen stalwarts Cornel Wilde, Jose Ferrer & Alan Hale Jnr. As a group, they raise and train Philippe, again Beau Bridges, the sibling separated at birth with the king not-yet-knowing this fact.

King Beau is a horror whilst the other is a decent sort but indignant at not being able to access his legitimate right to the throne. As the conniving Fouquet, Ian is involved in the struggle to keep Louis in power and uses anyone that will help sustain this, including Philippe, who will be substituted for the King and conveniently assassinated. This will enable the established King to miraculously return and show the people his divinity. As 'Louis', Philippe survives the attempt and is egged on by mediator Rex Harrison, his Musketeer guardians train him in swordsmanship. However, they get captured and sent to the notorious Bastille.

The King is no fool, "stop trying to look innocent. You haven't got the face for it," he remarks curtly to Fouquet early on. The latter seems to be a personal secretary and man with some authority beneath the King. We know he is a baddie due to the accompanying music when he comes on screen (if this were a silent feature children would boo him). We first see him in an oversized feather-trimmed hat and holding a cane with a silver tip, satisfied with the sculpting skills of an ironsmith moulding a crude iron mask for the fake monarch.

The nasty Louis is nothing like his stranger brother and a confused Ms Kristel, as Princess Marie Theresa of Spanish, is set to be joined in an arranged marriage but she is greeted at the quayside by the kind sibling initially and is perplexed when the other returns and proves aloof, behaving like a clod towards her.

Only marrying to sustain power and influence between the countries and for her dowry, Louis' real interest is Louise (Miss Andress). The horrid monarch is furious to hear that the fake one has survived and to discover that he freed all those imprisoned whilst briefly in 'power'; including the dreaded Musketeers! The latter awaits the heavy-browed Fouquet at his home and in character Ian tells them to take the impostor and leave. There is a history between them and he is not to be trusted at any cost so they tie him up and subsequently flee.

Subsequently, Philippe falls in love with Marie, the dreaded Fouquet tortures the benevolent Colbert and eventually, a switch is made on the wedding day of Marie and the French king: but who is it she marries?

Before this finale, more sword-fighting occurs including seeing Mr McShane battling whilst the warring brothers also clash in an outstanding scene of skilled swordsmanship resulting in the fatal slaying of Fouquet.

Sports-themed Yesterday's Hero (1979) opens with Ian McShane playing football at Maidenhead United's York Road ground in the cold and on a muddy pitch as Paul Nicholas (also in this as pop singer/ producer Clint Simon) chirps the title song. Caked in mud, it gets so bad that at one point you can barely tell that he is wearing blue and white stripes; oddly though, when the final whistle blows it's not so mucky!

As former golden boy Rod Turner, McShane is in a struggling side playing for Windsor United FC. Chatting with manager Mac (Mathew Long) on the coach back, they discuss pop star Simon's recent purchase of Third Division side "Saints" and their advancement in the F.A. Cup.

Back at his drab bedsit, echoes of his illustrious playing past are strewn around the place via photos and cuttings. But nowadays Turner is a boozer and goes on another of his regular benders until the coming day his sometime girlfriend Susan (Glynis Barber) arrives to find him in bed fully clothed and hung-over. This is a man who seems to spend his life in this state. It's a thankless role for the Dempsey & Makepeace actress and something she reflected upon on Twitter "One of my first ever roles….starring Ian McShane…and written by Jackie Collins. And it wasn't even saucy! Jackie went serious for this one."

He rushes off to the Ivy Leaf social club where his father Sam (the ubiquitous Sam Kydd) drinks and plays dominoes with his pals. Mac comes in and informs Roy that he has been sacked: a perennial occupational hazard for managers.

Always short of cash, he often asks his boss for a sub or to have his drinks bought for his dad and his cronies put on his tab.

Off to a boys' home, Roy regularly gathers the lads to take them to play football on the local pitches and seems to have been befriended by one lad in particular, Marek (Paul Medford).

Returning to the crummy flat he finds Susan there looking through his old photos. She wants him to move in with her but he's not interested. A few years younger than him, Ian was 37 in 1979, she leaves him to it and he lingers looking at the pictures and of one in particular of lost love Cloudy (American sitcom star Suzanne Somers). We cut to her grooving on stage with Clint (an always relaxed Mr Nicholas) performing some mediocre M.O.R. disco tracks Out of Love With Love & We've Got Us which will bring the duo major success on the pop charts.

Meantime Rod returns to his place which looks as awful in the dark as it does in the daytime. Susan is in his bed and he's drunk. Switching on his portable TV at the end of the bed, news comes of Clint's new club having an injury to their star striker.

With worries for the upcoming quarter-final cup game, in a meeting with team manager Jake Marsh (Adam Faith) and others, Simon suggests that they bring in Turner, "He was the best bloody striker in the business…he was magic." Marsh is unconvinced. Watching Ian's character playing in another match and defeated, again on a sodden pitch, Jake's summary of his old teammate to his Chairman is blunt: "Old. Slow. Drunk."

Visiting him in the dressing room, the cheery Mr Simon comes with an offer for his old hero whilst the veteran takes a swig from a bottle of whisky. And so begins his quest to get Roy to play for the Saints. This will take some doing. Dressing rooms were no place for modesty and we see Ian join his teammates in the communal bath!

Calling on football agent Georgie (Alan Lake), who uses an unidentifiable accent, he tells him that he is keen to play in the States. Bluntly told that if he was 10 years younger he might be able to scout a coaching role over there. Alan had memorably pursued Ian in Freelance but tragically took his own life in 1984.

With his options narrowing, Roy joins Clint and American singer Miss Cloudy Martin (Ms Somers) on their private jet travelling to Paris for a recording session. Clint notices that the two seem to know each other and Miss Martin confesses to him, a close friend keen to start a relationship, that as a young woman, she slept with Turner.

With her singing voice reminiscent of Olivia Newton-John, the old pro watches the recording whilst boozing away with others in the studio. Thankfully Ian doesn't have any numbers but he does have their song That's Not What We Came Here For in his head as an earworm and I suppose it is quite catchy.

Reluctantly accepting the offer after no immediate prospect of a job elsewhere, Turner's first training session sees a frosty reception from his new boss.

Out for a meal with Susan, he tells her that he needs to focus on his training and so that they should cool things for a while.

Mr Marsh (Faith) watches training in the snow and at another cold session, the arrival of the singing duo and asking Roy to join them for a photo adds to the manager's irritation.

On the day of the semi-final, staged at Portman Road, home of Ipswich Town FC, the production used the pitch before the league game v Manchester City, watched by a crowd of 20,773 on Saturday 31 March 1979.

Ian wearing the number 9 shirt as a centre forward "recalled from the soccer wilderness" as commentator John Motson chirps. After kicking off, Turner (McShane) wastes a chance before his side goes 1-0 up. He grabs the second, via an easy put in, watched on by Clint & Cloudy from their box. The team wears the yellow Admiral-made kit which was the Southampton away attire. In the dressing room at halftime, the seasoned 'baller' takes a sly swig of alcohol from his jacket. Observed by his manager, he is furious at him for doing this and squandering his talent. On the attack, Roy insults him by saying that he never had any. Tellingly his former teammate terms him "Yesterday's Hero"

Ian's real-life father, Scots-born Harry, became a professional football player after signing apprentice forms with Blackburn Rovers in 1937. After meeting a certain Irene Cowley, Ian was born on Tuesday 29 September 1942.

Onto Huddersfield Town before signing for Bolton in 1947, he also made his mark as part of the Manchester United squad in the mid-1950s (before leaving for Charlton Athletic). This resulted in the family relocating to the city. Harry made 207 appearances in total, scoring 20 goals, with admirably the majority of his games in the top division. When in the UK visiting family, Ian can often be seen at United's Old Trafford and as a lad, attended school opposite the ground. A scout for the club later on, with his own distinctive voice, Harry McShane was the official PA at the club in the 1960s. Remembered as a "really terrific human being," via his son in the Nerdist podcast, he died in November 2012.

Back on screen, the Saints run out winners with Turner tiring and back in the changing room the lads are in the communal bath. 'Motty' tries to conduct a live interview but doesn't get much from any of the victors before a grinning Clint gets launched into the bath; much to the delight of Ian and the others!

Afterwards manager Jake says that he wants to suspend Roy indefinitely but the owner is reluctant yet but swayed by the ultimatum of its "either him or me." As the Saints' manager is winning matches for him, for now, he acquiesces.

Later celebrating their success in a nightclub, all the players, manager, Chairman and the pretty American are seen having fun but Turner is blotto. Jake asks Cloudy to dance and works on manipulating her into getting Clint (Nicholas) to agree with him about Ray. She doesn't like him. Close by, a young woman pulls an unsteady Roy onto the dance floor and he accidentally bumps his old flame. He takes a missed swing at his manager and is removed by the other players. Cloudy takes him back to her plush pad and he sobers up after a shower (a shot of them at her home was used on the cover of the subsequent Cinema Group Home Video release). They talk about their past and the miscommunications towards the end before making love.

Walking back with him to his flat, he persuades her to come in but is thrown at discovering Susan there waiting for him. Uncomfortable, Cloudy leaves whilst he tells Susan that it is over, "That's one thing I never was: graceful, you know?"

At the social club later, Roy has now stopped the boozing and is enjoying grifting and playing snooker with Mac. Coincidentally, Ian would later act like a pro player in the TV comedy-drama White Goods. His calls to Cloudy remain unanswered.

Back at home, via the TV news, he learns of his suspension and hears the public insult by Jake;   declaring him past it and recommending that he retires from playing.

Calling at Clint's modern office, Cloudy is there but she discreetly exits until after he leaves. The determined footballer tells his Chairman that he wants to play. The fizzy pop stars' career is on the up and soon they peak at number 1 so are touring away but before she goes a distraught Roy calls at her place to reconcile but she says it's over.

Visiting the club to see his dad, Roy also continues supervising football sessions with the boys. Marek is absent, and he is told that he was disappointed with his supension but Turner says he will play in the final and has a ticket for the lad.

Engaging on a major health kick as Roy, Ian clears his flat of the many bottles of booze and we have the obligatory exercise montage of seeing him out running around the Windsor area (the scene outside the flat was shot in Uxbridge). In his real life, the actor would have a long-standing issue with alcohol which saw him sign up for AA in 1988. Of course, we also know that the film is a thinly-veiled story paralleling the life of one Georgie Best; someone befriended by Ian during his Old Trafford heyday (incidentally, he would narrate the 2002 BBC documentary There's Only One George Best). Sometime before shooting, Ian was regularly enjoying playing soccer alongside fellow acting pals including Tom Courtenay and Nicol Williamson.

Today Mexico, Tomorrow the World (1972) running at a little under half-hour featured them travelling to take on a local team over in Mexico during the 1970 World Cup tournament.

Back to Yesterday's Hero and in the film, he is a striker but Ian favoured playing at left-back. A natural left-footer by the look of it; onscreen Mr Turner also returns to training with the team: much to the surprise of his manager. Club owner Mr Simon wants Roy as a sub for the final staged at the old Wembley stadium. His manager sees this as a mistake despite having seen his efforts to get himself fit. However, he relents.

Facing a First Division side aka Nottingham Forest, Roy gets a call from Cloudy asking to meet but he is having none of it; upset by the whole situation, he declines, saying they can say their goodbyes now when she tells him she will be returning to the States after the final.

Yesterday's Hero proves a decent watch and lots of actual match day footage is used of the Southampton v Forest 1979 League Cup Final intermingled with Mr Turner senior accompanying Marek and a chaperone into the stadium. Sam (Kydd) is reminded that the last time he was here was a decade earlier when Ray scored a hat trick!

The match kicks off and the Saints fall 1-2 behind as we see Roy in his red tracksuit, seated next to Jake on the team bench. In the dressing room at halftime, he stands around idly listening to the manager's team talk before the second half. An injury necessitates a change and as Roy, Ian is told to warm up and with some 5 minutes or so remaining he enters proceedings. Here first-time director Neil Leifer inserts closely-cropped new footage of his star on the ball before he scores the equaliser. Fouled by the keeper, Roy takes responsibility for taking the resulting penalty: can he win the game in the dying seconds? Of course, he can! He strikes the ball and it flies into the net: 3-2 to the Saints. With supporters, Clint & Cloudy all seen erupting in joy, the screen cuts to a grinning Ian and freeze-framing as the closing titles appear. Surprisingly, the screenplay for Hero was provided by saucy novelist Jackie Collins. She visited the production on location and was photographed alongside a track-suited Mr McShane. Her husband, Oscar Lerman, co-produced the film with the legendary Elliott Kastner. Many years later, Ian was a guest on her 1993 This is Your Life tribute.

An 'A' certificate, the film was released in cinemas on Thursday 22 November 1979 and nationwide a few days later.

Fans could also buy the soundtrack album offering "20 sensational disco greats" too (see the cover below).

Ian's involvement in the HTV/ ITV film The Curse of King Tut's Tomb as explorer Howard Carter was curtailed this year after he and fellow cast member Eva Marie Saint were involved in a car crash whilst on location in Egypt. He had only been working on the project for a week. Miss Saint was uninjured. However, Ian broke his leg and took a year to recuperate after which time he returned to America and married. Robin Ellis replaced him. However, a still of him looking dapper in a suit and accompanying 'tache does exist.

3. Mini-series galore, Grace Jones & Lovejoy: The 1980s

A British actor now based in the States, Ian returned to the UK in 1979 to work on an intriguing and suspenseful project called High Tide (1980). Part of the esteemed Armchair Thriller branding, this four-part drama was made by the now-defunct ITV franchise Southern. Adapted by Andrew Brown, it was sourced from a 1970 novel by crime & suspense writer P.M. Hubbard. Sadly, he passed away almost a week after the opening episode was aired.

Freshly released from a 4-year prison stretch for manslaughter Peter Curtis (Ian McShane) is keen to savour his freedom. Intending to travel to the South Coast and buy a boat, he chooses to drive at night in a tale seeing the past intertwine with greed, passion, murder and more.

As Peter, Ian narrates his thoughts in an attempt to make sense of things as the truth unravels, "I was a free man feeling almost dangerously happy. The danger I felt was that the happiness might not last."

Staying at hotels, his sense of foreboding is proved right when he meets Matthews (Terence Rigby), someone who knew the deceased. His return in the final instalment will prove fatal for one of them. He quizzes Curtis about his contribution to the death of Evan Maxwell (Malcolm Terris) and we get to know that the two were involved in an altercation following Peter's beloved dog being run over by the speeding driver. Maxwell suffered a fatal heart attack and his final, gasping words related to a "high tide". For Peter Curtis, this will lead him to reveal events whose origins stretch back to France at the end of WWII. But as of now, he begins his quest to decipher the story and this will take him to Cornwall.

On the way, he offers a lift to a stranded young couple and afterwards, one of them; Celia (Wendy Morgan) joins him on his trip. But we soon discover that she has been paid to follow him by the mysterious Smith brothers; men not to be trifled with and associates of the deceased.

Thinking about his final words, Peter remembers more and makes a connection to a 9:52 flood tide pattern which brings him closer to discovering why the man had been out on that fateful day. He was heading towards a mysterious stone house perched on the banks of a river.

Peter (Ian) buys a small boat and the amiable Celia travels with him until he begins to doubt her motives. Did Matthews tell her about him? Who is she calling? A violent confrontation erupts and she vanishes just as he arrives in a sleepy village.

Heading straight to the local pub, he gets chatting with the friendly Cecil (John Bird) who invites him to join him and his wife, Helen (Kika Markham), for dinner. It is here that life changes upon meeting the beautiful lady and despite her being married, the two are instantly smitten.

Investigations take Peter back on the water to discover the lovely aforementioned house. Joining the dots, he ponders why Matthews was in such a rush to get here those 4 years previously. Snooping around outside the vacant property, he is met by the shotgun-carrying caretaker Fenton (Mike McKevitt) who tells him more about the place and its owners. He is unaware at this point that the man is an ally of the alluring Helen.

Heading away, Peter bumps into dedicated 'twitcher' Cecil (the aptly named Mr Bird) who asks him to supper. Convivial, he worries about his wife and her unhappiness with her life, apparently unaware of her concerns or involvements in past events which will soon resurface.

After previously calling to confess his feelings, Peter & Helen draw closer in a snatched moment during the evening and in the narration, Ian expresses his character's desire for her.

Compelled to return, in the evening light Helen comes to him and they kiss as the camera pans around them before they end up on the ground. A perspiring Peter lays next to her, post-coital, whilst his paramour stares into space.

Seeing Cyril whilst in the village, Peter finds a distraught Helen on the cliff tops. Acting oddly, she tells him to leave as she knows that he was responsible for Maxwell's death. He reluctantly agrees.

Spending a few hours in the bay, Celia returns and articulates her involvement in things whilst warning Peter that their safety is in question.

Come morning and in need of petrol, he rows his boat ashore only to discover her body floating in the water. Unwilling to contact the police, after all, who would believe a man with his recent past, he contains his anger at his current predicament.

Returning to Helen, he tells her all that has happened. It is here that she reveals that people are pursuing her because it was her French father who secreted gold bullion at the end of the war. Now Maxwell, Matthews and the Smith brothers want it and are prepared to kill or double-cross each other to get it. Maxwell was planning to do the latter when he had the incident with Curtis (McShane). Agreeing to take her to France on his boat on the next tide, via the voice-over he confesses his love for her and knows that Helen will be the one who decides whether they have a future together. It matters not, as he will do anything for her now and is compelled to help.

She later arrives at the stone house to rendezvous and they make love again. Returning to her car, now in the early hours, she is pounced upon by one of the brothers (Toby Salaman).

He leads her back inside and luckily Peter has hidden away. In a scuffle, he strangles the adversary. Revealed, Helen adds that there is another man nearby and so he goes to look for him.

In doing so, in the darkness, Peter is shot at by Matthews (Rigby) who chases after him down to the water. Cleverly, and with further shots ringing out, he leads him onto the heavy mud. Wading through, his aggressor becomes submerged by the quicksand and is gulped to his death.

Struck in the arm, Peter returns to the cottage to collect Helen. There with Fenton, she tells him that she is not going, as all those that were after her have been killed. For a moment the audience wonders if his life too might be in peril. In an excellent last scene, we see her face flickering in the light before she watches as Peter returns to his boat and rows away.

With its soundtrack nod to Hitchcock, High Tide was directed by Colin Bucksey; he and Ian would reconvene many years later on the U.S. drama Ray Donovan.

There have been many DVD compilations of Armchair Thriller episodes but High Tide had its own via a sketchy print on the Simply Home Entertainment label (2009) and there is also a cracking U.S. release from VCI Entertainment.

U.S. country singer/ songwriter Mac Davis was the headliner of the American film comedy Cheaper to Keep Her whose poster by-line read "A love story about women's rights...and lefts." Whilst another offered "Dekker thinks he's God's gift to Women!" He had written In the Ghetto and the fabulous A Little Less Conversation, both recorded by Elvis. And here is the handsome, newly-single Bill Dekker, a private investigator assisted by Tony (Art Metrano) in gathering evidence for alimony/ divorce cases offered by the uptight Locke (an appealing Tovah Feldshuh).

One of their cases sees them investigate therapist Dr Alfred Sunshine, who runs "...a combination sushi-bar and massage parlour for rich people at $100 a throw," as Dekker informs his new boss. It is a bushy-haired Ian who plays the Sunshine role for which he received another special credit name check on the opening credits of a film still set in the late-1970s (roller skating, anybody). Sunshine happens to be Locke's estranged husband, a fact that she fails to reveal whilst Dekker gathers incriminating information on him. The couple is in the midst of reconciliation but the PI discovers that Sunshine is selling up and preparing to leave with Laura (Gwen Humble whom Mr McShane would marry in August 1980 following 2 previous divorces).

Just what Ken Annakin was doing directing this nonsense is anyone's guess. He had worked with the actor on The Fourth Musketeer immediately released before this and enjoyed an eclectic career.

Back to the film, after visiting the therapist some 20 minutes in and his character, termed "Alfie" by Kate (Miss Feldshuh), returns later but the viewer sees how despicable he is but she doesn't. At brunch, amusingly Locke asks him, "How's the antique business?" (this in reference to him being seen kissing another woman outside a store, previously).

After investigating the doctor further and coming closer to his boss, Dekker subsequently learns that Sunshine is her husband. All the clients featured have their own motivations and in a plot rouse, an incognito Dekker strikes up a deal to purchase a vintage sports car owned by Laura who is planning a cruise with the duplicitous Sunshine (Ian). The trio agrees to conduct the sale at the quayside before the couple set off, with only the investigator knowing that Locke is also going to confront them.

This she does and Dekker's identity is revealed and it is here that the funniest moment in the film occurs.

A running gag sees Dekker as a seriously outlandish driver and it is a delight to see Sunshine and his lady friend freaking out at the hair-raising speeds achieved by the would-be purchaser when giving the car a test drive around the dock. Watch the petrified faces of Ian and Miss Humble's characters as the vehicle whizzes here and there. A forgivable continuity slip is exposed as we see the sunglasses worn by both appear and disappear during the sequence which ends with the car being wrecked.

The film ends on a high but it is Dekker and Locke who go on the cruise rather than Sunshine & Laura. Cheaper to Keep Her received a VHS release but has not had a DVD one. Davis is good fun in the lead, in only his second film appearance, via a screenplay co-written by Timothy Harris and Herschel Weingrod. Their first produced script together, the duo worked on other more successful projects subsequently after this.

"It was a dreadful film," recounted McShane to Lester Middlehurst in TV Times magazine (9 April 1988), "but good always comes out of something awful." Meaning his wife Ms Humble, they tied-the-knot on the Queen Mary (used in the film).

Following solitary TV and film roles the year before, 1981 found Ian not content with one guest appearance on popular crime drama Magnum, he enjoyed two: as different characters. His first; Skin Deep, arriving as episode 6 in the opening season and by far the better role, and Black on White, episode 3 in the following season.

Featuring the 'tach-tastic, Ferrari-driving Tom Selleck as the laconic private investigator resident in Hawaii, the unexpected news of the suicide of actress Erin Wolfe (Cathie Shirriff) finds the P.I. persuaded into working to discover exactly what happened to her by distraught former partner David Norman (Ian). Reluctantly meeting him again after declining to spy on her previously, the drunken Norman assures Magnum that she was murdered and that her unidentified lover was the culprit. A great deal remains unsaid.

Skin Deep relates to the title of the new film that the actress was about to start work on before her death.

Her agent speaks quite disparagingly of David, a man who helped shape the early career of Miss Wolfe.

The former tells Magnum that the "lecherous leech" made his client fear for her safety after the relationship broke down.

Working with Higgins (John Hillerman), Ian and Mr Selleck share a scene where the former technically explains that it was unlikely that the actress was able to kill herself with a shotgun. We watch as the beleaguered David (McShane) pleads with him to stop talking so graphically, with Higgins initially unaware of his connection to the case. Drinking incessantly and looking sickly, as Norman, Ian wears what looks like a ladies' blouse, whilst Magnum detects that the actress was murdered.

With the investigation continuing, a photograph of Ms Wolfe seen on a camping trip on one of the nearby islands leads Magnum to find its location. As he does, he is shocked to discover that David has moments earlier chartered a helicopter to take him there. Fortunately, Magnum's old Vietnam pal TC (Roger E. Mosley) has his own charter service and flies him there to confront the possible killer. But an oil issue with the engine sees the P.I. having to hurriedly make an unexpected jump from the chopper into the water below to reach the secluded cove.

He is shocked to discover that the actress is alive and furious at being discovered in her secret hideaway which she enjoys frequenting. Unaware of the news, Magnum tries to convince her to come with him until a shot rings out and strikes him. It is from David, who pursues them with a rifle.

It is revealed later that David shot 'Erin' when she was in bed but in a case of mistaken identity, it turned out to be his latest girlfriend who had gone there to talk about him. He covered up the error but its repercussions are being felt.

Rushing away, Magnum has a 'Nam flashback and orders Erin to pretend to be dead after she is also struck. Approaching her, the gun-toting Brit is pounced upon by Thomas and the two crashes into the water. It clearly wasn't Ian performing this stunt but it doesn't detract from the drama. T.C. arrives after letting off a flare to seek help and this is the last time we see Ian onscreen.

Safely back home, TC and Magnum chat and the latter asks if his old pal ever thinks of their combat days; TC lies and says no. The charismatic investigator also reveals that Erin is going to be fine after her ordeal. Skin Deep was broadcast for American audiences on Thursday 15 January.

Advancing to 1982 and the year proved to be considerably busier for Mr McShane, with a role in the American television drama The Letter sitting alongside The Quest & Marco Polo, both small-screen outings. He also acted on stage in two plays.

A popular 1949 American play written by the aforementioned Clifford Odets (see American Playhouse episode) The Big Knife played at the Watford Palace theatre in the UK with Ian as Charlie Castle in a revival directed by Michael Attenborough. Made into a film in 1955 with Jack Palance in the role of movie star Charlie Castle, here he is portrayed by Ian. As a play, it first ran on Broadway in 1949 but this particular revival played from Thursday 1 - Saturday 24 April.

Detailed on chaseside.org.uk, a review mentioned that "[Knife] may lean towards melodrama at times but it has a satisfying surging impetus as Charlie wrestles, not so much with his conscience but with his real nature, for he is a man of intellect and radical instincts. Ian McShane suggests his tough Eastern background and the sensitivity which has been sapped by the likes of Hoff, played with all the stops out, in the best Louis B. Mayer-Harry Cohn fashion, by Jeffrey Chiswick, and his sinister henchman Smiley Coy (Peter Marinker), the ex-officer who has completely sold out to the system and easily rationalises evil."

Later this same year Ian would return to America to star in Betrayal, a Harold Pinter piece, for no salary. Cast as Robert to American actors Penny Fuller, Lawrence Pressman and Michael Alaimo, Betrayal advanced to become a multi-winner at the 1982 L.A. Drama Critics Circle Awards; including Ian for Lead Performance. In the States, at the time Disraeli had been repeated on PBS under their 'Masterpiece Theatre' Sunday night slot after originally airing it in 1980 but with little notice but positive reviews. This time it was advertised prominently and got the viewers' interest. No doubt this helped draw an audience for this Pinter piece.

He had recently finished Exposed (released in 1983) and at one point during its run, departed to New York to shoot a film.

Returning for the third season of the popular Hawaii-based show Magnum co-created by the Donald P. Bellisario/ Glen A. Larson team, Ian features in the preposterous Black on White. The episode was broadcast on Thursday 28 October 1982.

As the ludicrously-named Edwin Clutterbuck, just what the writers were thinking of here remains a mystery.

All the Larson shows show a sense of humour and the author is hoping that this was the case in this absurd entry.

Ian is seen in the pre-credits highlights before arriving off-screen at the gates of the estate where Magnum (Selleck) is staying alongside Higgins (Hillerman). As Clutterbuck, Ian's character informs the P.I. that he is a soldier friend of Higgins from their time out in Kenya with the British Army in the 1950s.

An actor is only as good as his script and Black on White proves an embarrassment or is it all simply meant to be ironic? Poor Ian, in not one of his finest performances, has to play up the jolly Brit accent nonsense and his entry into the storyline has to be seen to be disbelieved. It is that embarrassing and riddled with stereotypes and clichés (he even smokes a Sherlock Holmes-style pipe!) After viewing the episode, one is left wondering if it was all a figment of Clutterbuck's troubled mind as he was one of the men affected by the tragedy, "A man can't run from his past forever," he had said to an uncomfortable Magnum earlier.

Regardless, plot-wise, Magnum creates a rouse to keep Higgins in the guesthouse thus avoiding his exposure to a prospective terminator who is killing former British soldiers involved in a retaliatory strike that turned into a tragic massacre involving women and children. Throw into this an agent or possible killer played by Lynne Moody and it hardly improves. After the joy of revisiting the first episode, this one has some good moments but a lot of it misfires badly. Add to the fact Ian's use of "wog" for the Kenyans makes for uncomfortable viewing in the modern-day.

All housed in the guesthouse, a distressed Higgins regurgitates the past but poor Private Clutterbuck has been driven to emotional collapse by his involvement. Just as in Space: 1999, Ian perspires profusely, particularly upon seeing an imaginary native tribesman about to attack him with a spear.

A heartbeat later he removes his shirt and trousers to reveal an ankle bracelet worn by indigenous people in Kenya and it is this link that enables the viewer to identify him as the one seeking revenge in what is the only decent plot twist.

On a balcony looking down at Higgins and a female friend, Ian is about to throw a deadly spear until a pistol-drawn Thomas Magnum bursts in. Pleading with him not to do it, Edwin (Ian McShane) looks to aim it at him but a shot rings out and he falls over the balcony and down onto the ground below.

As absurd as its reads, in the final moments after all this, Magnum even winks directly into the camera so the viewer can safely assume that this was all simply a jolly jape?

Shown in between his Magnum roles, American actress Lee Remick starred in ABC's The Letter, an Emmy-winning production that saw her nominated for a Golden Globe in the lead role as a murder suspect. Lee is Leslie Crosbie, wife to Robert (Jack Thompson) with Ian as Geoff, a dashing ex-soldier who becomes her lover until suffering a terrible fate. Directed by John Erman, he had previously won a prestigious Directors Guild of America award for his involvement in Roots.

Originating as a short story by W. Somerset Maugham, one of many, the work was fashioned into a stage play and is best remembered for the 1940 film version starring an Oscar-nominated Bette Davis. Based on actual murder events that occurred in Malaya, in 1911, we are asked to question whether it was self-defence, a lover spurned or something more. The American press advert for its TV premiere showed a simmering Ian with Miss Remick, with the by-line "She loved him. She hated him. She wanted him...and she killed him. Lee Remick. The Letter. Stunning. Shocking. Sensuous."

Told in flashbacks, this is somewhat of a rarity, in one moment, Ian gets to do his best Noel Coward singing voice impression as the sexual tension between his character and Miss Remick is palpable. Ronald Pickup, later to work with him on an episode of Lovejoy, co-stars. The Letter was shown on Monday 3 May 1982.

Many children loved The Quest, a short-lived American series that presented a role for Ian in its seventh episode: Hunt for the White Tiger. Broadcast on Saturday 4 December. Running for nine episodes in total, the show, which took two weeks to shoot each story, was cancelled by ABC after its final airing later that same month. The network invited viewers to come along and watch the 4 principal characters "they're off on running on a wild, madcap adventure that will take you around the world for the greatest treasure hunt of their lives…"

Press ads for Marco Polo proclaimed, "Tonight a forbidden secret is unlocked. The fury of Mongol warriors is unleashed in a life or death struggle." Ahead of its 9 pm premiere on the NBC network, viewers could learn of "The Man. The Legend. The Adventure." With its huge running time of some 10 hours, this Emmy-winning and multiple-nominee was shown in the United States nightly between Sunday 16 - Wednesday 19 May.

Playing Ali Ben Yussouf, formerly a humble Italian fisherman abducted and traded as a slave, Ian features in episodes 2 & 3 (of the eight) alongside his old R.A.D.A. mate David Warner. Trailers for the show saw a bearded McShane as "a renegade Italian turned Moslem warlord who releases the Polos' from prison... (TV Guide)" And in it, he delivers the line "by our law & the rules of law, you deserve to die." He looks incredible in his layered outfit, with a massive sabre at his side when granting Polo and his colleagues their lives and giving a long speech.

The first Western production to film in the Forbidden City and Ming Tombs in China (with Inner Mongolia, Fez and Marrakesh in Morocco also used) this was another humongous production with almost 200 speaking parts and featuring 5k extras. Newcomer Ken Marshall was cast as the world-famous Italian explorer/ trader. RCA/ Columbia released it subsequently onto VHS on three tapes, deeming it "An epic of war, love and intrigue as West meets East." A later DVD ran for more than 7 hours.

A beautiful music score was provided by prolific composer Ennio Morricone, with Marco Polo a huge national hero in Italy, his legacy was celebrated by a Panini sticker album accompanying the release of the film. Well-regarded by its audience despite some historical inaccuracies, a shorter version of a little under 5 hours was presented for European audiences.

Tasked with bringing the story to the small screen Vincenzo Labella was assisted by David Butler also involved in the writing. Ian had spoken his words on Disraeli and Mr Butler had also contributed dialogue to Jesus of Nazareth, previously. Look out for future Lovejoy guest star John Gielgud also in this.

"The society girl who became the most brilliant star in Hollywood. The star who became the most beautiful Princess in the world." That was ABC's Monday Night Movie slot describing Grace Kelly (1983), a made-for-TV feature lightly detailing the life of the actor before she gave it all up to marry Prince Rainier of Monaco in 1956. Charlie's Angels star Cheryl Ladd plays the lead covering the rise to stardom for the talented Miss Kelly who worked with the likes of Hitchcock, Cary Grant, Gary Cooper, James Stewart, Clark Gable and others. The recipient of an Academy Award at the 1955 ceremony, she despaired at the constant press intrusion and struggled with the Hollywood dilemma of a woman being allowed to have a career and a family life concurrently.

It was this dilemma that saw her introduced to Rainer whilst at the Cannes Film Festival in 1955. Photographed at the palace, they finally met and a romance subsequently blossomed. Miss Kelly was in her mid-20s, whilst the Prince was in his early-30s. It is from the hour mark in the film that Ian comes into the story, playing the monarch, complete with fake 'tache and neat attire.

After marrying the eligible bachelor, Kelly retired from acting to become Her Serene Highness Princess Grace of Monaco. Mr McShane is suitably suave-looking and sweetly, their wedding is shown, mixing actual footage with the actors. However, this is no tell-all-tale as Princess Grace was associated with assisting the producers of the telefilm. Look out for Lloyd Bridges, one of the swashbucklers from The Fourth Musketeer reunited with Ian as Jack Kelly, father to Grace. Diane Ladd also proves memorable as her mother. It was shown on American TV on Monday 21 February.

What a diverse year this one proved to be for Ian McShane, fourth-billed under lead Nastassja Kinski, ballet dancer Rudolf Nureyev and psycho killer Harvey Keitel in Exposed. Written and thrillingly directed by James Toback, this was another project in the eclectic 1980s film career of Miss Kinski.

Released in the U.S. in January, he could also be seen in the TV movie Grace Kelly and the cheesy soap Bare Essence. Both seen and heard in the trailer, Ian was cast as fashion photographer Greg Miller, with a penchant for sunglasses, caps and scarves, he discovers a sceptical Elizabeth (Miss Kinski) whilst she is waitressing in New York after leaving her University course in Paris.

Returning to the States, she has already been robbed and harassed daily and so isn't too convinced, "I just wanna make you rich and famous," enthuses the snapper after seeing her there, "is that a sin?"

After taking his number, Elizabeth visits Greg whilst on a shoot and he snaps away at her as he can see her potential. A subsequent photo session near the Twin Towers soon sees her on the cover of fashion magazines and a later job takes her back to France and another round of pictures by Mr Miller. But it is not simply the camera that is looking at her but mysterious strangers and we wonder why.

At an exhibition of Miller's photographs of his new model, Elizabeth briefly meets an enigmatic stranger whom she becomes smitten with. He is Daniel (Nureyev who was no actor).

He reappears later, spouts some existential gibberish and walks off down the street leaving her bemused. Breaking into her apartment and ordered to leave, we later learn that he is also staying in the complex. She is intrigued.

Walking in the freezing Central Park, she fails to convince Greg (Ian) that she is in love and the viewer wonders if Ian mentioned to Nastassja about working with her father back in the 1960s when he again played a man with a camera.

As the photographer, McShane's role is not at all involved in the darker shenanigans involving the terrorist cell led by Rivas (Keitel) whom Daniel is planning to kill. Elizabeth is disappointed to learn of his true identity and she spends time with Rivas and his team who are planning a hit. The author was a little confused by the plot but we do see Daniel show Elizabeth surveillance pictures and hear mention of a link to an Auschwitz concentration camp survivor.

Adeptly directed, Exposed whizzes along in scenes shot in the Paris wintertime but for all its efforts, it passes the time well enough, "It's an interesting film," Ian told L.A. Times reporter Roger Mann (25 Aug 1982), "an odd mixture of high fashion and terrorism...and the film has a really gruesome finale."

Sounding like cheap cologne, Bare Essence was a short-lived but still loved, American TV drama which nbc.fandom.com outlined as being: "....a soap opera starring Genie Francis (after she left General Hospital) about a young woman, Tyger Hayes and the intrigues of the perfume industry. Filmed between late May and early July 1982 it was ready to air that October.

Walter Grauman directed from a screenplay by Robert Hamilton based on a 1980 novel. The show originally began as a two-part mini-series shown on Monday 4 & Tuesday 5 October 1982 on CBS. Rating figures saw NBC pick up the show and the series aired on a Tuesday night from 15 February to 13 June 13 across 11 episodes. TV movie "Bare Essence: The Final Chapter" followed.

Ian featured prominently in the opening credits; chomping on a cigar, kissing a woman, slapping another (really) and grabbing at her. He received second-billing as Niko Theophilus. "The temperature is rising on Bare Essence," promised the press ads enticing viewers to tune in at 9 pm. Another offered "Love Her. Use her. Or Destroy Her. Everyone wants a piece of Tyger Hayes." As if that wasn't enough; "Bare Essence...is the love of power and the power of love". The ad campaign used an illustrated likeness of Miss Francis and beneath, small pictures of the cast including Ian. "He had to own the best. At any cost" was his character caption! Producers brought on the big guns in the form of Dynasty star Linda Evans & Donna Mills both in the first feature-length films which Mr McShane did not feature in.

Ian was fourth-billed in the 1984 Cannon film release Ordeal by Innocence, whose Spanish poster is shown opposite. A gorgeous, leisurely opening shot by Alan Birkinshaw and not the film's own director Desmond Davis, takes the viewer to Devon and the comfortable home of the Argyle family. We watch as Calgary (a lanky, bird-like Donald Sutherland) arrives there whilst we also catch an initial glimpse of Phillip (Ian).

The unexpected visitor is returning the address book belonging to Jacko (Billy McColl) unaware that his delayed arrival causes tremendous distress to all, including her husband (Christopher Plummer on fine form). Unbeknownst to Calgary, the former had been hanged for the murder of his mother, Faye Dunaway, seen in black and white flashbacks, some two years before. Shocked, he explains that the former could not have been the killer as he had been with him at the exact time of the event; unknown to the investigation at this point. Made unwelcome, Mr Calgary is perturbed to find that no one seems keen for the case to be reopened despite his own insistence.

As per usual, this is another Agatha Christie whodunit taken from her original 1958 novel, here adapted by Alexander Stuart. Sutherland shivers his way through the plodding story whilst competing with the incongruous Dave Brubeck jazz soundtrack in a picture that seems to have been beset by production issues.

The "man with the mission", as Mr Durrant (McShane) terms Dr Calgary upon meeting him some 40 minutes into proceedings finds Ian's dapper, a wheelchair-bound character being cuckolded by his wife Mary (the under-used Sylvia Miles) and curiously, and here is a spoiler alert, in the trailer, she is seen holding a pistol as her husband drops forward following the sound of a gun being fired.

Supposedly having an "instinct for survival", his fate is sealed later on as we wonder who'll be next in line to snuff it!

The casting in a big screen Christie outing is always enjoyable and here we see Ian in a supporting role in an expensively-assembled grouping directed by Davis, who never directed a feature film again after this. A former Camera Op, he stepped up to direct back in 1964 with the excellent Girl with Green Eyes. That film gave a role to the wonderful Rita Tushingham and should you wish to read more about her career, you will find my book about her of interest. Ordeal looks fabulous and has a film noir styling (although shot in colour) but a meandering pace. The film received a royal charity performance in February 1988 and Cannon repeated the same when they returned to the Christie fold with Appointment with Death in 1988 which featured Ian's old co-star Hayley Mills amongst its principal cast. The author released a guide to her career

the real mystery began...
Once the murder
was solved,

AGATHA CHRISTIE'S ordeal by Innocence 15

THE CANNON GROUP, INC. presents
DONALD SUTHERLAND SARAH MILES CHRISTOPHER PLUMMER IAN McSHANE DIANA QUICK and FAYE DUNAWAY
in a GOLAN-GLOBUS Production of AGATHA CHRISTIE'S ORDEAL BY INNOCENCE Director of Photography BILLY WILLIAMS
Music by DAVE BRUBECK Associate Producer MICHAEL KAGAN Executive Producers MENAHEM GOLAN and YORAM GLOBUS
Screenplay by ALEXANDER STUART Produced by JENNY CRAVEN Directed by DESMOND DAVIS
Released by Cannon Film Distributors (UK) Ltd.

in 2021 and I would again steer you to the references page. A '15' certification, Ian fans will find the best DVD packaging from the foreign language Optimum release of most interest as Mr McShane features on the cover as prominently as 5 others in the principal cast. The original theatrical poster sees Sutherland looming large and smaller pictures of six others beneath. The film received a prestigious Royal premiere on Thursday 14 February 1985 and a tie-in paperback released. Ordeal has now received a Blu-ray release.

Soon to be heard on a Grace Jones album, Ian featured in a music video for the Kim Carnes track You Make My Heart Best Faster (And That's All That Matters) taken from her LP Café Racers released the same year: 1983. Remembered for her classic Bette Davis Eyes, Ms Carnes proves a better singer than an actor in the cheesy promo which sees her and Mr McShane cosying up together. Just as in Exposed we see Ian snapping his lover (and vice versa) and generally swooning. The promo was partly shot at the Riverside Raceway in Riverside, California where we see Ian supposedly driving a car around the track. Notice his suit has the name patch of "Steve" and you will discover that it was pushed around by driver Steve Webb.

After enjoying a whirlwind romance with Jake (Steve Railsback), he and Lily (Pamela Sue Martin who had been in Dynasty, previously) become a couple but things soon start to change for them in Torchlight. Ms Martin co-created the screenplay with fellow cast member Eliza Moorman, and it was directed by Thomas Wright, a man who would soon work with Ian again in 1988 on Chain Letter. Aka Cocaine Paradise, Torchlight finds the reckless Jake bored with his working life as a business owner and wanting something new.

At a fellow artist friend's art exhibition, the couple meet Lily's old friend Guy (Todd Ruff) and she asks him who the man in the white suit is, seen nearby, "He's a real character...I guess you could say that at the moment Sidney specialises in artist block," quips the pal who indicates that the stranger might also be bisexual. With his ear pierced, (Mr McShane) is a drug user and supplier, enjoying freebasing cocaine and regularly partying at his rather luxurious home. Inviting the couple and various friends back, the peculiar Sidney passes on some of his product by breathing it straight into Lily's mouth! To freebase is the purest way of enjoying cocaine and many users would use it by lighting a bubble pipe and inhaling the smoke directly. This is what Sidney does, much to Jake's shock but the former simply tells him that this is the best way to enjoy its effect. It doesn't take much for both Jake (Railsback) and his brother, Richard (Arnie Moore) to partake too.

Creating a studio for his artist lover, the two soon clash with Jake bored by his idleness and deciding to visit Sidney.

A sweaty, dressing-gown attired Ian McShane invites him in, and their drug-taking friendship commences. Returning home with a small pipe, Jake asks Lily to join him in a smoke but she declines. He is rapidly developing a taste for the expensive drug.

With the unsettling Sidney in tow, the latter offers his understanding about Lily craving solitude within which to be creative and he also tells her that he is a fan of her paintings. Describing himself as a "consultant", Sidney will pull Jake into his seedy world.

Utilising that low, raspy tone, as Sidney, Ian welcomes Jake into his home with a kiss on the lips to pass on some second-hand smoke from his little bong. Drawing him into becoming an addict, Sidney is more than a little creepy with his attitude towards women. Somewhat aggressive and dismissive to his female guests, he simply uses them for sex and brings Jake in with him.

With her husband's personality affected by his addiction, the drug makes a person paranoid, eliciting a "psychological dependency" upon users, Lily takes Jake to the hospital in a vain attempt to wean him off the drugs. It doesn't work but she continues to try to care for him until things reach a crescendo.

Despite some inane dialogue delivered at times, Torchlight seems a well-meaning story and both Ian and Miss Martin prove memorable. The actor has since opined that the film is not that good but that he had enjoyed playing the character. However, he did attend a fund-raising screening in Atlanta to combat drug addiction; ironic in that the actor has freely admitted to passing cocaine use in his private life.

Ian's involvement in the storyline ends with a jump of some 6 months and Jake mentioning that Sidney (Ian), as Lily said, is "nobody's friend". We learn that the couple has split up and that Sidney "fucked him over" too.

"Your blood runs cold...your heart jumps into your throat." **91**
Too Scared to Scream film poster

The effete Vincent Hardwick (Ian) is one decidedly odd character, a man in his 40s who lives in the wealthy family home with his aphonic mother (the always watchable Maureen O'Sullivan); wheelchair-bound since a car accident whose tragic intentions will soon be revealed.

He is the favoured doorman at the Royal Arms apartment building, we know it's called that as it says on his ludicrously oversized hat that he wears as part of a 1930s type uniform last seen in movies of that time. But at least they were in black & white, here, his garish ensemble of U.S. cavalry-type trousers, gloves (a key component) topped off by a plush crimson jacket and a ludicrous bow tie is a sight to behold. He dresses like a rejected character for the Village People and try not to snigger as Charles Aznavour warbles over the opening credits.

A curious man, Vincent meticulously applys theatrical make-up in advance of stepping into his 'role' of concierge.

Made in 1982 Scream was not released until 3 years later. Fourth billed as "Ian McShane as Hardwick," it is also known as The Doorman (a more apt title). Regarded as being "...refined and a gentleman with the ladies," as one visitor tells fellow doorman

Edward (an entertaining Chet Doherty), things at the Royal soon turn black.

Lt. Alex Dinardo (Mike Connors) begins a murder investigation at the building once the body of Cynthia (Victoria Bass) is discovered stuffed into a washing machine after being stabbed by a gloved hand jettisoning out from her closet. This is the cue for some rather gory murders, leg slashing and a bit of salacious female nudity common to the horror genre. The teleplay by Neal Barbera & Glenn Leopold ticks many of the usual boxes and they supply a nice twist where their background in animation shows by the protagonist explainingtheir actions.

The murders are hilariously photographed by one-time film helmer Tony Lo Bianco, an actor known for cult classic The Honeymoon Killers and a role alongside Ian in the mini-series Jesus of Nazareth. Blaring music, slow-mo and legs slashed by a butcher's knife leads the police to visit Edward's family home and he seems the leading suspect.

Another death sees the needy Mrs Hard (Ruth Ford in her final role) as the victim and could the "crazy shit head", as a bartender terms him, be the killer? This is an unusual slaying as the perpetrator is hiding under the bed!

With a liking for quoting Shakespeare or prose, this is appealing to many female residents but the next victim is Blume (Sully Boyar) before his spicy lady friend is added to an already gruesome list. Ian's acting is a bit ropey at times and the author thinks that he seems a little miscast.

Coming on the scene is Anne Archer (hardly involved in things) who agrees to go undercover at the Royal in an admirable attempt to root out the killer. Coincidentally finding Vincent & his mother in Central Park, Kate (Miss Archer) chats with them and thus allows Alex & his partner to search through the Hardwick home for incriminating proof. Almost discovered, Alex finds a newspaper cutting detailing the car accident involving the mother and son; he believes that Vincent is their man but Kate is more sympathetic.

Vincent is arrested when evidence shows traces of his theatrical make-up found on Blume's body. The article mentions that both were involved in theatre and hence the connection is made. Jealous co-worker Edward doesn't seem to be a suspect.

Before this, Kate is put in grave danger back at the Royal and panic ensues with the discovery of a fellow officer seen swinging on the back of her apartment door. The killer attempts to force their way in, trusty butcher knife slashing at her from the doorway/entrance. However, she manages to fend him off before fleeing, whacking Vincent when she sees him on the stairwell.

Meanwhile, the detectives rush over to the residency where Vincent is seen in a state of panic and hastily packing a suitcase.

With the house silent, the detectives draw their guns and split up to begin a search.

Alex finds a bloodied and battered Vincent in a fabulous plot twist in which seems that the latter is dead but behind a 'woman' stabs at him. Here everything goes a bit Norman Bates as we notice the mother figure is taller and now standing up.

Ms Archer confronts the figure but gets a wheelchair pushed at her which results in her tumbling down the spiralling staircase. She gets up and a pursuit leads down to the basement.

Here the killer reveals themselves, "I don't understand," sighs Kate, as Edward removes his grey wig and proceeds to explain his past relationship with Vincent. He reveals that the latter had attempted to kill himself in the car 'accident'. Edward explains his obsession with tracking Vincent from the UK and the role his mother played in keeping them apart. He concedes that Vincent wanted nothing to do with him once he had been traced in America. Poor Edwards was jealous of the women residents' attention and so killed them all, or "fixed them" as he terms it. A struggle ensues and it looks like she is going to be killed until a shot rings out: it is from Alex, bloodied and exhausted.

Neither Scream nor Torchlight were critically well-received but the actor wasn't all disparaging when interviewed by Rosemarie Aguilar for the Daily Trojan (4 March 1985) whilst promoting his new play Inadmissible Evidence, "I enjoyed playing them for what they represent within each script and you're servicing the piece as a whole usually. Sidney the drug pusher in Torchlight…he was fun to play... you don't know who he likes. Vincent's mother-fixated, obsessive... he was fun as well, I liked him. They all retain a certain little piece of your heart."

Another busy year, 1985 also proved fruitful for Ian with a stage role saw him back at the Matrix Theatre three years after acting in their 1982 production of Betrayal, Ian was the star name in an award-winning production of John Osborne's 1965 play Inadmissible Evidence. Directed by Kristoffer Siegel-Tabori, his lauded central portrayal of solicitor Bill Maitland saw him win Best Lead performance at the 1985 Drama Critics Circle Awards (Siegel-Tabori and Designer A. Clark Duncan took home the others). The actor had a vague recollection of seeing Nicol Williamson play the role on the West End in London back in 1965.

"It's a very heavy piece," Ian told Susan King of the Los Angeles Examiner (4 February). My character never stops talking. It's a great part. Of course, you don't get paid, you can't. The one thing that you want it to be is right. Therefore, the people who have got to be paid are the technical people. Most of the best work you do is in the lower end of the pay scale. We're not doing a play for me to play Maitland, it's the play itself. If the play's no good, there's no point in doing it."

Opening on Friday 16 February after several previews allowed the production to be fine-tuned; this early-1960s piece received tremendous reviews, all of which highlighted his performance. Dan Sullivan, the theatre critic of the L.A. Times, offered "Osborne and McShane make Maitland a fascinating case, not so much for his murky midlife crisis (nothing new there) but for the commitment with which he is acting it out...this is a man who finds the human race, including himself, absolutely despicable...he still craves love.."

Chatting with L.A. Times reporter Janice Arkatov, the actor expressed his feelings about the role, "...a man...who's going over the edge," McShane said, "It's a very written-from-the-gut play. The character is confused and he's flailing. He has the idea that love between a man and a woman demands obligations, summonses, time-keeping. So that anonymous love, in this case, homosexuality, sort of excites him. On the other hand, he does want the comfort of a family and a wife, so it's the anomaly of ... things that he can't put together. An extraordinary piece..."

Meantime, a little later, Ed Kaufman of The Hollywood Reporter (25 February) added "As the aggressive and agitated Maitland, Ian McShane is absolutely wonderful - a man "on trial" for a way of life. As fine an evening of theatre as you could want."

Drama-Logue's Terry Fisher added, "Beetle-browed McShane brilliantly imbues the role...with a neurotic intensity that spews ugliness and disgust. McShane forces his rugged good looks into a grotesquery of all the agonies that haunt Maitland's empty life... [He] plays Maitland to the hilt with the force of a poisoned dagger stuck in him...slowly filling him with venom and draining his life of purpose, reason and fulfilment. This production has the stamp of excellence all over it." Variety (19 March) proved equally glowing: "McShane delivers a staggering performance as loathsome, loutish, disintegrating solicitor...[his] particular achievement is bringing an uncanny vein of sympathy to a man raging with hate, boredom and self-contempt, although there's no sympathy in the writing. McShane's character could be a self-pitying bore, but the actor's vigour and persuasion lift this cad to a...consuming interest."

"Smoldering [sic] passion. Hidden desire. Sacrificed love.
The story of a lifetime."

That was the press advertisement to promote the television premiere of Evergreen, a three-part series beginning on Sunday 24 February 1985 and running across 2 more consecutive nights. A popular 1978 novel by Belva Plain, it was adapted by Jerome Kass for NBC with Ian third-billed behind Lesley Ann Warren & Armand Assante and using a slight American accent to portray Paul Lerner, son of a wealthy businessman. In an L.A. Times interview that February, he termed his character an "erudite, quintessential New York banking Waspy Jew".

When housemaid Anna (Ms Warren) arrives, he is instantly smitten, as is she. Inviting her to lunch and returning to the house later they share a passionate embrace. However, he is obliged to wed Marion (Glynis Davies), the news of which she finds devastating. Anna subsequently marries (Armand Assante) and gives birth to a son; Paul is the father unbeknownst to him.

Time and decades pass and we later see them meet again and watch as Ian's hair is hilariously greyed! For Paul, his love for her never fades, "I made a mistake. I made the biggest mistake of my life and I've been paying for it every day since. I loved you then. I love you now. I just never knew how much....not an hour in the day goes by I don't think of you, Anna."

Do they get together in the end and make a new life in Italy? Who knows as Evergreen is another impossible-to-view Ian McShane project. A paperback tie-in featuring the principal cast members was published with a smaller photo of him on its cover.

Broadcast over 5 consecutive nights between Sunday 31 March - Thursday 4 April, the epic mini-series A.D. was adapted from the recent Anthony Burgess novel The Kingdom of the Wicked. Co-written by him with Vincenzo Labella, Burgess had previously collaborated with Ian McShane on Jesus of Nazareth. Its opening theme and the Lovejoy one composed by Denis King were included on the 1986 compilation album Telly Hits 2 (as was Miami Vice; another show Ian guest-starred on).

With its huge $300m budget the tie-in paperback proclaimed it "The Magnificent story of triumph, passion and a love that changed our world forever."

Coupling the New Testament with added fictional material in such a major production there was bound to be cast members that had worked with McShane either before or after and A.D. is no exception. In one of his final roles, Last of Sheila co-star James Mason acts with him; here as Tiberius to Ian's ambitious Sejanus. Neil Dickinson would subsequently be in The Murders at Rue Morgue whilst there is also a part for The Wild and the Willing co-star David Sumner and a major role for John McEnery, a friend of William Shakespeare in the TV series. Ava Gardner from The Ballad of Tam Lin can also be seen in amongst a huge, international cast.

A.D. ran for many hours and the first time that we see the actor is when he and Jack Warden return to see the ailing Emperor Tiberius on Capri. Wrapped in a burnt ochre-coloured toga and hair brushed forward, as Sejanus, Ian looks the part and delivers the clunky dialogue perfectly.

The modern-day Braker was a two-hour TV cop show pilot with Rocky nemesis Carl Weathers starring as Lt. Harry Braker. Shown on ABC in America on Sunday 28 April it was directed by Victor Lobl and co-written by James Carabatsos & Felix Culver. Not picked up, it saw roles for both Ian (as Alan Roswell) and his wife, Gwen (as Kate).

Ian is heard at the start of the music maverick Grace Jones' record Slave to the Rhythm providing the introduction "Ladies and gentlemen: Miss Grace Jones. Slave to the Rhythm". A classic, he appeared on her album of the same name reading a lengthy excerpt from Ian Penman's essay The Annihilation of Rhythm before the commencement of the opening track Jones the Rhythm.

Shot at Limehouse Studios, London, American Playhouse: Rocket to the Moon was a Channel 4 co-production with PBS in

America, and the latter screened it on Monday 5 May at 9 pm. They termed it "Clifford Odets forgotten masterpiece", a 1938 play adapted for television by Wesley Moore it became the penultimate work to be directed by John Jacobs. Set in the sticky New York heat of 1938, at a dental surgery, Ian is the rather amusingly titled Willy Wax (I imagine it caused him a few giggles, too) who arrives just on the hour mark as a patient to dentist Ben Stark (John Malkovich). The first of two roles in the playwright's work, Ian utilises an American accent as a smart-suited "lone wolf" musical producer who is excitedly welcomed by the tooth man's new Secretary Cleo (Judy Davis). She is attracted to his perceived, glamorous life and harbours faint hopes for a career on stage but becomes entangled with married man Stark and seems to be desired by every man that she meets. Australian-born actress Judy Davis is Ms. Singer, the lonely young woman looking for love and prone to fabrication that is also longed for by Ben's insightful father-in-law, Eli Wallach.

Flirting, Willy and Cleo the former's desire is of a physical type, the latter is looking to get a step up the career ladder only. Later, they are confronted by this realisation when Cleo resists his off-screen advances and scratches the predator's face.

During all this, Ben's equally unfulfilled wife Belle (Connie Booth) sees the threat of the younger woman and is devastated to hear him confess his involvement with her.

Ian is in a few scenes; with his final appearance towards the end of the play (it cannot betray its origins). "This is how you behave over a little pony that can't stand on its own two feet," asks an anxious Willy after Ben throttles him. Moments later Cleo arrives and forces the disbelieving Mr Wax away. This is the last we see of him before the couple have a heart-to-heart which Mr Prince (Wallach) challenges when presenting her with the least romantic marriage proposal ever heard.

Rocket was launched in the UK on Thursday 4 September 1986 at 9.30 pm.

Originating as an 1841 short story by Edgar Allan Poe, The Murders in the Rue Morgue had been filmed twice before Ian made an appearance in a 1986 TV film version starring George C.Scott & Rebecca De Mornay as father and daughter Auguste and Claire Dupin. Adapted by David Epstein and directed by Jeannot Szwarc, their Paris looks gorgeous.

Its 1899 and Miss De Mornay lives with her father, a pragmatic Mr Scott, a renowned Parisian police detective recently forced into retirement. But when her toadying fiancé Adolphe (Biggles star Neil Dickinson) is accused of the gruesome murders of two ladies in the fictitious area Rue Morgue, she pleads with him to help. Initially declining, he reconsiders and is assisted by godson Phillipe (Val Kilmer, given little to do) to try to find out who the real killer is.

Mr McShane arrives to investigate, resembling a snooker pro or magician with a long cape and period moustache. He and Dupin (Scott) have a mutual antagonism due to the latter having solved past cases which the Prefect, as Ian is known in the story, left unresolved.

With other slayings occurring, many locals fear going out into the shadowy Paris streets alone whilst Dupin and Phillipe begin their sleuthing. This leads Dupin to be confronted by the Prefect before he discovers the id of the killer & accomplice.

Calling at his office at the police station late one evening, Dupin startles the Prefect by attempting to throttle him and voicing his findings. Accompanied by many officers, the two go to arrest the culprits at night and the viewer has to stifle a giggle at seeing Ian dressed like a naval officer, complete with medals on his chest.

Trawling the local park where victims had been murdered previously, hilariously, Claire (a wooden Ms De Mornay) is attacked by a rather unusual assailant. Rather than reveal the moment, I would urge the reader to seek out the film.

"How can you stop what you don't understand?" asks the taglines on the original VHS sleeve. Who knows; but what we do know is that Mr McShane and director Mr Szwarc immediately reconvened for another small-screen project: Grand Larceny.

Before that, something rather special arrived this year on British television. Ian had been working on The Great Escape II mini-series when a fan sent him a Jonathan Gash Lovejoy novel, which he read on a transatlantic flight back to the UK.

Looking for a comedy-drama to work on, the actor thought it might make an interesting project.

It was either this or a project about biographer Boswell; so we think he made the right choice.

With friend and colleague Allan McKeown, they got Ian Le Frenais to write an outline for a TV dramatisation and so Ian met with Mr Gash (a pseudonym used by Dr John Grant) to discuss the idea. As already mentioned, he and McKeown, who sadly died in 2013 after a long battle with cancer, has since been acknowledged by the actor of learning a great deal from this sharp-minded man and friend. They had initially met on If It's Tuesday, It Must Be Belgium; with McShane acting and Allan the onset hairdresser.

Naturally, the TV version of Lovejoy (no first name) is quite a bit different from the printed version but none the worse for this. On the page, the seedy travails of the penniless antique divvy are told across 24 novels published between 1977-2006, many strands featuring in the telly scripts. For the uninitiated, a "divvy", is someone who has an emotional response to a genuine antique upon seeing it, antiques are everything to Lovejoy.

Antagonist Charlie Gimbert features in the books and is brought to life so perfectly by Malcolm Tierney, however, he does not feature in all the series.

The beautiful Lady Jane Felsham (Phyllis Logan) is absent from the novels too, as is young Eric; brilliantly portrayed by Chris Jury who provides great comedy relief as Lovejoy's dozy, over-aged apprentice. As for Tinker, barely recognisable in his TV rebirth ala Dudley Sutton, quite some way from the repugnant character so enjoyed between the pages.

Usually shot within a May-December filming schedule, the opening series came to BBC TV on Friday 10 January 1986.

Filling the 9.30 pm slot, the show offered 10 episodes. It didn't set the world alight and received little promotion with Ian not doing a great deal to publicise it.

Driving a Volvo, which the actor hated, here the technique of addressing the camera directly was incorporated and away from the UK, it was known as "The Lovejoy Mysteries".

The opening shows did wonders for the Long Melford area, with cast/ crew resident at the George & Dragon pub and often found enjoying a tipple in the nearby Swan.

A strong opening episode, taking its essence from a Lovejoy novel, The Firefly Gadroon was written by Mr Le Frenais (another was The Judas Pair, whilst essences of other novels also pervade

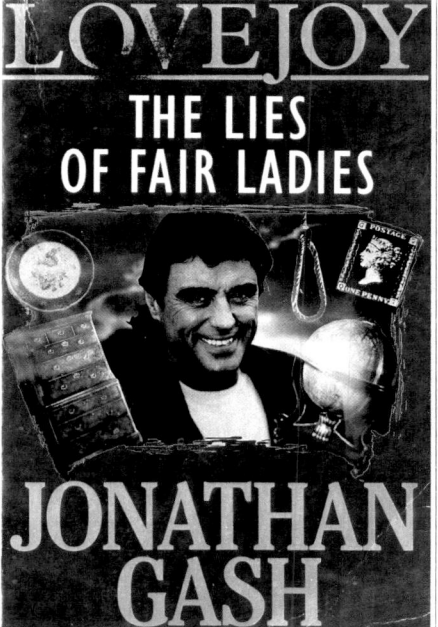 

series one). A learning curve for all, storylines were written by him alongside other writers. Many actors and directors that Mr McShane had previously worked with or would subsequently, feature in the opener i.e. Space: 1999's Zienia Merton, Anthony Jackson, Geoffrey Bateman, Anthony Valentine & most memorably, Ronald Fraser, making the first of his 2 separate appearances. Ian's old mate Francis Megahy scripted episode 7, too. In homage to Ian McShane's father, Harry, Lovejoy can often be seen drinking from a Manchester United F.C. mug.

Also this year, Ian narrated Village Voice, part of Open Space, another BBC programme.

Written by Jaws creator Peter Benchley, Barrington was an entry in the CBS Summer Playhouse series and shown on Friday 10 July 1987. It was a one-off story starring Matt Salinger in the lead and Ian as Marbury. Space: 1999 star Barbara Bain played Salinger's screen wife in this American anthology.

Second billed to the attractive Marilu Henner (of TV's Taxi fame) Grand Larceny (1988) was written by Peter Stone and directed by Jeannot Szwarc. Henner is 'Freddy', the estranged daughter of Charles Grand (Frenchman Louis Jordan only ever seen via a computer program wittily called DADD). Learning of his death, she travels to the South of France to clear up his affairs and it is here that she meets Flannagan (Ian McShane), a former friend and colleague of his who knew her father whilst both were incarcerated. Ian's character learns that Mr Grand was a thief, just like

GRAND LARCENY

Ian "Lovejoy" McShane in sun, sand and swindles on the Côte d' Azur

Starring: Ian McShane
Omar Sharif

Television Entertainment

Gems

former safecracker Mr McShane. However, both men had been involved in schemes that saw already stolen items being reacquired/stolen by the team.

The novel video program explained to her by Flannagan shows her father able to respond to certain questions that she might ask, with pre-recorded responses. It seems that Charles (Jordan) wants her to continue the family business and sets her a task to see if she is up to it. Flannagan expects her to fail and if so she will not receive all her father's assets.

The task is given to her by Morrison (James Cossins), another Brit abroad; Ian's character is supposed to be Irish but there's no hint of an accent present, employed by an insurance firm outlines that she is to locate a valuable stolen racehorse. Tanned and well-dressed here, McShane was 45 at the time of making the picture and the whole thing plays like a glossy TV movie.

Back to the plot and someone doesn't want her to investigate but nothing is quite what it seems in Grand Larceny. This includes the introduction of playboy horse breeder Rashid Saud (a typecast Omar Sharif) who takes a shine to the lass. .

Her attempts to purloin the horse, with a little help from Flanagan, look likes succeeding until Omar and his cronies scupper their scheme. She is locked in a cellar but fortunately gets rescued by Flanagan in the nick of time and the race is on to stop Mr Saud from transporting the valuable equine overseas. Ms Henner does well as the pace of the film thankfully grows too.

She eventually manages to outwit the others and things turn out to be something more in a fun, late twist. Larceny fittingly aired on British television one Saturday night in 1988 and the small screen seemed its right home (one its VHS covers is shown on page 101).

A classic slice of 1980s drama, enhanced by a silky synth theme by Jan Hammer, Miami Vice proved a mighty success in its day; running for 111 episodes across five seasons between 1984-89.

Often deemed more surface than substance, we follow suave Vice detectives Crockett and Tubbs, Don Johnson & Philip Michael Thomas, with their liking for expensive suits and cars, rolled up sleeves and pastel tones.

Ian was a guest star in 2 episodes, playing different characters but utilising the same hackneyed South American accent.

His initial role comes in Knock, Knock... Who's There? and was shown on Monday 24 October 1988. Episode 21 in the third 'season', it was followed by Freefall, episode 17 in the final season, airing on Monday 20 August 1990.

As Esteban Montoya in Knock, Knock, amusingly his character wears a dinner suit, complete with dickie bow tie, in all his scenes, most of which feature D.E.A. agent Colby (Elizabeth Ashley). We do get to see him with the leads at the start of the story when he is engaged in a drugs deal at his Club 78 venue. The duo is undercover but gets their arrest spoilt by the intervention of a bogus D.E.A (Drug Enforcement Administration) who steals all the money and gear. They take Montoya into custody but are unable to hold him subsequently and he is allowed to continue his shady dealings.

Aided by Colby, their first-seen meeting is hilarious; shot at night, Signor Montoya arrives by speedboat and the two chat on something that resembles a 1980s music video shoot. Indeed, the background music plays as Ian's man applies pressure on his police insider to keep tipping him off about raids.

Led by 'Sonny' Crockett (Johnson) he and his colleagues look to reveal who that person is, unaware that it is the wife of their old colleague. Under tremendous financial pressure to pay for medical treatment for their son, her husband is wheelchair-bound after being shot whilst on duty.

In a further chat with the stressed Colby, Esteban is again in his penguin suit only now with an added Dracula-style cape (later we see him in a long leather coat). He is keen to get details of Sonny's background as he has plans to eliminate him thus preventing him from making further money from drug deals. Calling him direct, Sonny is surprised to hear from him and his offer of a new deal.

They agree to meet in the crowded Little Havana district where extras mill about and enjoy glancing at the camera whilst a showdown begins as an elaborate stage show goes on in the background. Defiantly not one of Ian's strongest acting roles, the climax occurs after we see Crockett and his team mingling amongst the people and Esteban and his gorillas arriving with guns.

The confrontation commences with shots heard and people killed as Esteban flees, first holding a female stallholder as a shield before casting her aside and running off towards what looks like a hotel or something similar.

It's hard to tell, what with the soft pastel lighting and Sonny pursuing him. All faintly ridiculous stuff, as Esteban reloads his pistol, the hedgehog-styled, barnet-wearing Sonny sneaks up and points his gun at him. An anticlimax, a grinning Esteban Montoya surrenders. The best moment occurs at the close where Sonny reads the rights to a wounded agent Colby.

Yield of the Long Bond was a contemporary play by which Larry Atlas is known. Directed by former actor Andrew J.Robinson, its world premiere occurred on Thursday 14 May 1998 with the production running until Monday 13 July.

With all its 99 seats priced at $20, "The small Matrix Theater Co. is one of L.A.'s most reliable purveyors of quality revivals," offered Variety's Charles Isherwood. Ian was cast as "....Satan-the soulless Paul Rosario, a charismatic, impeccably dressed, morally bankrupt tycoon on the Verge of being financially bankrupt as well," as Debbi K. Swanson commented in the magazine Rave!

Robinson had won the L.A. Drama Critics Circle Best Director for The Homecoming and Endgame; the only double winner in the 30-year history of the Circle. Uniquely utilising two actors to alternate in playing the same role, Ian and Gregory Itzin, the show garnered rave reviews.

This year found Ian acting in a number of made-for-TV offerings including The Great Escape II: The Untold Story, a lengthy, two-part series made for American television which would air on 6 & 7 November 1988 on NBC.

Most of us would have seen The Great Escape on one of its annual Christmastime telly screenings or elsewhere, but what of this? Written by Walter Halsey Davis, it is not a docu-drama but a dramatised event of some actual events and so therefore I would steer you elsewhere to read about the actual escape.

Returning to the GEII, "75 men escaped. 25 made it. 50 were brutally executed. Now, it's payback time!" roared the press advert for the telefilm, which was also repeated on its subsequent VHS box cover. Released on the Vidmark Entertainment & RCA Columbia label almost 90 minutes was cut from these versions whilst a DVD release sadly remains non-forthcoming.

For Ian McShane fans, we need only concern ourselves with Part I, The Untold Story, as the actor does not feature in the concluding

The Final Chapter, as his character, pilot Roger Bushell is one of the men brutally murdered on the hour mark.

Superman actor Christopher Reeve, never the most demonstrative of performers takes the lead as Major John Dodge, cousin to Britain's war-time leader Winston Churchill, and would-be escapee at Stalag Luft III, mainly filled with R.A.F men like Bushell, and warmly welcomed back by the men at the start of the story. Ian's character looks resplendent in the iconic blue uniform, oversized cap and dapper white scarf. As the "Big X" he is the lead organiser of the ongoing escape tunnel known by but not yet discovered, by the "Jerrys" or "Goons" as the prisoners know them.

The cast certainly dresses the part, all in various uniforms, but everyone looks too clean and crisp for the 1940s wartime setting which might remind fans of his similar role in The Battle of Britain.

Many want to bring forward the escape date, with Bushell and Dodge agreeing that it will still go on. With civilian clothes and fake papers created for 200, that figure is way off come.

With darkness as cover, the duo is shocked to discover that one of the tunnels is short and that it comes out perilously close to a security position. Complicated by an ongoing air raid, we watch as Ian and many others utilise the trolley system to transport them along the tunnel. Yank Corey (Tony Denison) is discovered by a nearby guard enjoying a sly cigarette, before the alarm is sounded and they reluctantly leave their colleague.

It is revealed that 76 men managed to abscond, putting pressure on the Camp Kommandant who is confronted by a furious Dr Absalon (Donald Pleasance, who has also been in the 1963 film). A man with some influence, he informs him that the Gestapo is likely to dish out punishment to those involved.

Meanwhile, Dodge (Reeve), Bushell (McShane) and others, all dressed in civvies, board a departing train and sit silently as the atmosphere of suspicion around them proves palpable.

Forced to flee before pulling into a heavily manned station where they face arrest, Bushell loses his hat whilst running.

Elsewhere, an incensed Fuhrer employs Burchardt (Michael Nader with a comedy German accent almost as awful as Charles Haid's fake Brit) to eliminate those caught by joining Absalon.

Ian, Reeve and Denison find their characters initially aided by a friendly farmer before being betrayed and recaptured.

It is stated that 22 men have been returned but for the trio, they face a stay at the notorious Hartheim prison where many, many people were murdered during the war. Major Dodge (Reeve) asks Ian why they have been brought there as they are neither political prisoners nor high ranking officers. "Because no one has ever escaped from here: except in a coffin," is his curt reply. The men are in danger but McShane's Bushell is singled out by Burchardt upon reading his records. Looking at them, we see that his R.A.F. pilot is meant to be 24 but in 1998 the actor was 46 already!

Taken to a wood at night, Bushell and some other men are informed by Absalon that Hitler has condemned them to death and has already executed 2 escapees personally, the fanatical Burchardt shoots them as Ian's character and the others begin to recite the Lord's Prayer.

Back at Hartheim, Dodge discovers that the men have perished and he and his pals continue with their escape plans but their time is dissipating.

Filmed in the former Yugoslavia, the first part, The Untold Story, was directed by Paul Wedkos whilst the second was by Jud Taylor, an actor back in the 1963 original.

The concluding segment of the story consists of Dodge, Corey and others seeking those responsible for the deaths after the balance of power switches as war comes to an end.

Ian and attractive co-star Leslie Bevis featured in Chain Letter, a curious supernatural thriller for ABC television in the States which was broadcast late on Saturday evening 5 August.

The premise, created by William Bleich, was that a chain letter was sent out to various people presenting differing temptations. If they took the bait, it proved fatal. Ian is the Messenger of Death, with Ms Bevis his secretary, Miss Jones, for this unsold pilot directed by Thomas J. Wright, the man who helmed Torchlight back in 1984.

Winner of multiple awards War and Remembrance covers the period from the Japanese attack on Pearl Harbour in December 1941 through to August 1945 when atomic bombs were dropped on Nagasaki and Hiroshima.

The Herman Wouk novel provided the source material for 30 hours of prime time TV furnished by worldwide shooting locations and a top-notch cast.

A sequel to The Winds of War, Remembrance [sic] presented roles for many established actors including Robert Mitchum at its heart. John Gielgud, Brian Blessed (seen fleetingly onscreen with Ian) and Patrick Floersheim enhanced the McShane connection. Ian can be seen on the opening credits too. Our man is cast as journalist Phil Rule, a hard-drinking figure sited in Singapore, then British-controlled but on the edge of collapse to the marauding Japanese.

Reconnecting with father and daughter visitors Robert Morley & the shimmering Victoria Tenant, Rule knows them well. "Talky" aka Mr Morley, is subsequently obliged to relocate and give a propaganda speech from Australia, leaving behind the ever-so-pretty "Tudsy".

Seen in a white tux at one of the many parties, on Christmas Eve she subsequently comes to him and he declares that he still loves her. She replies that he hasn't changed and naturally they sleep together even though she has a soft spot for Mitchum's character (and he tells another person that she has a boyfriend in the R.A.F). Interestingly, we get a glimpse into his past as their previous liaison in Paris is mentioned as is his estranged Russian ballerina wife (who remains unseen).

With such a large cast of characters, Ian comes in and out of the story. Relocated to Moscow by 1943, we see him in shorts and shirt comfortably schmoozing with the British Ambassador whilst able to switch to a suit in the evening for a party invite.

Disappearing thereafter, his death is revealed by a letter sent by Pamela (Miss Tennant) to "Pug" (Mitchum) where she speaks of his passing via a menacing V-2 Nazi missile.

Costing a fortune to make, not surprisingly the Emmy-winning mini-series failed to recoup its mammoth $135 production costs (acknowledged by Executive Producer Brandon Stoddard, who also confirmed that 46k people worked on the series). Shown in chunks of 3 hours from November 1998 onwards, more episodes arrived in May of the following year. For the 2019 documentary Master of Dark Shadows which remembers Dan Curtis, director of War & Remembrance, Mr McShane provided the narration.

Not to be confused with either the 1967 or the 1985 war film, The Dirty Dozen was a short-lived telly series consisting of 11 episodes shown from Saturday 30 April, with Mr McShane as Lindberger in episode 9, Don Danko. Fellow cast member Amadeus August was also involved, and the two would soon be seen together again in the small-screen Dick Francis TV film In The Frame.

Set in Lisbon, Portugal in 1943 the "dirty dozen" set about stopping a Nazi-funding counterfeit money operation. Directed by the prolific Ray Austin and written by David Thoreau, Sitting Target director Douglas Hickox also directed several episodes.

In 1989 a succession of television appearances came for Ian both in the UK & the States coming in The Last Video Show; episode 4 in series 7 of Minder, a massively popular comedy-drama starring Dennis Waterman & George Cole, as Terry and Arthur Daley, respectively, by now firmly established as a small screen favourite with audiences.

McShane and screen wife Rula Lenska are rudely woken by an early morning police raid led by Inspector Dwyer (a beard-free Brian Blessed) and carted off to the local nick in a storyline when we used to watch films on videotape and actually visit a store to rent them.

Here, a saucy feature showing Dwyer in a compromising position with a young woman via a set-up created by renowned gangster Jack Last (Ian) is inadvertently mixed-up with some rental tapes from 'Daley Videos' situated next door to one of Jack's businesses. The snide Dwyer is calling time on his aiding and abetting the latter's criminal activity but the valuable tape is being used to persuade him to reconsider!

A sharp-suited, accented Ian and a heavy visit the store to retrieve it only to find former boxer Terry manning the desk. Initially friendly, Jack soon becomes irked upon hearing that the tape is out on rental to the sleazy Ken Campbell and he will have to wait until it is returned the following day. The heavy wants to give McCann (Waterman) a slap whilst the condescending Mr Last agrees to return but not before threatening to destroy the shop if his precious cargo is not returned. Dwyer and his partner follow behind.

A sterling cast also features future co-star Ray Winstone who enjoyed a recurring role as Arnie, a young man keen to make a few quid however he can and not necessarily via legal means! Also featured is Tony Vogel from A.D. & Marco Polo.

Come the morning and Terry arrives at the shop with Jack and his heavy following. Hooky videos being another Daley line of commerce being exploited by the businessman proves fortuitous as Terry cunningly makes duplicates of the incriminating tape after learning of Arthur also being threatened.

Looking like somebody is going to get hurt the condescending Ian pleads to get his tape back and asks if there is a back way out of the shop after having it returned. As Terry leads him through behind the counter, the heavy asks his boss if he can hit him and in a nice bit of fight choreography, a battle ensues. Terry whacks the bruiser first then Jack (McShane) lunges at him behind the counter and gets thrown over it and onto the shop floor in a sequence that is not performed fully by the actor.

Arthur (Cole), Arnie (Winstone) and others are miraculously released from police custody following Dwyer's sway with his immediate superiors and all seems well.

At home, Jack and his wife set about to watch the tape only to segue into some children's show before any adult scene was revealed. Flabbergasted, we see Dwyer (Blessed) and a crony discovering likewise and experiencing the same outcome. The episode, shown on ITV on Monday 29 January 1989, was directed by the veteran Roy Ward Baker who also helmed another dozen episodes before his final telly work in 1992 after initially starting as a film director. It was written by Andrew Payne, who also furnished scripts for 2 Dick Francis racing films starring Ian in 1989: Bloodsport & In the Frame.

Young Charlie Chaplin made for television by the now-defunct ITV franchise Thames was originally a 6-part series sketchily detailing the early life and rise of Chaplin across almost 3 hours. Released to coincide with the year of his centenary, most of us would be unaware that Charlie came from a theatrical family; with his mother, Hannah; 1960s model Twiggy and father, Charles Snr, as portrayed by Ian, both performers in the business.

With his young son watching in the wings, Charles plays to a music hall crowd wearing a tuxedo and top hat singing the popular comedy song Champagne Charlie and getting the audience to join in. Offstage, things were a little different, as his drinking and womanising caused a split with Hannah and a separation from his 2 sons, Charlie (Joe Geary doing a fine job in one of his few acting roles) and Sydney (Lee Whitlock).

In the opening episode, Charles (Ian) leaves for another woman and his family to tremendous poverty. As the emotionally fragile Hannah, Twiggy puts in a fine performance as she tries desperately to keep the family together despite enduring hardship and difficulties concerning her fragile mental health. Receiving a letter from her husband, with the audience hearing Ian's voice, it orders her to leave him alone and not to ask for money; a cruel thing to do and something for which the real Chaplin senior was arrested. Prone to be seen wearing a hat, Mr McShane is not suited to such attire and looks quite an odd sight.

Ian gets to sing several songs, miming to Champagne and others either on stage or in local public houses and tellingly, we see the aspiring talent Charlie taking some aspects of his father's routines to utilise later on in his career. Here though, both he and Sydney still have a love for their errant father who shows them how to get a free meal at posh restaurants   and struggles with his relationships with women. One of them, Louise, Georgia Allen regularly lambastes him and demands that he get rid of Charlie after he brings the traumatised youngster to their home following Miss Hannah's admittance to the local mental asylum (something that reoccurs). This talented actress would reconvene with McShane on a Lovejoy episode, subsequently.

The drama ends with Charlie being given his first step up the theatrical ladder via his father and about to head off to America and eternal worldwide fame.

But before then, Ian and master Geary combine well in demonstrating the affection between father and son via their scenes together. Young Charlie Chaplin seems to have been made with a nod towards the American market and some hackneyed scripting by Colin Schindler with Andrew Nickolds and Stan Hey. The former would subsequently reunite with Ian on both Lovejoy & Madson (writing an episode of the former and a producer on the latter). Director Baz Taylor would also work on a great many Lovejoy episodes.

By recommending his almost-teenaged son for a touring production helps set the boy on his career, seemingly bowing to Louise's demands to get rid of him.

When an elated Charles inherits a pub from his uncle, he is in his element singing around the piano with the customers whilst poor Hannah crumbles behind the bar under the pressure.

As Charlie, Joe visits his ailing father, wheezing and gasping for air, in hospital, in their final scene onscreen together. Sadly, it was common for many musical hall artists to succumb to alcoholism and Charles Senior was a case; he died aged 38 when his son was 12.

Not brilliant but an amiable watchable, Young Charlie Chaplin was nominated for a Prime Time Emmy over in America (as well as being recognised at the Chicago Film Festival) and was initially shown on Wednesday 25 January 1989. The production made the front page of popular TV listings magazine TV Times for the week commencing 21 January, with photos of the cast and Chaplin himself on the 40p cover.

By the time Ian arrived in Texas as writer/ director Don Lockwood, Dallas was into its twelfth season when his initial appearance was broadcast on BBC TV on Wednesday 5 April 1989. Filling the 8 pm slot, that classic split-screen opening and theme from Jerrold Immel helped make it a massive ratings winner and popular success. Detailing the antics, family and business-related, of the Ewing family at their South Fork ranch, its most memorable member being J.R. aka the inimitable Larry Hagman, who coincidentally also directed Ian's first episode: Comings & Goings. As an aside, TV Guide magazine voted Ian's Deadwood cowboy sixth in their list of all-time baddies, with J.R. naturally at no.1.

Looking like he has stepped off the set of Lovejoy, we see that Don favours blue jeans, a white polo shirt and a leather jacket ensemble upon being introduced to Sue Ellen (Linda Gray).

Ridiculously, she is seeking a writer to flesh out her "….Texas version of Citizen Kane", and he takes on the job after initially being a bit sceptical, "The man is an absolute monster!" Speaking with J.R.'s niece Lucy (Charlene Tilton), she reveals details about her uncle and many of his nefarious past deeds to the newcomer.

Seen across the final 13 episodes of the season, Don & the emotionally-vulnerable Sue Ellen soon become romantically involved. Constantly needing reassurance, virtually every scene with his new love ends with them kissing. There is warm chemistry between the two actors and Miss Gray clearly got on well with Ian as immediately after she made a guest appearance in Lovejoy.

Giving the widowed filmmaker her diaries to draw inspiration from, there is much humour in their fledgling relationship despite Sue Ellen being deeply affected by subsequently reading the screenplay and watching the filming. Ian does appear alongside Mr Hagman but only briefly as virtually all his screen time is next to Miss Gray. Most of those moments occur at the film studio, where the two walk around the sound stage or talk in his office.

Inevitably with so many episodes made, some of the acting is occasionally a little uneven; a particular instance seeing Ian's fury at discovering Sue Ellen having surreptitiously read his rough draft. Amusingly, Mr McShane is often seen pretending to drink from empty cups or mugs for which he is an expert here (take a look next time you see him).

Seeing major casting in place, Sue Ellen is overwrought by the sense of reality but for her, the motivation is to make public her ex-husband's wretched behaviour towards her and others. And with the filming advancing, she and Lockwood draw ever crosser. So much so that she arranges for him to meet her son, John Ross. Introduced at a restaurant, the young boy is frosty and seems hostile toward the Brit, initially.

With the production closing down after filming is completed, Sue Ellen is shocked to hear that Don has been offered a lucrative & possibly career-defining new job that will take him away for at least a year. Could this sound the end of their relationship? He thinks not and wants her to accompany him.

At the wrap party, Don chats with her and Lucy in the closing episode, Reel Life. Wearing a little cowboy hat, to distinguish himself from J.R, he declares his love and wants her to relocate to the UK with him. She replies that she needs to think about the offer and to talk with her son.

This is Ian's departing appearance in the soap and actress Linda Gray also left the show (but she would return subsequently). John Ross says that he doesn't want to leave South Fork and his family but agrees that she should go and that they can stay in contact with regular visits. The series closes with Sue Ellen showing J.R. a cut of the finished film and he is left astonished and furious by what he sees up on the screen. He demands that it be destroyed but a gleeful Sue Ellen declines.

A distinctly 1980s feel pervades the made-for-TV trilogy of feature-length stories coming under the Dick Francis Mysteries monocle featuring Ian as Jockey Club investigator (who knew they even had one?) David Cleveland.

Twice Shy, In The Frame & Blood Sport followed his various adventures across Ireland, Canada and Germany and the 1989 project could easily have been made into an affable, afternoon-type series. Sourced from novels published by former jockey Francis, he died in 2010.

Twice Shy kicks off proceedings with Ian over in Ireland following the death of a friend killed whilst climbing. David decides to visit the family following a round of golf with his boss (Patrick McNee given scant to do).

Over there, his nephew is a prize young jockey whilst Donna (Dearbhla Molloy) is the distraught wife being hounded by occupants of a mysterious car and whose closet contains things that she would rather be kept private: namely an affair with Ted (John Keegan), a pal of Peter who happens to have valuable computer discs (this is 1989, remember) containing the formula to a lucrative betting scheme. This is naturally sought by many including those that will do whatever it takes to retrieve them; including murder.

Delving deeper, Cleveland (McShane) visits Ted and discovers his involvement and his affair with his friend's wife before pressuring him to tell the truth. The latter confesses that he got greedy and altered the files whilst his visitor warns him that others will come looking for them.

These include Liam (a weak Conor Mullen), the psychotic son of Fitzgerald (Nial Toibin), whose horse David's nephew is riding in an up and coming race. There is always such an event occurring in the

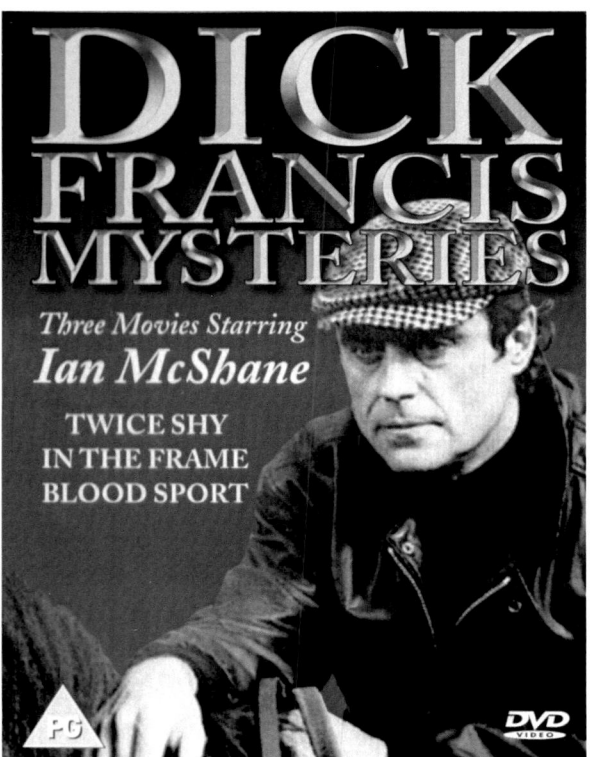

films although the equestrian plot link sometimes fades and they prove enjoyable viewing for anyone.

Another key event in each is the romantic life of the protagonist, here supplied by the pretty Kate McKenzie, Fitzgerald's screen daughter who runs the stables.

Come race day and David joins Cassie (Miss McKenzie) for a morning ride along and the viewer does acknowledge that Ian seems an able rider. He also has a penchant for a nice flat cap. As Cleveland, Ian portrays a creative man, familiar with using violence to protect himself.

A damn fine investigator, apart from the occasional awful suit choice, he also resembles Lovejoy, favouring a leather jacket and jeans and even doing the characteristic wink!

His delving is not always appreciated, "You should have been a policeman, Mr Cleveland," remarks a local copper. "Ah, but they wouldn't have me: insufficient charm," is his retort to the officious and tiresome plod.

Visiting the charming Mrs O'Rourke (Geraldine Fitzgerald) he cracks the case and discovers that her late husband had developed the scheme only to have it taken after confiding in Peter. She confides that it was Liam who took it. Subsequently contacting the police, he tells all and also informs them that he has the discs.

At the pre-race party, Keeble attends (McNee), expecting to see Cleveland there under the proviso of asking him to return to give a lecture somewhere. He arrives in a white tux after Cassie is kidnapped by Liam and his goon to use as barter for the discs.

Come morning and Cleveland and the police await a call. Liam orders William to bring the precious cargo to a secluded location. Placing a tracking device on him, the scheme fails once it is discovered and amusingly, Liam is written as if in a James Bond film. He also has a pistol which will have a fatal effect soon enough.

William is tied up alongside Cassie in a boathouse by a lake until Cleveland manages to find them after abseiling down the cliff face where Peter had died (clearly not the actor doing this). Finding them, Cleveland scuffles with one of the villains and Liam fires at the GARDA helicopter approaching. As they continue, he aims the gun but accidentally shoots his associate, "For crying out loud. You've gone and bloody well killed me!"

With the case closed, Cleveland returns to Mrs O'Rourke but is astonished when she declines his offer of the returned discs.

At a picturesque stone bridge, the investigator and Cassie stand together, "You're going to regret this!" she chides before he motions and throws the discs into the water, "Wanna bet?"

Twice Shy took as its source the original 1981 Dick Francis novel and was written by Miles Henderson. It received a VHS release and can be found on the DVD box set of all 3 films.

In the Frame, as the middle film, is arguably the strongest in the trilogy. Itself a novel from 1976, David Cleveland is in Toronto for a script written by future Lovejoy writer Andrew Payne. He had also written the Minder episode in which Ian had featured in recently, in a productive few years.

German director Wigbert Wicker takes over the production in this Canada-based story which then ventures into Germany.

Arriving at the mansion of his old pal Don (Lyman Ward) where he meets his friends including the gorgeous Marina (Barbara Rudnik who died in 2009) things take a sinister turn when the wife of one chap returns home to discover their house emptied before the place is blown up with her in it. Just who is the group behind it and why? "What's going on, David?" asks the lanky Bill, dwarfing Ian when occasionally shown next to him; Ward was 6' 3". Describing himself as an entrepreneur, his home is also emptied and the valuable wine in his cellar is also removed. Heavily in debt, Cleveland attempts to help his gambling-addictive mate.

In all the films, Mr McShane and other cast members are obliged to drive in and out of scenes and as we know from Lovejoy, the actor is quite swift on the pedals!

Investigations take him to Germany and a re-acquaintance with Marina who works for vineyard owner Hermann Forster (Amadeus August who had worked on Dallas when Ian was in amongst its cast). The two fancy each other and David warmly accepts her invitation to stay at her apartment whilst he visits gallery owner Wexford (Peter Saatman) owed money by David's friend. The horse riding connection is broached as Forster owns a racehorse soon to be competing in the country and a sub-plot involves an artist forging paintings featuring the creatures immortalised by Sir Alfred Munnings.

Don's unexpected arrival at Marina's place negates any development in the romance between David and their host and the duo set out to investigate further.

Visiting the art gallery incognito, with Ian putting on an abrasive accent to make himself known, he returns and is told that there are other pieces that he might be interested in purchasing. Left alone by Wexford to browse the works, Cleveland sneaks upstairs and goes through his private papers to find evidence. Disturbed by one of the owner's men, the snooper has to fight his way out and is chased around the town square until losing his aggressive pursuers.

Both Forster and Wexford are mixed up in a scam to steal from their mutual clients but meanwhile, Cleveland tells Don that he is going to return a painting to its rightful owner. He intends to do this on the day of the big race near the town which many locals attend.

The black leather jacket receives another airing and Wicker snappily directs a fun story.

Dressed in blue workman's overalls, David (McShane) busts into the gallery where the painting is stored, assisted by Don, who manages to get away from the racecourse in time to help. The two prove an amusing double act and successfully retrieve the artwork only to be chased by Wexford's thugs with the duo in a car and the others on a nippy motorcycle.

Meantime Marina discovers that her boss is in cahoots with Wexford and Don and David are adamant in wanting to sort this situation out before anyone else is hurt.

Hiding in a stunning rented property in the hills, Cleveland briefly returns to town to tell Marina to give Hermann his location: they will be expecting him and his cronies and so plan. Mr Cleveland is a resourceful character but things soon take a violent turn, when Forster arrives with Marina at gunpoint.

Wexford and his men also come along but David fixes them after another tasty fight with one of them. The kidnapper is furious and demands the painting, list of names and contact details of future theft victims and Wexford (who had been neutralised by Dan).

An amazing pursuit follows with Ian's Cleveland chasing after Forster who has Wexford in the back. Not to be outdone, the former is expertly able to manoeuvre downhill through a wood to get ahead of his assailant (who looks just as surprised to see him as anyone would surely be!) The German flips his car and the chase ends in an exciting onscreen moment. Kudos to the stunt people involved.

Exhausted and relieved, Cleveland stands next to the battered vehicle driven by Mr Forster as a police car pulls up and Marina and Don climb out. All are exhausted by their experiences and pleased that they made it through.

Speaking on the phone to Don, David is seen in bed and the two share an amusing exchange with the American hanging up as soon as the return of his and Marina's money is mentioned. She pulls him close and the two share a passionate embrace as we leave our Mr Cleveland's second outing now completed. As a novel, In The Frame took Francis in to double figures in books published worldwide.

Blood Sport (aka Power Play) is the final outing for investigator David Cleveland, opening with Ian, a horse-lover off-screen, with his latest partner enjoying a morning horse ride before he receives a call

to fly to Canada where a big race is due. Now involved with security, the organisers are worried about Munroe (Ron Van Hart) who intends to harm horses at events such as these.

Cleveland discovers him near one and there follows a speedy pursuit watched by startled onlookers at the track. It ends with the Brit head butting his assailant to subdue him! Not to be confused with the 1988

Van Damme feature of the same name, this Bloodsport received its own VHS video release and was again scripted by Andrew Payne.

Also in Canada for this one, Toronto, Ontario and other locations, Keeble (a devilishly underused McNee) mingles with horse owners including Teller (Kenneth Welsh) and persuades David (McShane) to join them for a jaunt on the lake the next day.

A wealthy individual, on his boat, Teller asks for Cleveland's help in locating his stolen $6m stallion called Chrysalis, which is presumed dead but he still feels is hidden away somewhere.

Out on the water on a jet ski, the millionaire is knocked off by a passing speed boat; but this is no accident rather a planned attack (later revealed to be by a couple involved with the kidnapping) intending to ward off any further investigation. Ian's character is a bit of an action man, diving in to save the injured Teller and bring him to safety.

He also discovers the abandoned speed boat and finds a clue: a matchbook advertising a chain of restaurants after steering another speedboat alongside it.

More expansive than the other stories, Bloodsport offers Mr McShane the chance to inject a little humour, especially in his interactions with insurance man Walt (a terrific Heath Lamberts, who sadly died in 2005).

Although David leads, Walt assists and they have fun dealing with the various situations that are met during the investigation after the Brit decides to stick around and help Mr Teller. This brings him into contact with the scrummy Linny (Carolyn Dunn), a younger woman who provides the libidinous Jockey Club investigator with some romantic interest and her sauce-loving stepmother Eunice (Jennifer Dale in full on vamp mode). She proves a little unstable, shooting at him and warning him about not treating Linny well after ruling out any physical contact between them. What is it about this man being so desirable to women? It is a trait common the films but the author guesses that like 007, bed-hopping is the norm.

Switching to Calgary, David & Linny have to visit all 34 venues in the chain to try to find clues to whoever was behind the wheel of the speedboat. He knows it was a man and a woman after video footage recorded the event. With no luck and only 3 locations remaining, their fortunes change when a bartender recognises the couple as Matt & Yola (a grouchy Timothy Webber and attractive Laurie Paton).

Visiting their dude ranch, Cleveland tries to look inconspicuous but manages to look quite amusing in a cowboy-type hat and blue coat and jeans. He bugs the telephone line and records proof of their involvement with horse breeder Offen (Lloyd Bochner). A scheme is in transit with the valuable racehorse being switched with a doppelganger and Cleveland is about to put himself in great danger, this being something that he seems to do frequently. David discovers the horse there and pretends to be a novice rider to join a trek run by Yola who mentions a treacherous track that leads elsewhere but is only passable by expert riders. He informs Walt and Linny as to his findings and a scheme is hatched to take Chrysalis back to its rightful owner: Mr Teller.

However, Matt searches his room and realises what he is up to.

Come morning and Cleveland snatches the horse and makes his way down the path towards a rendezvous with Walt. Unfortunately for him, Matt and others are awaiting him and the Brit is struck unconscious. Awaking to find himself tied to the horse, the beast is set off at speed whilst it looks like curtains for the investigator. But we know that he is a masterful rider and Houdini-like, he manages to free himself and guide the startled beast down the hazardous track and back.

Spotted returning to the ranch by Yola, he quickly speeds off in his car to meet Walt. Bruised and battered, David returns to Toronto and the Teller estate. Here we learn that the disgruntled Offen is involved in the kidnapping and proposed death of the foreign visitor.

A switch is in motion by his men and the others whilst Cleveland, Walt & Linny work together to follow the horse trailers and intercept them. A perilous task, one of the stud hands has a shotgun and it is down to David to subdue him and his accomplice before they succeed in the crossover.

Managing to take charge of them, Cleveland is then jumped by someone from inside the trailer whilst a reluctant Walt circles the disused farm location being utilised. Linny is also around but on her own. Following yet another scuffle, the good guys prevail but at some physical cost. "Limey jerk!" yells Walt before Cleveland replies, "Fat idiot!" They mean no harm but are relieved. Linny retrieves Chrysalis with the job almost done. Confronting Offen with the 2 horses, he confesses to his involvement and is arrested.

Shot in a hot summer, the incidental music is too prominent and often overwhelms. Having not read the original novels, the author had no preconceived expectations of the TV adaptations but it seems that there were many plot/character changes.

Ian later provided narration duties for the 1991 Dick Francis audio book Odds Against.

4. Into the 1990s: More Lovejoy & lots of other telly work

On into a new decade, 1990 saw Ian acting in some iconic American detective series: Perry Mason & Columbo. For The Case of the Desperate Deception, Mr McShane joined this feature-length episode in a supporting role as Andre Marchand, a small role where he once again can be seen smoking on screen. Amusingly, his accent fluctuates too and is joined in an entertaining instalment by Jesus of Nazareth actor Ian Bannen.

But before then, Ian next had dealings with another iconic and much-loved TV detective.

Like all good detectives, Columbo (Peter Falk) can be annoying but his dogged crime-solving skills eventually enable him to get his man (or woman). Rest in Peace, Mrs Columbo was a feature-length episode for the grubby, Mac-wearing investigator and shown on Saturday night, 31 March under the "ABC Saturday Mystery" slot. Episode 4 in its penultimate series, it is difficult to see that Bing Crosby was originally wanted to play the lead, and then Lee J Cobb before Mr Falk proved keen to take it on. His instincts proved right as the show won 5 Emmys and lasted for 69 stories across an incredible 34 years.

Show writer from the 1970s, Peter S. Fischer, returned for writing duties but Ian's role as Leland St. John is not that substantial. In another suit-wearing businessman role, he plays a married man engaged in a new affair with realtor Vivian Dimitri (Helen Shaver). Someone with a complicated past, her grief at losing her jailed husband sees her fractious mental health lead her to seek retribution against those that wronged him: namely, mentor Charlie (Ed Winter) and Lt. Columbo.

Arranging to meet Leland at a restaurant after seeing-off Charlie, she uses him as an alibi despite the two only knowing each other for six months after she sold him a property.

Columbo is called in to investigate the death and soon suspects Mrs Dimitri. Anticipating his next step, she confesses to sleeping with St. John (Ian McShane) on the evening of the murder. Necessitating speaking with him, the sleuth quizzes him on the links where he and his friends are waiting to tee off. Readers might recall seeing Ian also on the green in one of the recent Dick Francis trilogy of TV films.

After working on numerous cases and perhaps not instantly recalling them all, the Lieutenant is reminded that he had been responsible for previously arresting Vivian's husband.

At the hour mark, she receives a late-night telephone call from Leland revealing that his wife has found out about them. We see him in his lovely home; with a log fire burning in the background in another wealthy dwelling reminiscent of the one seen later in episodes of Ray Donovan. Drinking and in a melancholic stupor, she tells him not to call her again: consumed by grief following her husband's death.

Interestingly she begins to befriend the detective in an attempt to meet his wife. Why? To kill her and inflict the same sense of loss that she is experiencing. A bright spark, Columbo interacts with Vivian's physician and is warned that she is dangerous. But he realises this and gives her the necessary impression that she is the one manipulating him.

In a somewhat elaborate but rather predictable contrivance, he stages his wife's funeral so that she believes that she succeeded in poisoning Mrs Columbo. Ian's character is also present and in some clunky voice-over narration used to express the inner thoughts of each character, we hear him question his presence there (he does not speak with her or anyone). Afterwards, Columbo speaks with her and she offers to give him a lift back home.

At his home, she is delighted when a call comes through confirming that his wife was poisoned and she needs him to know that she is responsible. Eating the same spiked marmalade that she gave her, he play acts that he too has been affected (but in actuality, he switched the jar earlier after having its contents analysed). She gleefully informs him that he is going to die before outlining what she has done. In the final moments, Columbo's colleague reveals his presence after recording the confession: although how his little Dictaphone would do so from another room bemused me.

Superseding his first appearance on the show as a drugs businessman Ian returned to Miami Vice for the feature-length finale Freefall which aired on Monday 20 August. Here as portrays corrupt dictator General Manuel Borbon looking to leave his Latin America enclave of Costa Moroda for sanctuary in the U.S. provided he spills the beans on the drugs cartel that controls his country. With obvious echoes of Noriega, McShane's General is straight out of the stereotypical mode: military fatigues, cigar-chomping and enhanced here by his beloved Alsatian hound.

He also has fey detectives Crockett & Tubbs, dressed in their most ridiculous of fashions, begrudgingly tasked with covertly extracting him to the States. Into the fifth season, onscreen the detectives have become jaded and almost self-sacrificing but they retrieve the selfish leader and survive plenty of threats to their safety in doing so. Ian and the boys, Don Johnson & Philip Michael Thomas, share some brief screen time but the role is somewhat limiting for McShane.

After receiving a shot to the arm, an unconscious Borbon is secreted in a safe house in Miami. Unhappy about this, it is revealed that he has contacted those that support him to arrange his exit. Watched over by Vice until his clearance can be confirmed, the boys take a shift at security when the house is attacked and in the melee, the General manages to flee. A Columbian death squad is after him and those still loyal to him from home are also trying to help whilst others look to have him killed too.

The determined C&T manage to locate him subsequently after being given a clue by his daughter Bianca (Maria Stova) to a local bank where funds are collected for him. Many people are killed in this farewell episode which sags at times, particularly in the moments where General Borbon is mentioned but not seen on screen. Further shoot-outs occur before a sweaty McShane joins the detectives, now exhausted by their endeavours, being transported to another location. Stopped by law enforcement, dodgy drugs man Raymond (a youthful Greg Germann) shoots Borbon (Ian) and it looks like he has been killed.

However, in a sharp plot twist, discrepancies in his autopsy report see C&T discover that the General faked his death.

They locate his mistress, played by Anna Katarina, alone and dejected after informing the officers that he has since fled.

Following some poor plotting strands, they locate Borbon boarding a tiny seaplane and heavily guarded. Voicing their presence to him, the General orders his men to kill Sonny (Johnson) & Rico (Thomas) as he clambers into the plane at the waterside. Another shoot-out follows and the police manage to subdue his protectors, and more deaths follow. The partners both fire at the laden plane which explodes in midair watched on by its apathetic terminators.

Disillusioned by the corruption and aggravated by government departments, the boys ceremoniously throw down their badges whilst their boss, Lt. Castillo (Edward James Olmos) promises to support them.

Knowing this to be their last onscreen time, the makers of the show were able to include a surprisingly touching montage of scenes as Crockett & Tubbs depart. As for Ian McShane's contribution, after the earlier appearance in the third season neither prove to be his most interesting of roles as he is given scant to do. Also, the delivery of the script proves uneven, as does the style of interpretation.

"LOVEJOY IS BACK!" Featuring the perfect theme tune written by Denis King, and following an absence of 5 years, Radio Times listing magazine featured Ian on its cover for 5-11 January 1991 promoting the return. Shown on BBC1 Sunday 6 January through to 24 March, 11 episodes were presented after the actor had sacrificed a lucrative role on Dynasty to allow him to make more Lovejoy tales. After each series, Lovejoy is always somewhere new and in the books, he was regularly seeing the utilities cut off to his decrepit cottage while onscreen he lived in one of the properties owned by the Felshams or later, by nemesis Gimbert. Ian saw him as an outsider in the antiques trade, often faking them, as in the novels. Fans could also "win a date with Lovejoy" according to TV Times magazine 2-8 March.

The first series had been successfully repeated and so when the second started at 8:05 pm, the show made the cover of the aforementioned TV Times.

As Lovejoy, this year Ian also did a jokey skit for a BBC trailer promoting the new series of Antiques Roadshow which was on early in the day.

Opening with finding Lovejoy in prison, Anthony Valentine is in this series with his character playing a part in putting our favourite trinkets man there. Dick Clement joined writing partner Ian Le Frenais to pen the return, with actor Trevor Brown, Terry Hodgkinson, Steve Coombes and Douglas Watkinson all pitching in multiple scripts. John Woods directed the first of 4 episodes whilst Lee Whitlock from Young Charlie Chaplin, Warren Clarke from Sewers of Gold and Ronald Fraser make appearances and a return, respectively. Another blast from the past was a fun role for Aubrey Morris. And most amusingly, Malcolm Terris who was in the High Tide, where his character gets strangled by Ian, resurfaces in episode 4: Montezuma's Revenge.

Increased to 12 episodes this time, the show offered the first of writer Roger Marshall's 8 episodes contribution for a returning cast that now knew each other well. Ian and his team made the first series on the proviso that they could shoot 2 more. Changes at the BBC and contract wrangles meant that it was not picked up until 1990 when they began filming series two.

125

American soap star Linda Gray was the guest star across 2 episodes: Riding in Rollers & The Black Virgin of Vladimir, which were directed by Francis Megahy (one of his 4). She and Ian had been in Dallas together after he joined the cast in 1989 which by then she had been involved with since 1978. The actors made the superimposed cover of the 50p TV Times for 23-29 March which also featured Ian's old film co-star Jeremy Brett on its cover which detailed several shows. Other highlights included "Lothario with oils" Tom Wilkinson in a memorable entry, a recognisable Tony Selby from Villain and Celia Imrie, the go-to actress for snootiness, in the second story.

Series 2 was also noteworthy in that Lovejoy began using a different vehicle: Lady Jane's tatty old Morris Minor. Aka "Miriam", there is a collectable toy from Corgi available to purchase as a souvenir! A scruffy Toyota pick-up truck would feature in later series, driven wildly by the actor, as per usual. Mr McShane has said that he was fond of Brian Blessed's appearance on the show in "Vladimir"; episode 11 and shown on Sunday, March 24, at 8.15 pm.

Remembered as being a joy on set, this was the closing entry in a strong return series.

Written by George Eckstein, from characters created by Erle Stanley Gardner, the latest Perry Mason story was set in Paris and details the personal quest for justice sought by marine Captain Berman (Tim Ryan) to locate a former Nazi responsible for the permanent injuries to his mother and the brutal death of his 2 uncles back in World War II. Following the death of a witness identifying his whereabouts in modern-day Paris, it seems that there are others with a stake in this complicated case. Attached to the Unites States Embassy there, a lead sees Berman confront the man he thinks responsible but inadvertently facilitates his assassination by an unknown assailant and the former framed for murder.

Mr Mason is an old family friend and reluctantly agrees to investigate after agreeing to defend the Marine in court.

Beginning to piece the clues together, at a little before the half-hour mark, Mason visits a hesitant Marchand (Ian McShane) at his work. The latter is a former business colleague of the deceased, himself enjoying life in France with his younger wife Danielle (Yvette Mimieux). The reticent interviewee denies having embezzled a great deal of money from his associate but will later admit to having a relationship with the man's wife.

In Deception, Ian is only seen on screen a few times and it isn't much of a role for the actor.

As the investigation continues and the case brought before a court, several people are exposed by Mason as being duplicitous and self-serving with links to Odessa. McShane's final appearance is a brief one, obliged to attend the hearing (but never called) as justice is rightly served.

Chillers proved quite a contrast for Ian this year with the Mason episode shown alongside this UK television work made for ITV via the HTV franchise. Here he co-stars in a devilishly-good adaptation of a Patricia Highsmith short story titled Sauce for the Goose. Adapted by Andrew Hislop; one of his two contributions, it was part of a dozen self-contained episodes subsequently released on DVD. Aka Mistress of Suspense, the peculiar Antony Perkins offered an opening and closing insert about each story and his comments make more sense once the stories have been played out.

Broadcast on Friday 25 May, Sauce was directed by writer/director Clare Peploe and it won the Prix Publique award.

Ian features in the montage of clips on the opening credits as crooner Steven Castle, arriving in Porthcawl, a coastal resort in south Wales, for a performance, and in need of digs. In his cheap suit, bouffant hair, and a twinkle in his eye, he resembles disgraced 70s pop sensation Gary Glitter.

As Steven, he charms his way into the lives of hoteliers Olivia and Lawrence Emery, Gwen Taylor & Benjamin Whitrow and despite their Harbour House hotel being temporarily closed mid-summer, he manages to get allocated a room. The staid Mr Emery is not at all keen on the "smarmy" performer, with his stance proving right as Sauce proves to be a terrific story which proves catastrophic for all those involved.

Starved of affection, Olivia falls for the garrulous newcomer and soon declares her love for him to her astonished husband.

She and Steven agree to not see each other for a while, to discover whether their feelings are genuine. Bereft, it seems that the relationship might be over. However, Castle (Ian) has slyly coerced her into murdering her husband after disclosing to him upon their first meeting that Lawrence is well-off and doesn't need to work, struggling as he is with an on-going back problem.

A fatal, pre-arranged 'accident' is arranged for Mr Emery and following his death, Steven & Olivia marry and all looks well for the duplicitous duo. But poor, stuffy Olivia, as played by the always-brilliant Miss Taylor, finds her paranoia telling her that her amour is attempting to kill her off to enable him to get a hold of Lawrence's stash of money.

Sinister now, Steven fakes being supportive but he is planning to knock her off via a novel use of a walk-in freezer in This being a Patricia Highsmith story there is a twist.

Setting things up, the bolt on the freezer door slips down and accidentally shuts Steven inside. He had disabled the locking mechanism on the wall opposite, necessitating that the entrance is obstructed to allow a safe exit. He had gone inside to store the ice cream cake so favoured by his beloved, as the couple are preparing to spend an evening outside on this their anniversary.

Through the small window, we watch as he asks the tipsy Olivia to open the door but seeing the look in her eyes, the audience knows that this is unlikely.

Ignoring his pleas, she dances giddily around the kitchen as he starts to shiver.

Come morning and Olivia practices what she is going to tell the police and explain his accidental death. Looking inside, she discovers a frozen Steven. Previously he did an amusing, vexed impression of her there and had taken her owl-like glasses. Stepping inside to retrieve them, the door slams shut behind her. The burgeoning reality of what is going to happen dawns upon her and she lets out a scream. But there is no one to hear!

A fantastic piece, Sauce for the Goose is expertly played by the 3 principals. It is also a showcase for the signing talents of one Ian McShane. As the story opens, he is seen and heard crooning away in that relaxed style and he continues throughout the episode (even popping up on an audio cassette given to Olivia). Ian has a long musical history and had a single, Harry Brown, released back in 1962.

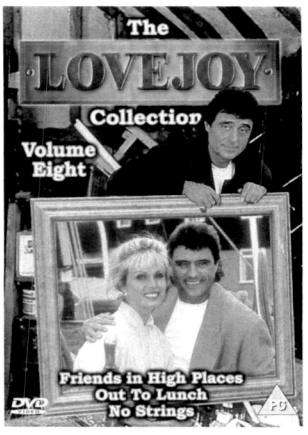

Commencing its run on BBC1 Sunday 12 January 1992 through to Boxing Day, 13 episodes of the new Lovejoy series found Dame Joanna Lumley (pictured opposite with Ian) co-starring in its opening three storylines as his love interest, Victoria. She had acted with Ian in that peculiar film The Ballad of Tam Lynn where they can be briefly seen in group scenes. Ian's wife Gwen had been in a stage play with her a couple of years before her casting as Lady Jane's friend.

Promoted by a rather waxy Ian on the 18-24 January cover of Radio Times, we get a glimpse into Lovejoy's past via his posh daughter and ex-wife. As for actors, Paul Rogers crops up; he had played the cuckold husband in The Wild & the Willing, Larry Lamb, Minnie Driver and old Hollywood star Donald Pleasance makes an appearance; the latter had memorably worked with Ian on A Journey into Fear. Jonathan Coy completed the first of his two 2 episodes and then-popular Irish band Hot House Flowers also feature in a fun episode. Not forgetting Tony Vogel who is in the opening story.

Steve Coolms received his second writing credit for the excellent Eric of Arabia episode (which was the first of 4 directed by Ian) and Dick Clement also contributed. Peter Barber-Fleming directed a couple and Francis Megahy another, and it gave Jeremy Paul his first writing contribution: one of 6. John Crome directed the start of a half-dozen episodes from series 3 onwards and a couple of days after Christmas, Lovejoy came to a close with the excellent Prague Sun. Directed by Geoffrey Sax.

Fans could also be tempted to buy the Ian McShane album From Both Sides Now released this year but it seems not many were tempted. Featuring 14 M.O.R. tracks such as Avalon & Drive, the former was released as a single and fans could see him performing the song on the lunchtime BBC One show Pebble Mill on Monday 9 November.

On the Saturday morning of that same week, he appeared on the kids show Going Live! (one of two appearances).

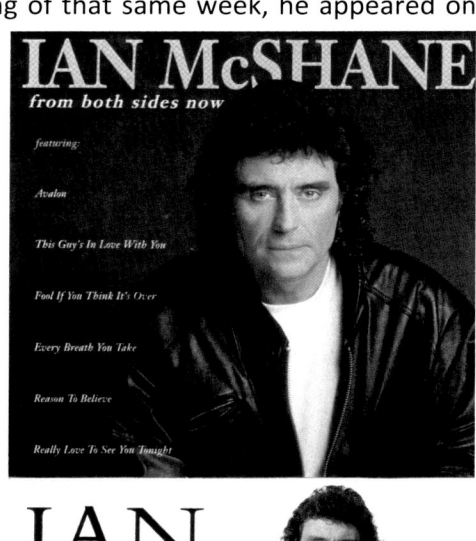

He would later be reminded of the Pebble Mill appearance via the pithy Jonathan Ross chat show, "Eat your heart out Brian Ferry!" guffawed the actor upon seeing a clip in 2013.

As a guest on the terrific Dame Edna Treatment back in 2007, his host had also teased him about his singing by getting him to autograph the album (as she intended to sell it on a popular internet auction site rather than savour it!)

A clip of him crooning The Police classic Every Breath You Take was also endured by all!

Being a long-term supporter of the Variety Club of Great Britain, Ian and the Lovejoy cast were thrown a tribute luncheon at the Hilton, London, on 15 December.

Remaining in the same year, Ian was the narrator of Prokofiev's classic tale Peter and the Wolf and accompanied by The Royal Philharmonic Orchestra, Sir John Gielgud, who made an appearance in Lovejoy, had been one of many actors to provide such duties previously. That unique voice could also be heard in a TV ad for Sainsbury's with Ian describing a favourite meal of salmon before he is revealed on screen; no doubt thinking about his fee.

Now switched to Saturday nights, series 4 of Lovejoy commenced on 10 January 1993 for a run of 13 episodes. Always starting strongly, this one was no different.

A raft of writers contributed scripts including Douglas Watkinson and Terry Hodgkinson, with a few actors returning to the fold and Ian directing episode 4: The Colour of Mary, which he has since termed "completely mad but wonderful". It was his second time as director and a couple more would follow. Richard Griffiths, later in a Pirates of the Caribbean sequel alongside Ian and T.P. McKenna; so good in Villain, return.

Lovejoy works for Lady Jane in sourcing antiques for her or her clients and he is assisted (or not) by his barker Tinker aka "Tink" and the aforementioned Eric Catchpole (Chris Jury) taken on because his father is paying for the over-aged apprentice to learn about antiques. The series concluded on Sunday 11 April.

Working solidly on the show, Lovejoy came back to British television on Sunday 5 September in the 7.30 pm slot with a noticeable cast change. "Meet Lovejoy's new lady" offered listings magazine Radio Times, showing a healthy-looking Ian on its cover alongside Caroline Langrishe who replaced the sadly-departed Phyllis Logan. Caroline was cast as plumy auctioneer Charlotte Cavendish, to spark off against the old rogue and proved popular.

Presenting 14 episodes this time through to 27 December, regrettably, another major cast member would also depart: Chris Jury as the ineffable Eric who leaves in episode 6.

As per usual, major actors were drawn to the show alongside some past working colleagues of Mr McShane; John Hallam, terrific in films Villain & Sexy Beast; Sir John Gielgud in the Christmas special; Freddie Jones from Sitting Target and Dallas co-star Ken

Kercheval all feature. Sir John, who could rarely get Lovejoy's name right reconvened with McShane after both had roles on the Marco Polo mini-series back in 1982. Coincidentally, the esteemed thespian had signed his R.A.D.A. certificate which Ian was awarded after missing his final term to make his first film.

Ian also directed episode 3, A Going Concern; his third time behind the camera, alongside Nick Laughland who helmed the first of his 2 episodes, Gordon Flemyng & Jim Hill doing likewise whilst Geoffrey Sax returned to direct one final time.

Illustrated below is a stunning likeness of the actor in the role. Created by Angela Beadle, see the thanks page for her full contact details.

Resembling Lovejoy and wearing blue jeans, a white t-shirt, mullet and suit jacket, this year Ian starred in another TV ad shown on UK television for Nescafe coffee. Interrupting the peace and tranquilly of a young couple out on the water, he arrives in a huge boat next to them and asks for a lift to shore. She offers him a nice cup of coffee and he purrs, "Mmm, Nescafe. No mistaking coffee at its best." He returns the favour and the following day they join him on his boat.

There are a couple of Ian projects that simply proved elusive to view and one of them was White Goods (1994). Ian is snooker player Ian Deegan, teaming up with disgruntled teacher Charlie (Lenny Henry) on a popular TV snooker-themed show ala Big Break where "...the pair have a major falling out when they can't agree how to split their winnings," according to memorabletv.com.

There is a widely-seen scene involving him with the rather lovely Rachel Weisz, as Elaine, a TV crew member, enjoying a hilarious sex scene with him on top of a snooker table with sports commentary amusingly echoing from the TV behind them in this upper quickie moment. Written by Al Ashton, also an actor and in this as Chris, it was one of only a couple of pieces that he directed. He died in 2007 aged 49. Larry Lamb is also in this after recently working with McShane on a 1992 episode of Lovejoy.

The sixth series of the ever-popular Lovejoy returned for a final batch of 10 episodes from 2 October through to 4 December 1994 in the perfectly-suited 7 pm Sunday night slot. Also this year, Ian narrated the first of his 2 documentary shows Natural World for the BBC (another followed in 1998).

As an thespian, Eric Deacon would appear in 5 episodes of Lovejoy as D.I. Hardwick he also wrote the opening story in the new series which his character also features in: The Last of the Uzkoks. This was Mr McShane's fourth and final time directing, joining Paul Harrison, Alex Kirby & Ian White all of whom steered a couple of episodes.

Wife Gwen Humble appears in an episode. And later, Clive Russell is also seen. He memorably acts with Ian on Game of Thrones. The marvellous Frank Finlay is in episode 6 after working with Ian on Sitting Target back in 1972 whilst Terence Rigby acted with him back in a 1980 Armchair Thriller batch of episodes.

Probably the same man, Martin Jarvis is also in an episode; they had acted alongside each other back in 1960.

Shown on Sunday 4 December at 7.10 pm after more than 70 outings we said a fond farewell to a much-loved show via a Dick Clement script titled Last Tango in Lavenham.

In the closing entry, many changes are afoot for Lovejoy & his pals. Chris Jury briefly returns as Eric, as does Phyllis Logan as Lady Jane; the beauty of their relationship being that despite it almost happening previously, it never became a physical one.

Baz Taylor was given the director's nod for his 18th episode.

Lamenting the close of the last series, fans could still enjoy hearing Ian narrate Lovejoy novels such as Paid & Loving Eyes & The Great California Game.

Lady Jane's house and Lovejoy's cottage seen on screen is Belchamp Hall whilst his workshop for the last two series is on its grounds; in use today as "Lovejoy's Holiday accommodation".

Working extensively on British television projects with the BBC, Soul Survivors was also a 1995 drama sandwiched between Lovejoy, another TV film and new series; Madson. Regarded as being great fun to make by Ian, it is virtually impossible to view nowadays. **133**

Shot on location in Liverpool & Manchester across 12 weeks, he stars as Otis Cooke, a Soul DJ who reunites the four original members of an American soul band. After travelling to the UK to reignite their careers via a tour and CD release, alas, the reality proves a struggle!

Written by Barry Devlin, he remembers in correspondence with the author, "I liked it a lot when I saw the final version. I had great fun on the shoot. I'm a musician and so is Ian, so we had a lot to talk about, under the hot Atlanta sun. He plays a DJ who loves the now-defunct Soul group, The Tallahassees. He wants to reform them for a European tour (minus their lead singer who was shot by a jealous husband) so he goes to America to find them. He succeeds and brings them back to Liverpool but imagine his surprise when the "dead" lead singer shows up. Isaac Hayes, Antonio Fargas (Huggy Bear), Taurean Blacque and Al Matthews: quite the combo. Ian seemed to like it a lot (the music). He was especially happy when the location crew set one of the railway track scenes in... Lovejoy Atlanta! No kidding."

Shown on Sunday 10 & 17 September in two parts, it would seem that it has never been repeated and only a still of Hayes with Ian is available.

Shot in a sparse monochrome, a moody piano theme accompanies the opening titles to Madson (1996) where we see a figure collecting up his law books and emerging from a cell and into the light of colour: that man is played by Ian McShane. "Madson was…about a man trying to discover the truth behind his false imprisonment," remembers Liz Friedman, who came up with the enticing solution to express the situation which for her efforts, pucked up a prestigious BDA Bronze Award.

"McShane IS MADSON: When John Madson is released from prison, after serving eight years for a murder he did not commit, he is determined to discover the truth behind his misarrest and false imprisonment." That was the BBC introduction to its new, six-part drama series which began its run on Wednesday 17 April at 9.30 pm. Following the news, a pensive Ian graced the tie-in novel by Rachel Silver but a smiling, short-haired actor could also be found on the cover of listing magazine Radio Times for the week commencing 13 April.

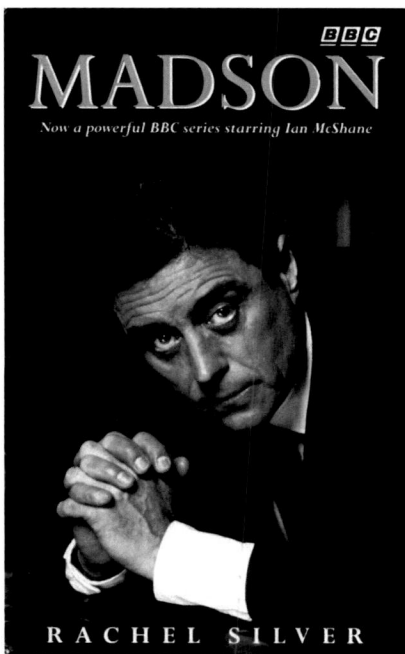

BBC

MADSON

Now a powerful BBC series starring Ian McShane

RACHEL SILVER

Co-written by Ian Kennedy Martin and Producer Colin Shindler, Rob Walker directed Ian alongside Joanna Kanska, Matthew Marsh, Thomas Craig, Charles Gray and others with Jayne Ashbourne as Sarah Madson. Released, Madson wants a job as a law clerk but it proves hard to find employment as an ex-con with storylines seeing him investigating blackmail; a woman being threatened by an errant partner; eviction; helping a youngster imprisoned and wrongly convicted & working with an international footballer accused of committing murder.

In correspondence with the author, writer/ PR expert Rachel Silver confirms that "My book was actually a novelisation of the series which was from a new story devised by McShane and his producer for the BBC following the success of the Lovejoy series. Such a long time ago! A shame it's not on DVD, no idea why though, probably if a show runs to a few series they are more likely to consider it a commercial prospect for release. I worked from the scripts. I was also the script editor and was based in White City at the time and was quite a privilege to work with the BBC veteran Ian Kennedy Martin (who penned three of the episodes). We did start to develop a 2nd series but it didn't happen ultimately."

More work for the BBC followed in the coming year, with Ian used to narrate Animal People: Dogs at War shown in September and on Traders of the Lost Scrolls & Q.E.D.

Returning to acting roles, created by Chris Thompson, 55 episodes were made of The Naked Truth: an acerbic American comedy series between 1995-8 starring the funny Tea Leoni as Nora, a newspaper reporter/ photographer.

Ian appears in 2 episodes as Leland Banks, her ex-husband in i) Things Change & ii) Bridesface Revisited.

The first opened season three on 22 September 1997 & the other, episode five, on 20 October.

Their divorce is mentioned in the first episode and Ian's appearance in Things Change sees him briefly re-enter her life. She has a new job with the Inquirer paper and Leland (McShane), a media tycoon, wants her back. "So do you go out on the Ides of March with that haircut?" quips Jake, a new work colleague upon meeting Leland. Ian does wear his hair tightly oiled and the remark proves quite amusing in a show that the viewer gradually warms to once you get past the exasperated delivery. Getting on well with her, Leland, with the actor seen wearing a tuxedo, something he does in many roles, offers her a job on his paper but she declines.

Returning in episode 5, with a further 12 in the final season left to run, Nora is invited to Leiland's wedding to wife number 3. In an event full of celebrities ranging from the sublime to the ridiculous; Virginia Mayo to Morgan Fairchild, Ian is once again outfitted in a tux. Their onscreen relationship is such that she speaks freely to him and is amused to discover that his bride looks a lot like her and that she, in turn, resembles the first wife, who is also there.

In his adventures in Space: 1999, Ian was driven insane by an alien force and here in this 1998 feature-length Babylon 5 TV film, he is pursued by ETs called the Soul Hunters. Led by Martin Sheen, resembling an oversized, bald Robert Duvall, it has been said that he was originally cast in the role of Dr Robert Bryson (the part that Ian took on). In retrospect, the plain-speaking Mr McShane has stated that his role was probably the worst thing that he ever worked on.

And it is true, there is a lot of mumbo-jumbo dialogue spouted but B5 is not devoid of humour and proves an appealing watch regardless of whether you are a sci-fi fan (the author most definitely not being). Bryson is an earnest archaeologist obsessed with his study into immortality, "life in death: life eternal". After surreptitiously secreting one of the glowing globes discovered within a vast whispering gallery alongside innumerable others, such an action will have major repercussions which will be seen soon.

Seen at the start of a sci-fi franchise well-loved by fans, The River of Souls was written by the show's creator J. Michael Straczynski. River was the fourth of six feature-length episodes in a project that had stretched to 5 seasons.

The story is set in 2263 and arriving on Babylon 5, he is introduced to Lochley (Elizabeth Scoggins) whilst attending a pre-arranged meet with his new boss, Garibaldi (Jerry Doyle), who wants to know about his work and whether or not they will provide future

Photos: Author's Collection

funding for his Life Eternal (L.E.) project. Transfixed by the power of those contained within the globe, many thousands of distressed souls never gave their permission to have their thoughts recorded at the time of their deaths. Collectively entombed for more than 10,000 years, many want vengeance, "Evolving not dying," as their representative declares to Lochley. Manipulating Dr Bryson, he is used as a vassal, a conduit to the outside world and their presence is gathering strength, "Better to destroy the station. Embrace the darkness… than go back there."

Looked for, they eventually locate the doctor and Ian's final scene sees him transfixed by the glowing globe and contained within a hologram, seated in the lotus position, as he watches on as Sheen gives a long speech full of regret. The well-meaning Soul Searchers, who travel the universe to gather the souls of individuals as they are about to die, is represented by Sheen, considered a youngster within his society, who comes to realise the harm done to the unwilling souls trapped for eternity. Offering himself as a sacrifice to the malevolent force, moments after the danger passes, Bryson is released, dropping to the ground but Sheen's character is a victim of it all.

A glossy TV production whose soundtrack is too loud, D.R.E.A.M. Team (1999) offered another "Starring Ian McShane" name check plus an "And Martin Sheen" credit.

There is little originality here but proceedings prove enjoyable and the fateful climax is pulsating. Shot in Puerto Rico, this is not to be confused with the Michael Keaton film or the series "Dream Team" which came out at the same time.

Written and directed by Dean Hamilton, Mr McShane makes a startling entrance via a helicopter, as disgraced Sir Oliver Maxwell with his Executive Assistant Lena (Traci Lords). Developing biological weapons on his private island hideaway known as "Pirate's Keep", we are immediately entering into 007 territory. Former KGB man Corzon (Paul L. Smith in his final role) and Irish terrorist Murphy (James Remar) are assisting in the scheme which is being secretly monitored.

Garrison (Sheen from Babylon 5) creates the D.R.E.A.M. Team = Dangerous Reconnaissance Emergency Action Mission Team and recruits Bond wannabe Zack (Jeff Kaake) to go undercover with Kim (Angie Everhart), Victoria (Traci Bingham) & Eva (Eva Halina) in working to prevent Maxwell. The latter is an amoral man who is aiming to sell his findings to the highest bidder for somewhere between $5-10b.

Offering another opportunity for Ian to get his golf clubs out, Eva catches the attention of the well-dressed businessman with the team using her to draw him closer. But Sir Oliver is a cautious person and so has his minions check out the credentials of his new acquaintances. "He certainly holds your attention," quips one of the girls. "So does a cobra!" shoots back another. Continuing his scheming alongside the Russian, Maxwell is yet another titled Brit role for the Blackburn-born actor.

As an aside, by 2012 Ian would become the recognised voice of ESPN's British Open, narrating several evocative short inserts much enjoyed by fans.

Flattered by the young woman's interest in him, Sir Oliver feigns enthusiasm but secretly he is involved with Miss Brant (Ms Lords). Indulging Ava in her request for the team to stage a photo session on the island (the girls are incognito as models), here Zack sneaks off and discovers the Anthrax-processing lab. Maxwell & Lena are aware of this as the group flies off. From here the action increases following the abduction of Eva by Maxwell's men. He calls the team and orders them to do nothing for the next 48 hours or she will be killed by them.

However, he knows that there will be a rescue attempt and is simply trying to buy a little time. As is de rigueur for villains such as Sir Oliver, a powerful man, he indulges in a taste for a good Stogie.

Eva is rescued but taking over a local observatory, Maxwell & Lena instigate their dastardly plans and the D.R.E.A.M. Team has 10 minutes before a detonator will set off a huge explosion. Showing his true colours, after Sir Oliver is given activation codes by Murphy 5 minutes are remaining and in a moment of delight, he tells the Irishman that there is going to be an explosion especially: with him in the car. Arriving outside, lots of fighting occur; Ian's Brit and Zack (Mr Kaake) and another between Lena and one of the girls. With the timer showing less than 120 seconds and wearing his nice suit, Sir Oliver is karate kicked through a window and crashes down to his twisted death below. In a tense few moments, the team manages to deactivate the detonator with only seconds to spare and U.S. missiles are aborted before striking the location.

A made-for-TV film pilot which was lazily termed a Charlie's Angels rip-off, a resulting series never happened.

Voice work presented itself for Ian with a job narrating the BBC Hollywood Greats documentary in 1999 and on the 2000 special Jack and Bill.

5. 2000+ More films, theatre & some classic TV

The success of Sexy Beast (2000) put Ian's name back on the lips of TV execs and this led him to be approached to audition for Deadwood, subsequently. Directed by newbie Jonathan Glazer, Beast went on to win a load of film awards and was also nominated for many others. Co-written by Louis Mellis & David Scinto, the duo would also furnish similar duties on 44 Inch Chest; a project that offered roles for both Ian and Ray Winstone.

The sight of a rather rotund and rapacious Mr Winstone in nothing more than small yellow pants, sunning himself in the Spanish sun is not particularly appealing but this is what we are greeted with at the start of the film. As retired criminal Gary 'Gal' Dove, he and his beloved wife Deedee (Amanda Redman) enjoy a sedate life in a villa in a small isolated village with local friends Aitch (Cavan Kendal) & Jackie (Julianne White) reminders of their past.

News comes that a job is being planned by "Mr Black Magic, himself," Teddy Bass (Ian McShane) with recruits being rounded up by his trusted second-in-command, the psychotic Don Logan (Ben Kingsley in Oscar-nominated form going against type). Dressed in all black, Teddy had met Harry (James Fox), proprietor of a safe deposit box establishment, at a sex party and has been planning the job for six months thereafter.

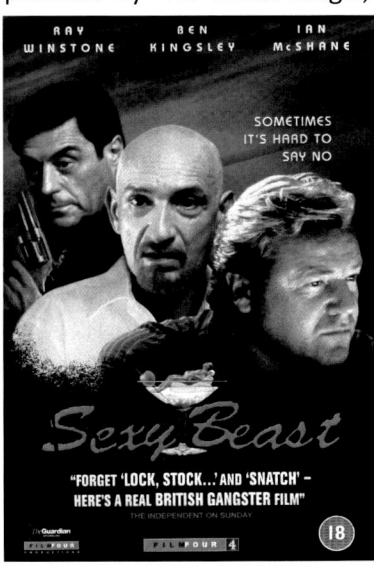

Destroying the previously-relaxed atmosphere, Logan is due to arrive in Spain the following day. Gal assures Deedee that he is not going to accept the role, after turning his back on crime but he has little choice other than to speak to Don and carefully thank him for the offer and respectfully decline.

However, the latter is not a man to say no to or even look at the wrong way and his arrival is not welcomed by any of the 4.

As Don, Kingsley is manic, violent, offensive, rude, sensitive, feared and a liar in equal measure and poor Gal is battered by him into submitting to join the team whether he likes it or not.

Forced to return to the UK to link up with the crew, Gal also meets Teddy who puts him up in a luxurious hotel and meeting him subsequently at breakfast, asks him where Don is as he missed the flight back. With beautifully coiffured hair, as Teddy, Ian is superb; resembling Bryan Ferry and not a man to be trifled with. Initially thinking that a demonic March Hare is going to kill him in his nightmare, he is rightly frightened by him but Mr Dove cannot wriggle out of things and is forced to participate.

Around to see another heavy-duty break-in ala Sewers of Gold, this time Ian's character hasn't to do any of the labour, only observing as Ray Winstone and the others take the novel approach of breaking into the vaults by flooding the place.

With the job a success, the gang celebrates at a restaurant/ club where Teddy takes Gal aside. The latter informs him that he is catching a plane back home later in the morning and is obliged to accept a personal lift from Teddy.

Accompanying him in his Porsche sports car, the driver declares that he has to make one stop on the way to a posh location. It is here that he tells Gal to come in with him and we meet Harry (Fox, brother of Edward from The Battle of Britain) from earlier. Surprised to be awoken in the early hours, the host offers Teddy a drink but is shot dead in an intense onscreen moment that proves unexpected. The tension is palpable and Gal pleads with Mr Bass that his involvement in this kind of thing is not what he does anymore.

Back in the car, the fear barometer is sky high; Teddy insults Gal by giving him a £10 note (and asking for change from £20) after asking how much Don (Kingsley) had offered to pay him for his involvement in the robbery. Merely a ruse to mention the missing nut job, he lets Gal know that if he cared a jot about Don then he too would be a dead man by now.

The passenger is told to get out of the car and it speeds off leaving a traumatised Gal relieved to be allowed to leave.

Left at a deserted bus stop, he takes out a ruby ring from his pocket, the spoils from the robbery that he managed to hide away.

An amazing film, Sexy Beast has a clever screenplay with stunning imagery and wordplay remaining with the viewer long after its closing credits. Ian is not so much involved but is pivotal in his Teddy character orchestrating seeing Gal (Winstone) involved in the robbery and all its connotations.

Theatre maestro Cameron Mackintosh presented a world premiere of The Witches of Eastwick an adaptation of the 1984 John Updike novel at the historic Theatre Royal Drury Lane, London. Following 3 weeks of previews from Saturday 24 June, its opening night arrived on Tuesday 18 July 2000. Ian's former acting colleague from the late-1960s, Ian McKellen attended.

Telling the tale of a trio of divorcees living in the town of Eastwick, Rhode Island, USA, its adaptation and lyrics were created by John Dempsey and composer Dana P. Rowe, who saw their work play the Prince of Wales Theatre, also in London, between 23 March 23 – 27 October 2001 but minus Ian McShane. As Darryl van Horne, the role so fantastically played by Jack Nicholson in the 1987 film, Ian was top-billed and made his first foray into musical theatre ably supported by prime talent Lucie Arnaz, Joanna Riding & Maria Friedman as the witches.

Smoking a cigar a foot long, van Horne sets about seducing his way through many of the ladies before being banished at the end of the story. An ITV documentary followed the making of the show.

Costing £4.5m to bring to the stage, the pressure was on for Mackintosh, whose last production had flopped. A mix of the book, film and its composers, the producers had seen many people before Ian came to audition. They needed someone whose speaking voice was the same as their singing voice and after Lionel Bart had told Mac that Ian could sing, he was in the frame for the lead. Requiring stamina to be able to perform in the show, vocal teacher Mary Hammond worked with the actor to bring him up to standard. The large cast gathered for its initial read through on Monday 17 April and Ian was there, complete with his reading glasses on!

A soundtrack CD featuring Ian and the original London cast was recorded that September at Whitfield Street Studios in advance of its release on the First Nights label in 2000. It sees Ian perform 8 songs, commencing with I Love a Little Town and closing with The Wedding. At some point during the run, he sang I Love A Little Town on a UK TV show. Elsewhere, Britain's Most Terrifying Ghost Stories had Ian's lovely tones added as narrator for a TV show.

Thieves was a short-lived U.S. series co-starring John Stamos & Australian actor Melissa George as career crims striking a deal with the FBI to help bring in others instead of going to prison. Airing on ABC in the 9 pm slot, its premiere arrived on Friday 21 September 2001 with Ian featuring in Jack's Back, story six of eleven, as the man in question. Shot in Canada, the show filled the same Friday night slot and his offering could be seen on 9 November.

Moving onto 2002 and Ian made a guest appearance in The West Wing, playing Russian negotiator Nikolai Ivanovich in Enemies Foreign and Domestic, episode 19 of the third season. Shown on Wednesday 1 May, McShane is only in a few scenes, working with negotiator comrade Kazlovsky (George Tasudis) in liaising with Sam Seaborn (a miscast Rob Lowe). The trio is arranging a first meeting between the new Russian President and his American counterpart, President Bartlet, as played by Martin Sheen.

Wishing to stage-manage it into a perfect event Ian is seen early on as a studious advisor who has more to offer than simply sorting out the logistics of the Helsinki meeting. Wanting to pass on a statement to President Bartlet, the contents of which are far-reaching as it relates to nuclear proliferation.

Early on in the storyline, the American secret service had learned of the Russians being involved in building a rector for Iran which can develop nuclear weapons, but the new incumbent wishes to distance his regime from this.

A pedigree, award-winning American series which ran across 7 seasons, this elegant political drama detailed the working lives of those involved in serving the President from the West Wing of the Oval Office in Washington D.C. Mr McShane is convincing in utilising a heavy Russian accent too.

Set in a contemporary London Asian community where tradition sits alongside the modern, Bollywood Queen finds pretty nineteen-year-old Geena (Preeya Kalidas) living a life guided by her own "music of destiny." A love letter to the colourful 'Bollywood' film industry, this breezy feature combines all its fantasy, naffness and exhilarating effervescence entertainment and proves a fun watch.

Geena respects her cultural traditions but also seeks to live a modern life, hence her involvement with an aspiring R&B group. But when Jay (James McAvoy) enters her life a mutual attraction proves problematic for them both. He is new to the capital and gets a job working with his brother, the gruff Dean (Ciarán McMenamin), at a textile factory, where he soon becomes innocently embroiled in the rivalry with an opponent who just happens to be Geena's family. Unaware of this, they develop a relationship and soon she submerges him in her world, including taking in a Bollywood feature. She asks his opinion about the film, "Mad, bad and I dunno... beautiful," replies the Scots actor (using a West Country accent).

Discovered together at a club by her over-protective brothers, one who has his own secrets, the lovers are kept apart and we get to see how they feel via musical numbers, "Real life isn't what they show you on the silver screen," is one of the lovely, willowy lyrics sung by Geena after being stood-up by Frank's son. Ian doesn't sing a number, his character, Scotsman Frank, is estranged from Jay.

Naively coerced into ransacking their rivals factory and clothing templates, protecting his brother, Jay is unable to prevent him from a scuffle that sees him hospitalised.

It is here that the estranged father and son meet. Frank, a little grubby and dressed in a black leather waistcoat and unshaven, is there already when Jay visits Dean. Little is said but the two have unresolved issues. Jay seeks to escape with Geena and the viewer wants the youngsters to have a happy ending via a screenplay by director Jeremy Wooding and Neil Spencer.

Bollywood Queen had started as a short film called Sahri & Trainers, with the characters school-aged.

Ian had recently been in the West End and took on the role of Western-obsessive Frank as he was pleased to be involved in a production that steered away from the usual London-centric gangster films common to the time. "It's a very good script, it's a nice story, you know," commented the actor. "Very sweet. Very, very sweet. It's a charming script." The producers were wise in decreeing that having someone like Ian bringing a raft of acting experience behind him, could only benefit the film.

Bollywood Queen has a rich vein of humour and we get to see him on screen subsequently when the young lovers return to confront those that have worked against them. This sees Jay call in at the home shared by his father with Dean and then Geena to a family wedding.

Meeting Frank for the first time, he reveals to her that 'Jay' is actually James and that next to his sibling they were named in tribute to cult actor James Dean. Money is returned and reconciliation occurs between Jay and Frank.

We will see Mr McShane once more, following Geena's appearance at an Indian wedding where she performs a number with her two friends. Initially, it seems that her ailing father is also looking to rebuild a relationship with his daughter but when he declares that the family name has been dishonoured, she and Jay leave. He is distraught and confides to his wife that perhaps they will not see her again. She replies that they will and that she is a feisty character just like her father.

Seeing the various characters getting on with their lives, including Frank & Dean working on a market stall together, we leave them as we hear more thoughts from sage Uncle (Renu Setna), "The stars, they merely guide us, Geena. The rest is up to you."

There are some sparkling moments of poignancy in Man and Boy (2003), a BBC TV adaptation of the Tony Parsons novel, despite some unconvincing early performances. Even Ian's brash TV talk show host Marty Mann proves a little unconvincing at first. However, if you persevere, the acting improves especially when Pauline Collins and Jack Shepherd come into things as parents of producer Harry (Ioan Gruffudd), supporting him through a marriage breakdown thanks to their son's one night stand with attractive new co-worker Jasmin (Shelley Conn).

Harry is the producer to wide-boy host Marty who enjoys mixing it up with his guests (winking directly into the camera at one point) and revelling in his media coverage. Whilst away from work, the former is left with a five-year-old son to bring up whilst his estranged wife, Natasha Little, departs for Japan.

As Mann, Ian is the demanding star who causes controversy by attacking a guest during a live show and being disappointed by the subsequent lack of press coverage. Running through his script on autocue at the studio, the petulant Marty is easily annoyed but has his attention drawn to the capable assistant producer, the aforementioned Jasmin.

At a subsequent meeting between the star and producer, Harry (Gruffudd) tells him that the network wants a 15 minutes delay for the live show to iron out any more issues occurring. However, Marty has other ideas and fires him after informing him that he wants Jasmin more involved and that she is his replacement. "You'll thank me for it later," offers Marty, adding "No hard feelings, eh?"

Ian features in a few scenes of this relationship drama, later bumping into Harry and his lady friend Cyd (an appealing Elizabeth Mitchell), whilst out schmoosing with rising star Eamon (Jason Barry), an Irish comic being groomed to present a show to rival Mann's. Watched on by Cyd, Marty congratulates Harry on his new job and the former colleagues briefly chat after we notice the seasoned host at another table with Jasmin. Greeting the young comedian, Marty suggests Eamon guests on his show whilst the comic jokes that he wants him to come on his new show! A tale detailing the complicated lives of couples with children, Man and Boy premiered at 9 pm on BBC 1 television on Saturday 30 March.

Remaining in 2002 for a moment, not many remember In Deep, a BBC police drama that stretched over 3 series and 22 episodes made across 2001-3. Popular TV faces Nick Berry and Stephen Tompkinson co-star as undercover detectives Liam and Garth, posing as drug dealers in a bid to capture Jamie Lamb, a big-time cocaine importer aka Ian McShane.

He had been finishing shooting Sexy Beast before taking on this new job and it seems he knew Executive Producer Mal Young who convinced him to return to British TV.

"It's after he jacked in the antique business and before he became a cowboy," quips co-star Tompkinson on the DVD commentary. Berry's popular series Heartbeat would compete directly with Lovejoy from 1992.

Untouched, was enticingly shown across consecutive nights in the 9 pm slot, with the Peter Jukes storyline directed by past Miami Vice and future Emmy-winner Colin Bucksey. Ian had worked with him back in 1980 on the mini-series Armchair Thriller: High Tide.

As so-called family man Lamb, Ian's character is one serious business figure and also a person not to be crossed; as his ex-partner Monica (Kate Gartside) discovers.

Ewan Stewart as ex-Scots copper Neil is his security advisor tasked with carrying out all the dirty deeds which Mr Lamb declines to get directly involved in.

Investigated locally (the story is set in Manchester but hardly being shot there in actuality), he lives in a large, detached property with his pregnant wife and daughters and always seems one step ahead of the law. This is where Ketman (Berry) & Garth (Tompkinson) are brought in; to ingratiate themselves with the bid dealer and work alongside him.

Mr Lamb is a canny man but he does get taken in after Monika had recommended the duo but only after being arrested and obliged to work with them in gathering verification against her former partner.

As Lamb, Ian is seen running and also enjoying his home and family, with the trappings of wealth including a snazzy Range Rover car, regularly hops on a lawnmower to maintain his spacious lawn and also enjoying a dip in the pool. The cast and crew spent a week on location at the house for the double episodes which ran for an hour each.

Initially meeting Lamb at his club, the undercover lads begin their task of gaining his trust but soon enough things start happening which demonstrate Lamb's ruthlessness. With the police watching his home, Jamie is surprised to have Monika call and inform him that his nemesis DCI Geary (Ken Bones) is determined to arrest him once evidence has been gathered.

Photographed, the images will later be used to provoke a chain reaction in proceedings that result in the murder of his wife Tania (Joanna Roth).

Initially, she is unaware of the extent of his dealings but her significance proves catastrophic; with even police officer Carli exasperated by her behaviour.

The boys visit Lamb at his home where he becomes infuriated upon learning from Neil that Monika has cut a deal with the police and so he demands that the newcomers kill her. This is a test for him to be willing to do a business deal; offering them a discount from £500k down to £400k after they do as he asks. The canny Scot wants to witness the killing but Tompk's character manages to avoid this and fake Monika's death.

Meanwhile, Mrs Lamb is sent the provocatively incriminating photos of her husband with Monika and leaves the family home, taking the children with her. Upon discovering this, Jamie loses control only to be slyly supported by Liam (Berry) who attempts to keep him focused on the deal. The businessman appreciates this and asks the duo to take care of his wife, also!

Berry & 'Tompks' are very watchable together and have great onscreen chemistry.

Exacerbating Jamie's temper by sending a solicitor's letter and demanding half his assets, a disbelieving Tania is distraught to discover that her husband now wants her dead. She decides to visit a private clinic with her actions proving her downfall.

Aware of Neil's covert skills, Liam & Garth have to make the staged murder of Jamie's wife convincing. This they do by snapping Polaroids and bringing him her decapitated finger with his Nan's ring still attached before he throws it onto the fire.

Meanwhile, the deal-making arrangements continue but a new demand is made: Jamie wants the duo to return his daughters to him. This throws them but they manage to convince Mrs Lamb to agree to allow the case to continue. Her husband proves a real Jekyll & Hyde type, agreeably described by his creator as being a sociopath.

Still adapting, he tells Liam that he cannot do business with killers Liam & Gath after seeing the fake pictures of his 'dead' wife and orders him to dispose of them once the children are returned. His deputy is a formidable man; also carrying a pistol, which is recognised by the undercover detectives (they also carry firearms).

A time is arranged for the exchange of drugs/ money and youngsters but both sides prove edgy and a location change occurs.

The fellow officers shadowing proceedings lose connection with the boys and this places them in real jeopardy.

Astonishingly, during all this, Jamie's wife calls him and confesses that they are undercover police officers about to arrest him. She wants to return home but he is barely interested.

He continues and whacks his car door into Tompkinson before grabbing the children. In the meantime, he says nothing to his deputy about what he has discovered. With no backup, Liam batters both men and is about to shoot until a weakened Garth manages to get his gun to work!

Afterwards, Geary and his fellow officers go to request that Lamb accompanies them to the station to answer questions but things are not that simple. He is waiting for them, with a solicitor at his side and a signed letter from his wife, who comes down the stairs, outling her being illegally coerced into acting against him. He is still not beaten but tragically, a hint is made about his wife feeling better after her procedure.

Subsequently returned home and seemingly getting away with any involvement, Jamie joins his wife in the luxurious pool as the police discontinue watching them. However, Kelly (Miss Norris) says to Garth that he might have evaded arrest but his family life is about to be rocked. The two male detectives cannot believe that she has done this and after we see Ian on the phone with the clinic, questioning the fee required, something is about to happen.

They observe as he at first greets Tania warmly only to dunk her head underwater with his fury unravelling. It is a hugely affecting scene and terrifically paced and shot by the creative eye of Mr Bucksey. Garth and the others realise what is happening and they all rush over to the house. Kelly dives into the pool but Mrs Lamb is already dead. We see an incandescent Jamie roaring away as Garth draws his gun on his head from the edge of the pool. Music is used in a stylish moment and having watched the DVD, on the episode commentary, Mr Tompkinson explains that Ian was shouting "I'm untouchable!" with Garth screeching back, "Consider yourself touched." None of which is heard in a bit of a De Palma moment.

Ian was back working for the Beeb with Trust, a set of six, 1-hour episodes detailing the lives of lawyers in a busy law firm headed by Alan Cooper-Fozard in 2003. Aka P.G: "The Power & the Glory" he is a tightly-oiled corporate lawyer and one tough cookie running the company created by his father. Also in the firm are TV favourites Robson Green and Sarah Parish (who would later work again with an in The Pillars of Earth). Popping in and out of each episode to advise the other characters involved in the storyline Trust was presented on both BBC1 and BBC America with his role was termed "the eccentric megalomaniacal head of the firm."

Recent mid-afternoon repeats of Lovejoy brought the actor to the attention of a new audience.

Screened at 9 pm from Thursday 9 January through to 13 February, each episode cost a million pounds; inexpensive television according to Mr Green! Pretty much forgotten nowadays the show was released on DVD but is rare, its cover showed the full cast in suits with the line "Making deals, at home and at work, is what we all do in our lives every day."

After finishing work on this project Ian got the call to audition for a major new U.S. series.

But before that, in the kids flick Agent Cody Banks, Ian was directed by Dutchman Harald Zwart, who also had a hand in the screenplay with Scott Alexander & Ashley Miller, the latter wrote the script for Ian's episode of The Twilight Zone (also this year and detailed below).

A closely cropped Mr McShane is the head of E.R.I.S. whose Hong Kong HQ is where we find him keen to utilise the previously untapped powers of nanobod technology developed by the unwitting Dr Connors (Martin Donovan). However, the naïve doctor sees his creation about to be utilised for nefarious purposes rather than the humanitarian one he had intended.

This leads the American C.I.A. led by Keith David, who like Ian, has also lent his voice to many projects, including Coraline, to call for the activation of a special agent.

That person is 15-year-old Cody Banks (Malcolm in the Middle TV star Frankie Muniz) who is to be used to gain the trust of Connor's teenage daughter Natalie (teen singer Hilary Duff). Unlike James Bond, this agent is no master at talking to the ladies in a well-paced and entertaining feature which doesn't have a bad bone in its body. Like a progeny 007, even the soundtrack has obvious echoes of Bond. A surprised Cody eventually agrees to go undercover at the elite Prep school attended by Natalie after being advised by his handler, the rather attractive Ronica (Angie Harmon).

With Ian now seen in a smart black oriental outfit, he and his trusty henchman Molay (Arnold Visloo) are also at the birthday party thrown for Connors' daughter at their lavish waterside home (just how much does he earn?) Also, there is Master Banks, a young man who soon shows Natalie that there is more to him than his bumbling first impressions. Having made a grand entrance in a mini hovercraft from his boat in the bay, Dr Brinkman (McShane) observes Cody defending himself against a gang of school bullies also at the soirée and he soon suspects that he is an agent sent to spy against him.

Having his cover blown, his C.I.A. bosses abort the mission and warn Banks that he could be in danger: which proves to be correct.

Back at the E.R.I.S. thermo lab, we see a tanned Ian in a white outfit furious to hear that Connors refuses to be involved in any malevolent use of his creation; this makes no difference to the former who orders the hulking Molay to kidnap his daughter. Whilst doing this he and his men find her with Cody who tries to tell a disbelieving Natalie of his true identity. Despite his best physical efforts to fight them off, Cody is knocked unconscious and Natalie is taken to be used as a bartering tool.

When he awakens, Ronica orders him to forget getting involved and to let the agency find her instead. After discovering the tracking advice which shows that she is somewhere in the stunning Cascade Mountains region, the secret base housing E.R.I.S. here the film ventures into 007 plot land.

After managing to get himself captured along with Ronica, having located Miss Connors and her father, Cody is able to flee but with only 3 hours remaining before the nanobots are introduced into society via ice cubes.

Will he be able to prevent this?

Brinkman thinks not.

During a diversion created by the bright young agent, in the resulting melee, Natalie (the pretty Ms Duff) surreptitiously pops a cube into the gaping mouth of the evil Doctor Brinkman. As it slowly begins to take effect, he begins to disintegrate!

The base collapses around them, the heroes need to escape quickly and a helicopter is used but Cody is left behind. Does he manage to get away in time? Of course he does.

Ian's role in an episode of the latest incantation of The Twilight Zone feels very-1980s but was actually produced much later (there was an actual revival before this) as part of the often-baffling but equally entertaining cult classic show which was first broadcast in 1959. Ian co-stars in Cold Fusion; entry 35 of a mammoth 43 episodes making up the one season. This particular story from the second revival was shown on Wednesday 2 April.

A swift running time of less than half-hour, Fusion finds Ian as the mysterious Chandler, head of a small team in Alaska working on the secret Gemini programme. Communications have mysterious been cut so physicist Dr Paul Thorson (Patrick Flanery) is sent in to unravel the situation and return the programme to working status. However, once there things prove most peculiar.

Co-scripted by Ashley Edward Miller and Zack Sentz, the latter provided the screenplay for Agent Cody Banks.

Discovering that only 3 remain of the original 12 crew, Thorson meets them all and each seems obsessed with their situation and being spied upon. "Dr Chandler, the guy who thought up Gemini. He went nuts. We gotta stop him," demands the crazed Cmdr. Gordon (Gordon Michael Woolvett) believes the programme is a bomb. Attempting to discover the code to allow access into the secure lab, think along the lines of the T.A.R.D.I.S and you won't be far off, he then meets Morgan (Nancy Sorel) obsessed with writing out space & time calculations.

Next comes the disinterested Sykes (Keith Hamilton Cobb), adding to Thorson's frustration. A call on the phone features Ian's dulcet tones are heard all around the base and seem to be driving the now gathered occupants quite mad, "Hello Paul. Dr Chandler here. You wanted to talk to me. Well, here I am. Let's talk. About you and the end of the world." The good doctor initially resists but soon enough he loses control. Manipulating everyone, the malevolent voice continues, "Look at them, "they're all insane," begins Chandler before a scuffle ensues and ultimately Thorson shoots each of the others who all vanish. The secure door clicks open as he does this and he enters the lab.

Once inside, the actor emerges, sporting a goatee, Chandler reiterates that none of the others are real; but composite parts of Thorson's personality.

Things take a sinister turn once the former attempts to convince the visitor that he is the creator of the Gemini project; a bomb whose use would have devastating effects worldwide. Chandler tries to convince Paul that he should end things, "take the bullet" and kill himself. Instead, shots are fired at Ian's character and he falls to the ground only to morph into…Dr Thorson.

Ian received another "and Ian McShane" screen credit for this entertaining role which was directed by Eli Richbourg, one of only two credits. He died in 2012.

A nice change of direction in the feature film Nemesis Game (2003) marked Kiwi writer-director Jesse Warn's debut. Shot in Canada (for its tax breaks) across a month for NZ$6m utilising an international cast, Ian is seen right from the start of this so-so drama. Portraying police officer Jeff Novak. Complete in a suit and with a bit of an American twang to his voice, he features in a pre-credits scene interviewing killer Emily Gray (Rena Owen); "What the hell happened?" he asks. Second billed after Carly Pope as his screen daughter, college student Sara, they are somewhat estranged since his marriage to a second wife following the death of her mother in a car crash.

Keeping herself from other students, including randy Dennis (Brendan Fehr, who suffers a terrible fate here), she prefers to hang out with Vern (Adrian Paul) at his comic store. Enjoying puzzles, Sara naively responds to riddles left in the underground and becomes drawn into a dangerous game that proves fatal for a number of those involved. As a detective, Ian's Novak crops up whenever his daughter gets into trouble and one such instance is after Dennis is found hanged.

Also significant to the story is the release of Miss Gray after an attempt to drown a young boy. She is interrogated by him and seems to know a lot more about Novaks than he feels comfortable with. Who is being set up here? Is it Sara and Vern?

After Emily is arrested for killing a student at Sara's college, she and Vern discover more about a character called Nem Nem found in her copy of The Enigma of Metaphysics.

Executed, his followers subsequently devised a game now being recreated. Unbeknownst to Sara, Vern is playing a much deeper part in proceedings than he seems.

Interviewing Emily, Jeff (Ian) is concerned for his daughter's safety once the killer reveals pertinent information about them. Calling Sara, he asks her what she knows about a 'design' and the game. Requesting that she go to a safe place, the tension mounts nicely via Warn's screenplay.

Intriguingly, a young man who frequents the comic book store is awaiting her in the car park and a scuffle ensues; he reveals that he was the boy that Emily Gray attacked. He turns a gun on himself and it looks likely that Sara could be implicated in it all in the best part of the film. Consoling his daughter at the crime scene, Sara manages to wander off and back to the disused building where she had discovered her college friend dead. As for the final moments, well, the author will leave the reader to watch Nemesis Game to find out what happens.

Known as Paper, Scissor, Stones when Ian was filming, the film was subsequently recognised at the 2003 New Zealand Film Awards, taking away four prizes.

Primarily reluctant to take on a new television show as he was enjoying making Lovejoy and other projects in the UK, once Ian learnt of those involved with Deadwood he jumped at the opportunity to audition. A canny operator, McShane knew that it was likely to be a success and would do his career some good due to its wide exposure via HBO in America. Going in and feeling super confident, he took charge and received a call a couple of hours later offering him the role of Al Swearengen Enjoying a quick turnaround, Ian was filming 3 weeks later, after replacing an ailing Powers Boothe prior to the pilot being made (but he would appear in the show as a rival business owner sited opposite his place).

The Emmy-winning pilot episode directed by Walter Hill, who Ian already knew, and written by David Milch was made in 2002. In August of the following year, filming commenced on the first season of 12 episodes and by March 2004 it was on television. "Gunsmoke it ain't!" joked Ian of Milch's scripts, assisted by others, which often gave long soliloquies for the actors to perform. The latter had created NYPD Blues, previously.

As a historical figure, playing bar/ brothel owner Swearengen made Mr McShane love the show and the autonomy the team had whilst making it at the Gene Autry ranch, an old movie studio in

California. Changes were easily facilitated and the approach provided the actor with the most creative experience of his career.

In the burgeoning town of Deadwood, South Dakota, during the gold rush, Ian's pragmatist runs the Gem Saloon, there was seldom a finished shooting script, "It was the only thing I have made that I watched when it was on television, as I genuinely had no idea how it would turn out," he told The Off Camera Show, "because we would never finish making an episode without having started another one. We...were based only half an hour from the set, so there was a real feeling of closeness to the project." An organic process, Mr McShane had great empathy for his profanity-strewn character and regards Milch as a genius. The Brit abroad saw the show as echoing the story of America.

Assisted by W.S. Farnum (William aka Billy Sanderson), he fears the wrath of his boss but proves useful to Al and is endearing in amongst a busy company whose behind-the-scenes team were top-notch professionals. As Jewel, actor Geri Jewell is constantly barracked by Swearengen whilst her character is seen cleaning the bar area, whilst off-screen she has acknowledged that Ian and others were all supportive of her working on set whilst combating her cerebral palsy. Ms Jewell returned for the TV film, subsequently. Later working on Ray Donovan with Ian, here Paula Malcomson is Trixie; his best girl at the brothel and a woman who shares Al's bed regularly. Despite beatings, mistreatment and how bluntly he often speaks to her, she is devoted to him and they have a relationship amidst the wretchedness.

Set in 1876, at the Gem Al proves territorial and is a man who will stop at nothing to protect his interests; these include bribery, violence and even murder. He might not always get his way, initially, but he works on it and is constantly scheming to sustain his status in the town from internal & external bothers. With many visitors arriving as prospectors, money is there and the coarse Swearengen, hair centre-parted and sporting a bushy moustache, wants it.

With his and seemingly everyone else's favourite cussing word "cocksucker" in regular use, often amusingly so, the season closes with Al looking down at the bar from the landing above. His performance saw Ian recognised with a Best Actor nod at the Golden Globes, "Best gig I ever had," smiled the actor upon receiving it whilst adorned by his Deadwood moustache.

Accompanied by Gwen, the Globes were important in the industry and took place at the prestigious Beverly Hilton in January.

Offering a brief glimpse into the lives of very different women in modern-day Los Angeles, writer-director Rodrigo Garcia's Nine Lives (2005) proved a hit on the film festival circuit which led it to receive a limited theatrical release. Shot across a mere 18 days, Ian is seen in the trailer and features in the fifth story: Samantha.

Appearing a little under the hour mark, for 10 minutes we follow Sammy (Amanda Seyfried) who lives with her parents Larry (McShane) and Ruth (Sissy Spacek who would reconvene with Ian as a screen couple in Hot Rod. They both want her to get a good education by going to college but she worries about them.

As Larry Ian uses an American drawl, with a scruffy, greying beard and is wheelchair-bound. Mad for crosswords whilst wheezing away, Sammy moves around the apartment talking to each of them separately whilst internally struggling with things. A recent relationship breakdown and the demands to help her father are affecting her whilst our visit ends with her returning to her bedroom in a fragile emotional state. Coincidentally, her room is full of stuff including a panda bear soft toy on the bed; Ian would later lend his voice to animated gem Kung Fu Panda.

A beautiful looking production despite its drabness and brown hues, Deadwood returned for a second season in March 2005 runningth through to May, with Ian attending its premiere at the world-famous Grauman's Chinese Theatre in Los Angeles, that same month. He also presented the Best Actor Golden Globe, after winning it previously, to fellow Brit, Hugh Laurie.

Characters still regularly drop the f-bomb and more and the opening couple of episodes are distinctly cruder in both dialogue and action. Show creator David Milch penned the opening story which sees Al (Ian McShane) swearing immediately at the introduction to the camp of a telegram system.

Despising the interfering lawman Sherriff Bullock (Timothy Olyphant), the crime lord is once more annoyed at things going on around him. There is some flowery but baffling dialogue delivered by Ian and a truly horrific fight with Bullock which sees them flop over the Gem's balcony, a keen viewing point for its proprietor, and down into the mud below.

"Welcome to fucking Deadwood!" gasps Al to the startled stagecoach of new arrivals. In Deadwood, violence is regularly dished-out or a gun is drawn, to protect or attack.

In poor physical condition after his battering, Farnum's regional accent is perfectly aped by the disgruntled Swearengen and we discover that rival Cy (Powers Boothe) is just as disparaging about his sex workers as Al (who now displays his tendency for oral relief provided by one of his employees).

With his face resembling Frankenstein's monster, Al subsequently resists retaliating against the younger Sherriff and allows things to settle between them. Utilising trusted gofers Dan (W. Earl Brown) and Johnny (Sean Bridges) Deadwood may seem like a man's world but women here play a pivotal role. Sarah Paulson is introduced, an actor who would work on American Horror Story Asylum when Ian guested.

Some comedic moments are present in the second season particularly when poor Al has an excruciating case of gallstones which render him speechless. Tended to by the overworked and unstable Doc Cochran (Brad Dourif), he excretes plenty of whining and yelling, whilst the medic and Al's lackeys hold him down with the latter seen alone in bed with a relieved facial expression that proves hilarious.

His recovery proves slow, what with having been battered and the operation, and so Al watches over his domain via the bed. A man who will use anyone to get what he wants; he converses with Cy to keep it so.

On the macabre side, Swearengen takes delivery of the decapitated head of a Native American whilst allying with Merrick (Jeffrey Jones), newspaper publisher/ local printer,

His peculiar association with Wu (Keone Wong) proves most amusing also.

However, the verbiage scripting is overly complex at times and little wonder that some of the characters (and the viewers) look perplexed and baffled by it. E.V. Farnum is guilty of this as much as many of the others but actor Billy Sanderson is such a delight that this can be forgiven. Exceptional as the local hotelier and now, mayor, is a wonderful creation and excellent in interactions with Ian.

Season two is not as strong as the opening one perhaps due to the many different writers employed.

In the early-2000s Woody Allen lost his way, making pictures that nobody watched but with the occasional gem sparkling brightly. High calibre actors still wanted to work with him and Scoop (2006) is one such offering. The best in his trio of UK-based films, Ian is fourth billed behind leads Scarlett Johansson, Hugo Jackman and Allen himself, back when he enlivened his stories with a role (and all the wittiest lines).

Friends and colleagues eulogise the passing of newspaper journalist Joe Strombel (Mr McShane) whom we first meet aboard a boat accompanied by other recently-deceased people and a silent Grim Reaper. Perplexed upon learning that rich Brit businessman Peter Lyman (Jackman doing his finest English accent) could be the serial killer responsible for the deaths of several sex workers, he jumps ship to flesh out the truth. A fun murder-mystery, pretty American journalism student Sondra (an uber blond Ms Johansson) is to be the channel through which this will be explored.

Attending a magic show at the Shepherd's Bush Empire with gal pal Vivian (Romola Garai) and friends, Sondra is invited up on stage by seasoned conjurer Splendini aka Sidney (Allen, on great form) to help in a disappearing trip. Placed inside his "dematerialization" box, who should manifest himself but Joe, offering the ambitious but startled young woman the "scoop of the decade".

Returning the next day, she relays her experience to the sceptical Sidney that a killer leaves a Tarot card next to his victims' bodies by way of a calling card. But who will believe her ponders the grizzled magic man when her source is a man who died 3 days earlier! Uniquely, Mr McShane appears throughout as a ghost offering clues and leads for the twosome to follow.

Dragging a reluctant Sidney along to locate the suspect, Lyman (Jackman), after a false start they eventually discover him at a private members swimming pool known to Sondra's affluent friends. The suave Peter naturally takes a fancy to her and so begins a clumsy investigation. The only developing problem is that Sondra finds him hard to resist.

Scoop is a fun tale with Johansson and Allen an incongruous screen coupling. His latest muse, she is no Diane Keaton or Mia Farrow reincarnation but is amusing nonetheless. The film offered roles for many recognisable British actors but sadly, most have little to do.

Kevin McNally, who would work with Ian on Pirates of the Caribbean: On Stranger Tides is in this but alas they share no scenes.

Sidney is reluctantly and wittily obliged to act as Sondra's father when attending a soiree at Peter's fancy city apartment. Investigating in his Music room; looking for clues, the duo is moments from being discovered by their host.

But is Lyman the killer?

Sneaking back down later, Sondra discovers some Tarot cards hidden there and we do wonder.

Stromboli reappears to Sondra and urges her to carry on investigating despite her acknowledgement that she is falling for the handsome businessman. Meantime, the murders continue.

As the plot thickens, Stanley & Sondra are out for a birthday meal when the latter sees her beau passing by in the street outside. Odd in that he said he would be away on business. Another person is killed nearby, with a Tarot card left and it looks like Peter might be responsible.

"It's about time I take my story to a real newspaperman," concedes the young woman to Stanley, "one that's living." And they pay a visit to journalist Charles Dance who reveals that the Tarot Card Killer has just been found and it is not Peter Lyman.

Subsequently struggling to hide her deceit in telling him that she was investigating him, Sondra confesses all but Lyman accepts her explanation freely, adding that he bought the Tarot cards as a gift for her after she expressed an interest in them when they first met. Peter also tells her that he was negotiating a big business deal and hence his cloak and dagger behaviour.

The seasoned hack (McShane) manifests for a final time to Sidney and they share what he told her about thinking that Peter is the killer. Before vanishing, Joe (Ian) tells him to check Lyman's Tarot cards to see if one is missing.

Now chief investigator, Stanley delves deeper and reveals the necessary proof but Sondra refuses to hear him, stating that the case is closed. She is at the Lyman country estate, enjoying a weekend away with Peter and presently on the lake with him.

Deciding to drive down and save his friend, Sidney reluctantly ventures out onto the British roads but is confused by having to drive on the left and off-screen, a crash is heard.

Meanwhile, Sondra hears Peter's confession that he did murder the last prostitute and that he is now going to do the same with both Americans. Her cries for help go unheard and following a struggle, he pushes her into the water. Thinking that she has drowned, he returns to the house and calls the authorities saying that there has been an accident. After the police arrive, and his emotional speech has been delivered, Sondra miraculously reappears. She concedes that she is an expert swimmer and so managed to survive.

The story is published by Dance's newspaper and Sondra acknowledges Joe and Stanley in revealing the truth.

Elsewhere, as Stanley, Woody Allen is found on the same vessel as Ian previously, repeating his tried and tested stage patter on his fellow travellers.

We are Marshall is another sports film so beloved by American audiences but this one has its basis in true life; namely a 1970 tragedy that claimed the lives of 75 University football players and staff travelling home on a chartered plane returning to West Virginia following a game.

Ian is the straight-laced (and equally straight-haired in his 70s get-up) Chairman of the school board whose son, Chris, Wes Brown, was one on the University's American Football squad and sadly a victim of the crash. Visiting his local restaurant diner Boones daily for the past 30 years, Paul Griffen even has his own booth and is always there when not working at the local mill.

Members of the University board believe that the season should be suspended whilst the few remaining players such as Nate (Anthony Mackie) feel that they should continue as a tribute to their lost colleagues. Whilst attending a meeting alongside President Dedmon (David Strathairn), Nate calls on them and says those outside the building have something they would like to express: en masse in a truly breathtakingly poignant moment, the mass of youngsters and locals stand and look up at them chanting "We are… Marshall! We are…Marshall!"

Bowing to the collective call, the struggle to find players and a new coach proves almost too much until exuberant family man Jack Lengyel (Matthew McConaughey) convinces them that he is the man to take the project on.

Meanwhile, Paul (Mr McShane) becomes closer with Annie (Kate Mara), his lad's girlfriend who works at the diner. She offers to return the wedding ring that Chris gave her, which had previously belonged to Paul's late wife but he tells her to keep it and think of his son. A snippet of the scene features in the trailer for the movie.

At a press call to announce the new coach's arrival, in the background we observe Paul.

For the opening game back, lots of locals listen via radio, including Ian's character and after losing, Coach Leygel visits the restaurant. Disappointed that Paul instigated the firing of President Dedmon, the bereaved father is upset by his observations of the photo of father and son next to the booth. "This is not about a game," begins Griffen (Ian using another American accent), "This is about what happened to this town." Right now, winning is not what is important.

Aware of his son's plans to relocate to California with Annie, it is touching to see them together and the former encouraging the youngster to leave, "Grief is messy," he offers.

As Paul, Ian lives at the Frederick Apartment complex and a publicity still captured the actor there.

Listening to another Marshall game, Paul reaches into his pocket and discovers the returned ring.

The ending of the film is hugely affecting as Annie's voiceover tells us about the real individuals portrayed in Marshall and what happened to them subsequently. However, there is no mention of either her character or Ian's; this is because neither existed. Both are composites used as dramatic points to express the immense grief shared after such a monumental loss. Knowing this does not detract from the emotional impact produced by watching.

Another hectic working year, Ian and Gwen did manage to make time to attend several premieres of not only his work but also of various films.

Advancing to Sunday 11 January and the opening episode of the third and final season of Deadwood is broadcast. Coming less than a week since Ian, David Milch and others had attended its premiere at the Cinerama Dome in Hollywood.

Ian would join others for the dedication of Milch's Hollywood star and the actor also gave a speech.

By Sunday 27 August, the 36th episode, Tell Him Something Pretty, aired and that was that: cancelled. This came as a surprise and disappointment to the cast and crew who had assumed it would return. Ian had been at show creator David milch's Hollywood star unveiling in June.

We once again see blood on the floorboards at the Gem saloon and observe Al scrubbing it off after another fatality: men are regularly beaten to death and in actuality; the site averaged a murder each day. He continues to watch all life go by from his balcony above the main drag as "pain in the balls Hearst," as Al terms him, as played by Gerald McRayne, sees his stranglehold on the camp tighten but not without resistance. Taking a beating by him and one of his boys who proceeds to chop off his finger!

Fabulous to see a very old face from Ian's past; Aubrey Morris features in some episodes. As seen in If It's Tuesday, It Must be Belgium, the TV mini-series Disraeli & Lovejoy previously, they had worked on the latter in 1991. Sadly not sharing any scenes here, Mr Morris died in 2015.

Al has been deemed as being an honourable man but his diligence sees him administer fatal retribution to those that have been assaulted in the camp. On Election Day in the closing episode, he murders one of the young sex workers by slashing the throat, something he had done before. We contrast this with him heard singing a little ditty called The Unfortunate Rake in his empty bar whilst the community attends the nearby amateur night organised by Brian Cox & his troupe. Scots-born Mr Cox had appeared with Ian previously in Kings and they play in brief scenes together here: two actors at the top of their game.

Hearst (McRayne) leaves the camp during a tense final moment after which we once again see Al cleaning blood from the floor. Not intended to be the last look in at Deadwood, differences between Milch & HBO saw the show abruptly end here. Mark Tinker directed episodes this season and another for American Gods, subsequently. Cast member W. Earl Brown, a close ally to Swearengen, contributed a much-maligned script. This is where we leave but the journey is not quite over.

"Kill 'em all! Except for the fat one."

So orders a raucous Captain Hook aka Ian after joining forces with a disgruntle Prince Charming in Shrek The Third (2007), this outing for the lime green creature was loosely based upon the picture books created by American cartoonist William Steig. An actor whose rich speaking voice has brought him many jobs, Ian has also ventured into film & TV work which utilised his vocal talents only. But it was Shrek the Third which presented him with his first experience of being involved in an animated project. After playing the infamous Blackbeard the pirate he now stepped into the shoes of Hook, alongside Eddie Murphy, Cameron Diaz & Mike Myers for this fabulous piece of fun.

Employing an enthusiastic, stereotypical pirate accent with lots of "ayes" and so forth, Shrek the Third followed the popular 2001 original and its 2004 sequel in being a box office smash. However, critical comments proved unkind about the film.

Ian attended the première on Monday 11 June at the Odeon Cinema in London's famous Leicester Square following its L.A. one back in May.

A comedy overflowing with charm and good nature, The Hot Rod (2007) was lambasted by critics upon its theatrical release but found its home on DVD in America. Having since attained cult status, Ian didn't see it when it came out but caught up with it on cable subsequently, as many did. In a recent interview, the actor confessed that he was happy to get recognised for his role as Andy Samberg's father.

With his mother (Sissy Spacek) now married to former military man Frank (Ian having lots of fun), Rod Kimble (comedy man Samberg) habitually seeks his approval and respect via physical battles with him ala Clouseau & Cato. Ian can be seen in the hilarious trailer battering a frustrated Andy!

Holding on to a treasured photograph of his late father with 70s daredevil Evil Knievel, Rod believes that he was a stuntman and so continues the family tradition. Unfortunately, he repeatedly proves his ineptitude with various jumps proving a flop. He is more akin to Pee-Wee Herman than Knievel and is also hampered by an inadequate pedal moped to perform on!

Mr McShane had recently wrapped on Deadwood when he accepted the role of the well-meaning stepdad and the actor relished the opportunity to do something funny, regarding his involvement in slapstick comedy.

Their first scene together sees Frank batter poor Rod who in turn is ordered to take out the trash! Here he reconnects with old pal Denise (the scrummy Isla Fisher, later working with Ian on the grubby Grimsby).

Using another American twang accent, Frank reveals that he needs a heart operation which will necessitate finding $50k. "But I still need to kick your arse," whines the stepson as their mutual antagonism continues, "How can I do that if you're dead!"

Samberg is terrific as the petulant lead and when his character decides to raise funds for Frank, we know that they are probably going to fail.

A movie night featuring footage of the daredevil shot by his younger brother Kevin (Jorma Tacconne) is screened at a local cinema and attended by a poorly Frank, wearing a lurid velour tracksuit and bucket hat and accompanied by his wife. Unfortunately, the invited audience only laughs at his daredevil efforts and Rod, ever the trier, forfeits all the money raised after freaking out. And to confound things, his mom tells him that his father wasn't a stunt performer at all.

Deflated, he quits and the proposed jump is cancelled. His support team (including Bill Hader) ask him to reconsider and he subsequently agrees.

Seeing Frank (Ian) at home on the sofa, Rod lies about the fundraising going well and they have a heart-to-heart with the older man telling him that he is only tough on him as he is priming him in readiness for becoming the man of the house once he has passed. But the youngster still admits to wanting to beat him in a fight in a very funny scene between them. With a spanking new bike and accompanying leathers, and enthusiasm for his team, he is ready for the huge jump but we know that he will probably flop. He does.

All the while Frank and Marie listen in on the radio alarmed to hear that Rod has come off his bike. Wonderfully, donations flood in and the 50k is reached.

However, there is one epic fight remaining and it proves epic. The filmmakers clearly love 1980s films as we watch Ian in his green tracksuit and a determined Rod slug it out, crash through walls and garden fences until we freeze frame with Rod finally proving victorious ala Rocky. Shot in Canada, in Cloverdale, a small town outside Vancouver, Rod was released in the US on 3 August 2007. Originally a Will Ferrell vehicle, the Pat Brady script was reworked. Amusingly, cast member Jorma Tacconne admitted that Ian smelt lovely in a scene where Frank is comforting his son after his health worries are made known.

For The Dark is Rising aka The Seeker, Ian rejoined his fellow Battle of Britain cast member James Cosmo as part of the self-titled "Old Ones", a gang of immortals consisting of Mr McShane as Merriman Lyon, Cosmo, Jim Piddock and Frances Conry as time travellers seeking to uphold "the light" of goodness trait.

Developed from a series of books written by Susan Cooper, between 1965-77, Dark was the second story, published in 1973. Bizarrely, Trainspotting writer John Hodges contributed its screenplay. "Ian has got his booming voice and this incredible presence," offered director David L.Cunnigham who utilises a good mix of acting talent. Location filming commenced on 24 February 2007 in Bucharest with other locations in Romania including Transylvania, used to replicate a town supposedly somewhere in the UK for another project giving an "and Ian McShane" acting credit.

Its opening scene sees Merriman (Ian) introduced as the driver to Miss Greythorne (Ms Conry), with an invitation to visit them at Huntercombe Manor for a Christmas gathering. Will (Alexander Ludwig) accepts on his family's behalf and soon we will discover there is something special about this seemingly ordinary teenaged American boy having relocated to the UK.

Mr McShane features a goatee and beard combo and dresses as if he has come straight out of a Dickens novel. "I'm used to dealing with warriors, not boys," he bemoans once Wes and his brood attend the festive gathering. The poor boy is unaware of what powers he possesses and is pursued by a highwayman-like figure demanding the "sign" from the bemused lad. Christopher Ecclestone is fantastic as the pantomime Rider, on the side of the dark (evil) and shot in slow-mo riding his trusty and equally intimidating stead.

The Fab Four arrive to help and it is they who will try to protect and steer the boy into locating 6 signs invaluable to both.

"Walk with us, Will....through time," requests the amiable Merriman, leading the group from the cold through to a sunny forest and the Great Hall where they are at their most powerful.

Here they attempt to explain to him that they are outside of time and that he is a sign seer; they serve the light and the scary Rider, the dark, which is rising in strength as they speak.

A disbelieving Will has been tasked with finding the signs within the next 5 days or the world will be lost. As a teen, he is naturally flabbergasted by all this, scared and not wanting such a burden.

The mystery of the disappearance of his twin brother Tom as a baby is unknown to him at this stage, with the Rider later revealing that he took him to use as a pawn to break Will's spirit. Each sign, bringing the "power of the light" consists of stone, bronze, iron, wood and water with the final one hidden in a human soul. The Fantastic Four need Will to find the signs and Mr Lyon (McShane) informs him that he has great, untapped strengths to fight against the dark forces, including time travel.

This takes them back to the early 13th century and a scene involving a sea of snakes to contend with whilst hunting for another sign. Ian and the "Old Ones" are enveloped by the ugly reptiles and it looks like quite an uncomfortable scene to have acted in. Thankfully Will discovers the sign.

As Merriman, Ian's character is often tasked with encouraging the doubting young man into believing in himself and they share many heart-to-heart moments. With 2 signs gathered and 3 days remaining, a frustrated Will calls upon Merriman. Coincidentally, Ian is seen besides a fireplace with another poker at his side ala Ray.

With more time travelling resulting in the gathering of an additional sign, Merriman is furious with Will upon seeing him vent his frustrations. "Even the smoothest light shines in the dark," opinions the soothing warrior.

Will the Seeker have enough guile or time to gather the remaining signs? Miss Greythorne and Mr Lyon seem uncertain.

As the eerie Rider, Ecclestone is in great form and proves a memorable villain.

Snow is sent to the town by the cunning Rider whilst young Will manages to find another of the signs after his family take refuge at the mansion where he has a battle to protect them.

After the snow and cold there then comes flooding and the moment when Will's reserves are challenged by the pretty young woman Maggie (a sly Amelia Warner) befriending him and using her femininity to manipulate the smitten teenager into giving her the signs. But she is in cahoots with the Rider and is desperate to succeed in getting the signs to satiate her own needs.

A swarm of ravens charge the windows of the house as an ocean of water sweeps inside and engulfs Merriman and the others. Amidst this chaos and danger, Will finds the next sign whilst a disgruntled Rider rides of moodily in a beautifully menacing fashion.

It is not over yet.

Advised to return to the Great Hall whenever he feels in danger, Will joins the Gang of Four only to be emotionally manipulated by the Rider mimicking the pleading voice of his family from outside. Merriman pleads with the boy not to open the doors as it is a trick but the distressed youngster cannot resist and unintentionally lets in the deceitful Rider.

A terrific finale shows the Gang unable to prevent the intruder from attacking Will and each is blown up into the air and away. The Rider is unrelenting and preys upon Will's insecurities in an attempt to take the signs. It's always about the signs. Tension mounts with Will unable to find the sixth until he realises that he is the final one: he is the soul able to unleash the power of the light and thus save the world. This he realises via the conviction heard in Ian's voice as Merriman. For now, they have the upper hand against the darkness.

Reunited with his lost twin, Miss Greythorne bemoans to Lyon that Will should know how much they helped him. "He's only 14," offers a deadpan McShane, "It's a difficult age."

An enjoyable story and a film that deserves to be appreciated once it can find its right audience, The Dark is Rising warrants becoming a firm family favourite in years to come.

This year Ian acted in a succession of child-friendly fantasy films, another being The Golden Compass, adapted by director Chris Weitz from the Philip Pullman book Northern Lights.

An award-winning movie as well as receiving multiple other nominations, we step into a world of talking animals or 'daemon' as they are oddly termed (not intended in the malevolent tense/ sense but representative of the soul or self).

However, this is not Dr Dolittle, with Lord Asriel (a fleeting Daniel Craig) setting forth, investigating the origins of 'dust'; the essence of the spirit or soul. It proves a dangerous thing for him with those in the established religious status quo, including Derek Jacobi, reacting violently to his challenging of their belief system. The gorgeous Nicole Kidman as Mrs Coulter; a role expressing the gravitas of an exceptional actor ala Charlize Theron in Snow White & the Huntsman, may look delightful but underneath she is quite the plotter. Just as in many other stories, youngster Lyra (a debut role for Dakota Blue Richards), Asriel's niece, is a child with special abilities, for she is one of a chosen few that can read the symbols found on the face of the Golden Compass. One of the last remaining artefacts, it is therefore of great value and so its powers are much sought after by the likes of Mrs Coulter, who shows her true colours despite taking Lyra as her assistant.

The Golden Compass looks terrific and is enhanced hugely by its thoroughbred cast consisting of many British TV faces; including Jack Shepherd from Man and a Boy and Jim Carter. That charming American Sam Elliott is involved also.

Grabbed by a team of mystery men, Lyra is later brought to meet the King of the Ice Bears: Ragnar Sturlusson (lots of the characters in the story have Scandinavian surnames). He is voiced by our Mr McShane whom we are introduced to a little after an hour.

Convincing him that she is the daemon of his arch-enemy Iorek (Sir Ian McKellen, who had worked on stage with Ian back in the 1960s), she persuades the King to fight him once again after defeating him previously to gain the royal presence. She agrees to become his daemon afterwards.

It is amusing hearing the actor vocalise the huge white bear and we see them do battle to the death in front of many others. Spoiler alert here: after seemingly looking like the victor, Ragnar goads his exhausted opponent who glances at his dear Lyra, gathers some strength and succeeds in killing him.

The story continues and was left open for a sequel to follow.

Another enormous production involving hundreds of animators/ creative artists meshing together to create the world of The Golden Compass, flying witches, talking ice bears and more, was a project with a perceived shelf life. A great amount of official merchandising including a Playstation 2 game, Panini sticker album, board game and figures were available but alas, The Golden Compass failed to ignite the box officeseeing its sequels shelved.

However, a big noise in the industry, the film received a London premiere on Tuesday 27 November in advance of its December general release.

Finally this year, Ian returned to the stage and a revival of The Homecoming, a shocking black comedy regarded as Harold Pinter's best work. Written in 1963 it was first performed by the RSC in the following year. Playing the 1k+ Cort Theatre over in America's "Broadway" district from Tuesday 16 December through to Sunday 13 April 2008, with McShane in the role of Max. Coincidentally, it marked the 40th anniversary of the play and also since Ian had first performed in the States in the ill-fated The Promise. First previewed on Tuesday 4 December, the production ran for 137 performances and subsequently received a 2008 nomination as best show. Ian's Wild and Willing co-star Paul Rogers had won a Tony Award in 1967, as Max, and a revival came with Roy Dotrice subsequently. Playing Ian's horrid stage son Lenny, Raúl Esparza termed the play a "very sick comedy" when he and Mr McShane chatted about their involvement at the Cort on the TV show Theatre Talk (4 Jan 2008).

Jammed into the middle of animated delights Kung Fu Panda & Sponge Bob, writer-director Paul W.S. Anderson was a fan of the 1975 film Death Race 2000 and of a certain actor, "McShane is a particular favourite of mine," offered the creative on the making of the film, "he's such a tremendous sort of father-figure to everybody." When Anderson's mother, also a fan, visited the set of Death Race, she saw Ian as the biggest star involved with the project.

Third-billed in the reboot which was an unusual film for him to get involved in; location filming took the cast and crew to Canada. Fellow Brit, whispering Jason Statham, is the lead in the David Carradine role, as Jensen Ames, framed for the murder of his wife and daughter and sent to Terminal Island, as grim as it sounds, where prison warden Joan Allen runs things.

Here, skilled convict drivers compete to the death in the hope of gaining their freedom after notching up 5 wins.

In the food hall, a dangerous place for newbies, Coach (Ian) is seen seated, wearing tiny Mr Pickwick-type glasses, long slicked-back hair, watching as Ames is confronted by the local badass. After successfully battering a group of his men, Coach quips that he clearly didn't like the dreadful porridge either.

By now, Ian was in the character actor role where he would often chip in with the witty barb. It is not revealed as to what offence Coach has committed but later, in a heart-to-heart with Ames, he reveals that he could have been released years earlier but that he is so institutionalised that he prefers to remain.

When the warden offers the former driving ace a chance of freedom; the only catch is he has to win a race as an undisclosed replacement for the recently-deceased 'Frankenstein' masked driver. Both Hennessy (Ms Allen) and her second-in-command, Ulrich (a suitably horrible Jason Clarke) manipulate and cajoles him into accepting the premise of competing in 3 races staged across 3 days & broadcast live, all controlled by the warden, "The ultimate in auto carnage all available via subscription."

Coach and his crew of Gunner (Jacob Varges) & Lists (Frederick Koehler) support Ames with the former instructing him via a headset and each driver being joined by beautiful female navigators to please the paying viewership. But even here, Ames' new partner, the shapely Case (Natalie Martine) is being manipulated by Hennessy to sabotage his chances.

Finishing last in the opening race, pressure is put upon Ames and he learns that his family were murdered just so he could be brought in to drive for the death race event. It is here that he & Coach chat and the former acknowledges that he sees that Armes is no killer.

Stage 2 arrives with only a half-dozen drivers remaining after the death of others, the onscreen racing is well-delivered and proves most entertaining, even if this isn't ordinarily something you would be interested in. Cranking up the excitement, Hennessy introduces Mad Max-type armed vehicles to eliminate the disposable drivers whilst the bloodthirsty audience watches on. Ames plays along and succeeds in completing the race; "Now that's entertainment!" extorts Ian as Coach following the destruction of one of the armoured vehicles.

With several drivers dead, the day of the final race arrives. In the pit Coach quips "Gentleman, This should be interesting," as the race commences. However, the team is being sabotaged throughout and this continues with Ulrich disabling the gun on his customised Mustang, in a film set a little in the future.

Throughout Death Race, we watch Coach, Ian, forever looking into a mysterious little black book and at one early stage, we watch as he and the others duck down after a particularly loud explosion on the course.

Ulrich sabotages Ames' car and the driver realises that neither he nor Joe (Tyrese Gibson) is likely to be given their freedom should they win. His opponent has won 3 races already and is prepared to do whatever it takes to win the remainder as 70m viewers watch.

Containing lots of inane chatter and splatter-gun dialogue delivered in single sentences, it is all faintly ridiculous stuff but a nice twist at the close proves enjoyable. Joe & Ames work to escape whilst Hennessy and the audience watch a pre-recorded race.

It looks like Case is caught but not even that is what it seems as Hennessy realises that she has been duped. Coach, aware that Ulrich had placed a bomb under his driver's car, removed it before it could be utilised and we look on as the Warden receives a gift only for him to ignite it from a remote control from outside. "I love this game," he grins as the building above explodes.

Death Race took 14 years to be developed, with changes made to the screenplay before it was finally shot. And casting and production were lengthy for a good looking film that saw a new ending added once it had been shown to a test audience. Before its release came a delightful animated feature.

"Sometimes great courage comes most unexpectedly," and this is certainly the case for the happy-go-lucky Panda "Po". Trained in the skills of martial arts by the wise Shifu (Dustin Hoffman) and assisted by the "Furious Five" he is confronted by the returning Tai Lung (as voiced by Ian McShane) in the delightful animated feature Kung Fu Panda. Subsequently spawning sequels and shorts, we need only focus on the introduction of the Kung Fu-loving Panda, as voiced by Jack Black. Released on Friday 6 June under the DreamWorks umbrella that also made the Shrek films, Mr McShane lends his voice to the aforementioned evil snow leopard.

His third voice-only engagement following Shrek the Third & The Golden Compass, this one came before his film role in Death Race and a voice-only engagement in Coraline.

Acknowledged as the greatest Kung Fu warrior, Tai Lung also happens to be the main antagonist to the dopey young Po in a hugely-enjoyable outing. After defeating the "Five" Tai arrives in the valley where the frightened residents are seen scurrying away. Keen to confront Po who he believes has wrongly been termed the Dragon Warrior, first he is met by his former master and the two engage in a fierce battle in which the younger, more powerful tiger (Ian) is victorious.

After running off, Po returns and says he has the scroll that shows he is the main warrior. Ian, in a masterly delivery of incredulity gasps, "You? Him? He's a panda. He's a panda. Whatcha gonna do big guy: sit on me?" Another epic and complicated confrontation then erupts and once Tai Lin subdues Po, he opens the scroll and is bemused by its findings. Po rises and defends himself admirably against his much stronger foe. The disbelieving tiger is defeated by his opponent producing a key move.

The villagers return and the "Five" bow down to their new master in a fabulous feature. Seth Rogen from the Shrek movies also contributes to this Academy Awards & Golden Globes nominated film feature.

Ian was in London for the Thursday 26 June première at the Vue Cinema, Leicester Square in the heart of the West End whilst Mcdonald's latched on to the film including a free figure of Tai Lung given away via a purchase.

Closing the year, Ian guested in series 6 of the phenomenally popular cartoon show for Nickelodeon, SpongeBob Square Pants. Shown on Friday 28 November, he features in the opening story of episode 14: Dear Vikings where he voiced a burly Viking who replies to the super-keen SpongeBob's letter asking about their way of life. Taking him and fellow worker Squidward aboard their longship, where all the crew are called Olaf apart from his: whose name is Gordon!

Coraline Jones is a curious young lady who moves into an old, subdivided property now called Pink Palace Apartments. Her overworked parents seem to have little time for their blue-haired daughter who is told by her father to explore.

Director/ writer Henry Selick adapted the dark fantasy novella by Neil Gaiman and Coraline (2009) proves to be an atmospheric, charming and enchanting work.

A creepy affair at times, Ian would reconnect with Mr Gaiman on the TV series American Gods. The canny Mr Selick brought in McShane for the role of Russian circus man and beet-eating connoisseur, Mr Sergei Alexander Bobinsky. "He's got chops, that guy," laughed the stop-motion wiz, "There is a bottomless well to his voice. It's a stellar performance." The actor regarded a job such as this as a liberating way to work. The film received an Academy Award nomination, won a BAFTA and other animation-specific awards and also has a 3D version, like several other Ian projects.

Ian's character is ushered in around 24 minutes in upon finding the youngster outside his door. A most peculiar man with long arms and legs, potbelly, and a wide moustache on his long, pale face, he's also very agile. Exercising, he introduces himself thus as "The amazing Mr Bobinsky...but you can call me Mr Bobinsky because amazing I already know that I am."

Discovering a small, papered-over doorway in the house, Coraline is told not to go inside. But in her dreams, it takes her into an alternate reality where, naturally, things are not quite as ideal as they first appear. Her 'parents' are found there and Bobinsky is seen as the MC at a circus with tiny performing mice!

Here he is more colourful, with a bushy blue moustache and not pallid like before. Later, Coraline will see a pale imitation of the entertainer and realize that she needs to rescue her parents whilst also taking looking out for herself.

"Be careful what you wish for" is the tag line of the film and Ian also had something to say to his young audience, "It may be great out there; there may be wonderful stuff but your real mum and dad, if they are good they'll be really good to you and you should trust them."

Echoes of The Wizard of Oz ring through in a film with fabulous production values (an estimated budget of $60m) Coraline was released in the UK at the beginning of March.

Mr McShane acknowledged at the time that Bobinsky was his favourite piece of voice work thus far.

In contrast, Kings premiered on NBC in America on Sunday 15 March 2009 via an elongated 2-hour initial offering. Consisting of 13 episodes, each was said to have cost around $4m to make. An attractive, intelligent religious-themed drama, Michael Green retells the biblical story of David in a modern-day setting, scripting

6 stories, with scope for an unmade additional season. He would later co-develop American Gods; Ed Bianchi, a director here, later also worked on Gods, too.

Shot in New York, Mr McShane was pleased to be involved, "Like all Kings, he thinks he's benevolent and wonderful and great but power, of course, corrupts....." he told Jay Bobbin for an American TV magazine. Fresh from Deadwood and interested in working on network TV (something he would later regret); he added "I like that format of 10 days' quick work, working in a very concentrated way. I like going back and forth from films and television, too. It will be interesting to see what happens."

Looking statesman-like in a suit, as King Silas, Ian portrays an important figure at the heart of Gilboa, whose capital Shiloh, aka a disguised New York City, is set sometime in the near future. A man driven to succeed, the actor puts in a flawless performance. However, at times the plot proves tricky and it is difficult to tell what is meant to be perceived as literal and what is not. This is the case in The Sabbath Queen, episode 8, with a riveting appearance from Saffron Burrows. Visiting and watching his ailing daughter Princess Michelle (Alison Miller) Silas is reminded of previously striking a deal with Death (Ms Burrows). He also has a son in the military, Jack (Sebastian Stan), whose life is saved early on by David (Christopher Egan) who immediately but temporarily becomes like a second son.

Far from perfect, Silas has a secret child with another woman other than his wife, Queen Rose (a superb Susanna Thompson). He also has to contend with an ongoing war perpetuated by his nemesis, Cross (Dylan Baker), a disloyal General (Wes Studi) whom he stabs to death and the pre-eminent Reverend Samuels (a terrific Eamonn Walker who has some intense onscreen moments with Ian). Regularly seen attending events in a penguin suit, aka a tux, Ian was perfectly cast in what was his solitary TV work this year.

Dipping into soap opera territory at times Kings produces an entertaining climax with the ousted Silas returning after a failed assassination attempt.

Via a great twist, when the hollow inauguration of his son as king begins, a breathtaking moment sees Ian walk towards the civic building, dressed all in black. As armed soldiers take aim outside, behind him comes the rumble of a half dozen tanks.

Reinstalled, Silas acknowledges a perceived sign from God and calls for David & tells him that he should take his place: that this is meant to be. Whilst the embittered and exhausted king continues, the latter is seen running away and the story can continue.

A lengthy 13 episodes but enthralling stuff, regretfully Kings was lost in the scheduling and seeing its religious themes quietened in publicity materials, the show struggled to find an audience and consequently flopped. Alternate DVD releases are available, one featuring Ian prominently, with his head turned sideward next to uniformed co-star Chris Egan and another without any cast members on the cover.

As an actor, Ian was impressed by the talents of his Case 39 co-star Jodelle Ferland, who portrays the demon child in the film and he has also acknowledged that the cast members were comfortable with the capabilities of their methodical director Christian Alvart; pertinent in the psychological horror drama.

174   The delicious Renee Zellweger plays Emily Jenkins, a caring but over-worked Social Worker for Child Services who becomes emotionally attached to Lily (Ms Ferland playing a few years younger than her actual age), whose case she is given to investigate. A cute if subdued child, Lily's parents seem cold and detached but this is no ordinary investigation as will soon be revealed. The youngster is soon unravelled as being something quite, quite different to what she seems.

Just like McShane, Miss Zellweger has a distinctive and immediately recognisable voice, a raspy tone from the Texas-born actor and the two gel well together onscreen.

Ian comes into the story after 15 minutes as a friend and police connection of Miss Jenkins, who shares her concerns about the lack of intervention offered by her department head (Adrian Lester).

The sympathetic Detective Barron (McShane) tells her to bring him proof and he will then act but not until then. Utilising another deep drawl, Ian later receives a distressed telephone call from her and races over to the home of the little girl after Emily receives a worrying call from the child fearing that she is going to be harmed by her parents, Edward & Margaret, Callum Keith Rennie & Kerry O'Malley. As a couple, they might not seem as crazy as they act.

Barron & Emily find the girl having been forced into a gas oven and with the couple attempting to ignite it! Brandishing a gun, the detective fights off the husband before disarming the wife, whilst Emily rescues the hysterical child.

With the ten-year-old Miss Sullivan (Ferland) taken into the care system, she pleads with Emily to foster her but gets rebuffed; the busy professional has no time to look after a child, have a relationship or little else as her career is all-encompassing to her. However, she relents and is allowed temporary care until a foster family can be found.

Returning to the family home to collect some clothes, Emily notices that the couple's bedroom in the battered-looking property has bolts on the inside. So we wonder: just who are the terrified ones here?

When a fellow child unexpectedly murders his parents, Detective Barron gently interviews Lily to ask if she called the boy's home in the early hours before he committed the heinous act. Police records show a call made from Emily's residential number and he thinks she did call but the youngster denies this.

Barron and Emily ponder why the boy should kill his parents and once she speaks with him, the terrified Diego (Alexander Conti) reveals that the call was from a man.

Elsewhere, after a worrying chat with Doug (Bradley Cooper playing against his Hangover type), he fears for the child and his safety after she threatens him in the most subtle of ways. Romantically linked with Emily, she subsequently seeks Frank's assistance following Doug's gruesome death, telling him that he didn't take his own life.

Mr & Mrs Sullivan know that Lily is the vassal for something evil, with Edward believing that she rightly possesses the "soul of a demon".

Beginning to lose control, Emily seeks out Frank (McShane) at church whilst he warns her to get a grip.

The viewer wonders if Emily is in the midst of a breakdown but frightened, the Social Worker installs bolts on the inside of her bedroom door as little Lily glides around the apartment displaying a strong sense of malevolence.

Now both in danger, Emily visits Barron and he agrees to help her kill Lily. Following an early hour's call he received and following Emily's visit to Edward Sullivan, who tells her that this is the only way to stop the demonic presence.

Unfortunately for Frank, he will play no further part in proceedings after we see him leaving the police department with a sawn-off shotgun under his coat and making his way to his car. Creeped out whilst passing a snarling dog, he continues to his vehicle only to discover another vicious-looking beast in the back seat! It attacks him by biting his neck but he manages to draw the gun and shoot only for a gush of blood to be seen splashing onto the interior side of the window. Written by Ray Wright, there was a more horrifying and truly terrifying death scene involving Ian's character which differs from the one seen. Personally, the author feels that the alternate version of finding him pursued by innumerable spirits with mangled faces is much stronger than the one chosen.

Returning to her home, Emily (Miss Zellweger) discovers all her case files strewn over the floor and a pinboard with pictures of those already murdered including Detective Barron. However, she is too late to warn him as news of his suspected 'suicide' is revealed to her. Completely losing it, she yells and demands that Lily leaves only for the girl to speak in the voice of a male, demonic one!

An absorbing finale follows and the ending is pure hokum but is fantastic. Case 39 was released in the States theatrically on Thursday 1 October. The film's qualities were recognised by some award nominations including one for Ian. "Some cases should never be opened," declares the DVD cover but do watch and enjoy.

Co-written by Louis Mellis & David Scinto, the team behind Sexy Beast, the screenplay for 44 Inch Chest offers a very different picture that had been floating around since those days before being shot at Elstree and on-location almost a decade later.

A valuable 3 weeks of rehearsals allowed the cast to develop their characters and learn the often lengthy dialogue in the "world within a world", as cast member John Hurt termed the film. First time director Malcolm Venville used a single camera for a story centred upon the cuckold Colin (Ray Winstone on fine form), a man bereft after his wife Liz (Joanna Whalley) announces that she is leaving their marriage after 20+ years. Ian portrays Meredith, a single-minded gay man devoid of sentiment, "I choose to live my life without entanglements," he tells his friend, "without turmoil." He lives in a luxurious apartment overlooking London's Tower Bridge and dresses well. 1 of 4 pals called upon, each leads a very different life from the other but they all have one thing in common: Colin. Old Man Peanut (the superb Mr Hurt) is foul-mouthed and keen for vengeance to be reaped upon the young man involved whilst mother's boy Archie (Tom Wilkinson from an episode of Lovejoy) still lives at home and Mal (Stephen Dillane) is quite the nasty piece of work willing to do whatever his mate wants.

As a group, they kidnap the unfortunate man (Melvil Poupaud) from his waiting job at a restaurant and bundle him in the back of a van, where we have the pleasure of seeing Ian and his old mucker Hurt, and away to a derelict house. Locked in a wardrobe behind them, the group discusses what Colin wants to do next. Amusingly, it is Meredith that arrives last and the banter between him and Peanut proves a delight. Winstone is superb as a man experiencing a breakdown and in deep shock.

Simultaneously angry, devastated and overwhelmed, Colin asks Meredith what he should do. And at the toss of a coin, it is decided that they will deal with the situation.

Bringing him out, "Loverboy" has his hands bound and head cloaked, and is seated at a chair in the barren living room. The group verbally goad and attack him as Colin watches on, cringing. Peanut, with Hurt all greased back hair and often speaking in one word exclamations when not spouting calls for retribution and the shattered Diamond (Winstone) to sort things; he wants his friend to exact revenge slowly and painfully. This is a very different film to Sexy Beast but equally as affecting. Colin asks the others to step out whilst he speaks with the man alone. Long imaginary scenes play out in his mind including seeing Ian in uniform as a chauffeur complete with cap and kinky boots.

Sharing some moments in the hall, the friends wonder what is happening inside and return to see that the situation appears the same. Peanut seems disbelieving; an almost constant state for him whilst a mellow Meredith asks what should be the outcome for the man and Colin's wife. Mal offers that it is not too late for Colin to change his mind about letting their captive go but that is what he decides and the film ends rather abruptly with the boys leaving, switching tact swiftly and heading off whilst Colin lingers for a few moments alone with his thoughts. He then leaves and we feel that his intensity has passed. In fact, during a panic attack earlier, it is Meredith that succeeds in calming him.

During the film each of the actors gets a chance to tell an anecdote or to give a glimpse into their lives & one hears Meredith

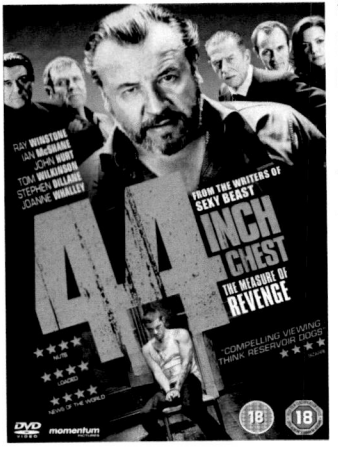

tell them that the previous night he came home with £40k after winning multiple bets against the manic Tippi (Stephen Berkoff) a gambling nut whom he bumped into and visited a casino with. The money is won not on the roulette wheel personally but by Tippi's desire to bet on winning at the table against the always relaxed Meredith.

Unravelling like a play, 44 Inch Chest is very well suited to home viewing and features an evocative soundtrack from Angelo Badalamenti and 100 Suns.

Released in North America in July 2010 The Sorcerer's Apprentice came under the mighty Disney banner, with Nicolas Cage starring in this kid's flick which features Ian as the narrator in voice only. A mainly modern-day New York retelling of the short featured in the 1940 animated classic Fantasia, Apprentice was shielded by a huge $150m budget, and the film advanced to become a box office hit taking $215m.

"The war between Sorcerer's was fought in the shadows of history," begins Ian in the pre-opening title credits. Setting the story in 740 AD Britain, he continues, "And the fate of mankind rested with the just and powerful Merlin. He taught his secrets to Balthazar, Veronica and Horvath. He should have trusted only two." Yet despite his extensive contribution Mr McShane receives no mention in the closing credits either. In a case of déjà Vu, the actor would later perform the same duties on Hellboy where Merlin is also name-checked in the story but he also gets to appear on screen.

Anyone who has read author Ken Follett knows that his books are lengthy. And the task for The Pillars of the Earth was how to transfer the essence of 1,400 pages into 8 hours of epic drama. John Pielmeier managed to do this and director Sergio Mimica-Gezzan steered proceedings across a shooting schedule of only 113 days. Filmed in Hungary for its tax relief benefits, Ridley & Tony Scott were Executive Producers for an engrossing production that keeps the viewer hooked.

Ian's name is first on the opening credits for a story spanning 40 years and set in the 12th century. He plays the oddly-named Waleran Bigod, a man of god not averse to profiting from others, including poisoning and artful manipulation.

The suspicious death of King Henry's son sets off a tumultuous chain of events and power struggles. Many battles between forces loyal to the King, then Stephen, are opposed by Maud (Alison Pill), the Earl of Gloucester (a doomed Donald Sutherland, whom Ian had acted with, in the 1984 film Ordeal by Innocence) and others, with the church placed firmly in the middle. In god-fearing times, it holds great power and is almost as significant as the royal lineage.

Many gory hand-to-hand fights, love interests and more make Pillars play out a bit like a Shakespearian tragedy. It is a fantastic series and hugely enjoyable.

With the story stretching across 40 tumultuous years in Britain, Ian is seen immediately amongst the cast at Winchester Castle, home of Henry I. Wearing robes, his hair long, centre-parted, he also has the tonsure; a bold patch to show religious devotion. Immaculately dressed throughout, he looks the part.

This epic tale begins with the King learning of the death of his son due to a fire and subsequent sinking of a boat that he and others had been travelling on. Jumping 18 years, we are introduced to the principal characters including a feisty Hayley Attwell as Aliena, daughter of the Earl of Gloucester. Rufus Sewell proves memorable as Tom Builder, whose wife dies in childbirth and later he is tasked with building a cathedral, something that changes the lives of many.

Stephen (Tony Curran) takes over the royal throne following the suspicious death of his uncle whilst his cousin, Maud, will play a major part in the unrest across the country for the years to come.

She joins forces with Gloucester and others in opposition but if she is victorious, it will be detrimental to the church and corrupt individuals like Bigod (Mr McShane).

Now a Bishop, Phillip (Matthew MacFadyen) tells him of Maud but Bigod is spooked at seeing Tom (Sewell) and his family and travelling group outside and orders them to leave. His reasons for doing so will be revealed much later. A man who beats himself at the altar, something he does throughout, as Bigod, Ian has ambitions and is adept at manipulating. Leaving a service for the appointment of a new prior, it seems that he has likely poisoned the previous one. Costumed in robes, this man is sly and lets Percy (Robert Bathurst) and his wife (a superb Sarah Parish) know that forces are gathering to oppose the King. Gloucester's castle is attacked and his fate is sealed.

Philip sends word to Bishop McShane of a fire at the building site and that Tom is going to take charge of the construction despite the setback. He visits String where Aliena and her brother are hiding and greets the Lord Bishop on horseback. Dressed in a black, hooded outfit set off by black leather gloves, as Bigod, the actor speaks slowly and deeply, initiating many manoeuvrings to get what he wants, no matter at what personal cost to others. He and Phillip have an antagonistic relationship but their paths remain entwined.

The Bishop agrees to an order for Tom's attractive lover, a sultry Natalia Wörner as Ellen, to be arrested and tried as a witch. Her connection to him reaches back to the man who got King Henry's son and his partner away from the burning boat previously. However, he witnessed Bigod stab and throw the young prince overboard with Regan stepping in to do likewise to his partner (whilst Percy hesitates), also in that boat. Ellen was the wife of Jaques, who was burnt alive by a committee which included Bigod.

She sets a curse on him which haunts him.

King Stephen promotes Percy and gives land to build a cathedral. The infuriated Bishop storms off vowing it will never succeed. The latter wants control his own church. Having befriended Tom and his family and subsequently become his lover, Ellen is condemned for being a witch at a hastily arranged trial conducted by Bishop Bigod. Freeing herself from her shackles, she approaches the seated Bishop and squats down from the tabletop and urinates in front of him. He looks on bemused as those behind him gasp in astonishment at her insult. She also stabs him. Indeed, all of the women are formidable in The Pillars of the Earth.

At Winchester, the Bishop (Ian) has survived, "A mere foot soldier's wound in God's battle against Satan, dear Regan…." He continues siding with her and Percy and this now includes changing the location of the new cathedral.

Visiting the priory to see the building work, the King and a smug Bigod arrive only to see masses of people helping despite the latter being told by his 'spy' Remigus (Anatole Taubman) that things were going badly. He grimaces at him, whilst the King is pleased with the progress. However, His Majesty is an unstable man and loses his sanity, seeing visions of his murdered uncle and under great pressure due to the altercations with opposing forces. All this occurs in front of everybody before Bigod observes a hooded figure glance at him and then move away.

War now ongoing for the past 4 years, personal advancement also shows itself by Regan killing her ineffectual husband and engaging in an incestuous relationship with her son, William (David Oakes). The progeny will ultimately prove her downfall but what a memorable screen character.

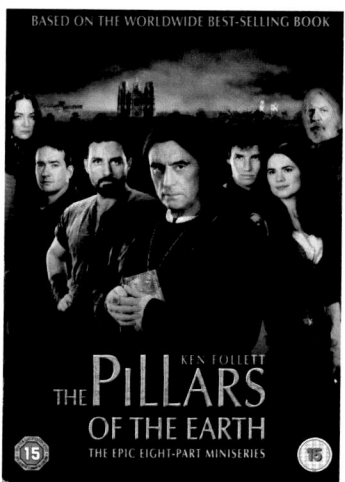

Meanwhile, Bigod stirs things up with the agitated Philip by continually trying to cause him problems and delays. They are always at loggerheads and the latter can barely hide his contempt for the corrupt Bishop. Visiting the site, Bigod sees the structure developing and speaks with Jack (Eddie Redmayne), son of Ellen, who is also a builder/ stonemason.

With Maud's forces proving victorious after yet more conflict, Bigod, Regan and William go before her and she allows the former to be the go-between in facilitating her half-brother's return. King Stephen is imprisoned and being visited by him, Bigod (Ian) continues scheming; deceitfully stating that he is on his side but that the defeated leader must concede that Maud is now queen. Poor Philip is also captured and he gives the order to torture and kill him once he has confessed. The Bishop has blood on his hands during all this and there is no level to which he will not stoop.

Wishing to become Archbishop of Canterbury, Waleran (Ian) continues orchestrating things to his selfish advantage. Jack & Philip miraculously survive, this being necessary to drive the plot, and Bigod is shocked to discover them in front of the Queen. Maud is stern but grants mining rights to enable the Cathedral to be completed on the proviso that her brother is returned. An exchange occurs, witnessed by the Bishop and others but this merely allows the inevitable warmongering to recommence. That suits him but after Maud has been duped, she orders the substituted child to be executed. Bigod is startled by this and is seen once again punishing himself at the pulpit.

Following the killing of Tom and Maud's forces having failed, she flees to France and Bigod continues to self-flagellate. Regan and her son are particularly ruthless but as he corrects her, "I need you to serve me, not command me." With the Bishop seeking to become Archbishop, he uses her to tell the incumbent one of his plans before she pushes him to his death!

With William at her side, she threatens Bigod, demanding a new title and all that this will bring. Pillars travels across decades but the one thing that remains constant is the development of the Cathedral. A disaster there sees many killed but not before Bigod speaks of his new title in front of the King and guests. Ian looks incredible in a hat and cape combo but his screen persona is denied when the monarch believes that the disaster is a sign from god. Bigod is pleased that Phillip's plans have proven disastrous but later continues with the self-harming; now cutting himself.

Paying a surprise visit to Philip and offers him the position of his representative whilst he is off to Rome to represent the church. Philip is not keen and later articulates his views about the putrid and evil man, declaring that he would never serve such a person.

Plot-wise, his identity as the murderer of the young royal in the opening episode is revealed amongst more battles being fought once more.

Further deception follows, with killings and power struggles peeking all around and it closes with Bigod despairing at his god, with his scarred back on shocking display.

Advancing a decade, Ian's character is now Cardinal, after having returned after 8 years in Italy. Now clad in red outfits, he receives a poison pen letter (or scroll in this case). Richard has returned and has his father's title back but the scheming continues.

Cardinal McShane continues his cunning ways but implores Tom's son, Alfred (Liam Garrigan) to provoke Jack (Redmayne) so that he can be arrested.

He also works with William to advance things against Ellen and she has her vengeance planned.

Arrested, Bigod leads an open trial of Jack with the executioner being sent for before the hearing has concluded: such are the times. Found guilty of murder, after Bigod had given Alfred a poisoned dagger, Jack is about to be hanged as the crowd looks on.

Ellen arrives with startling proof of Bigod's act of treason 35 **183** years ago. She brings evidence that her late husband had been employed to escort the young royal and his partner and had managed to get them into a smaller boat to escape the fire onboard. Ensconced in the water opposite them, he witnessed the murderous actions of both Bigod and Regan described previously.

Photo: Author's Collection

A flabbergasted Bigod denies all this to the crowd, decrying it as a lie but Ellen shows him the ring that Jacques retrieved as it slipped off the finger of the tragic prince that night. It was used to seal the scroll and was deemed lost but had been secreted away by a youngster and recently returned.

Consequently, it is William who is put into the noose after he confesses all about his parent's involvement in the same events by scuttling the boat. A startled Bigod looks on at the disclosures and begins to move away into the throng as the young man is put to death. The times saw people driven by a fear of god, or a perceived higher force and people like Bigod use this as justification for their often wretched doings. Or "holy ambition", as someone aptly describes it.

Jack rallies the crowd whilst Bigod runs off towards the newly completed Cathedral to claim sanctuary but this proves a fruitless demand as the place of worship has not been blessed.

He rushes inside, climbs up some scaffolding and along a narrow pathway on the roof.

Attempting to flee, he foolishly clings to a wall, as the crowd below looks on and Jack follows. The beads on his outfit get entangled and Bigod falls, only to cling to one of the figureheads shaped by Tom's son. Losing consciousness, the older man sees images of Jacques as the figure looks like it is weeping and as Bigod, Ian has that look in his eye that this is the end. He will die here now.

Every actor enjoys doing a death scene because the emphasis is purely upon them and Ian performs the passing of his character well. Declining Jack's help, he releases his grip and crashes down onto the ground on his back.

With blood oozing out of his nose and mouth, in a final show of contempt, whilst Philip offers the last rites, Bigod spits at him.

An ambitious project, Pillars received numerous award nominations and won one prime time Emmy, with Ian recognised via a Golden Globe nomination for Best Actor in a mini-series.

Shown on Channel 4 in the UK, a tie-in paperback was also published, and a board game and its dramatic soundtrack by Trevor Morris all saw a release.

"The biggest badass pirate of all time: Blackbeard"

Ian, Pirates of the Caribbean: On Stranger Tides (2011)

Coming under the all-powerful Disney branding, this was the fourth big-screen outing for Johnny Depp as Captain Jack Sparrow and his Pirates of the Caribbean franchise. It is initially tricky not seeing Rolling Stones guitarist Keith Richards when watching Depp in the lead role and amusingly, 'Keef' pops up in a brief cameo as his dad early on! This time Captain Jack is on a quest to locate the Fountain of Eternal Youth, something in which many parties share an interest. Jam-packed with stunts and sword fights, we also have Ian's beautiful Grimsby co-star Penelope Cruz in a major role here as Sparrow's former lover and the daughter of the infamous Blackbeard: Mr McShane.

Everyone seems to be doing an accent with lots of rotten/ gold-capped teeth and "ayes" all over the place but it is all such good-natured fun that the sceptic can sit back and enjoy. Amusingly, both Depp & McShane have major eyeliner situations going on!

185

After reacquainting himself with Angelica (Miss Cruz) and being duped by her, Jack awakens to find himself part of the crew on Queen Anne's Revenge, a ship whose captain is the notorious Blackbeard and he soon discovers that its First Mate is the gorgeous Angelica. Blackbeard is nowhere to be seen but we know that he

Photo: Author's Collection

wants the elixir to fend off his perceived impending death via a man with one leg; that stranger is represented by his badass old nemesis Barbossa (Geoffrey Rush enjoying himself). King George (Richard Griffiths) also wishes to locate the Fountain and sends him to lead a party to it until Sparrow manages to flee. But they still have Gibbs (Kevin McNally) who has a map until burning it and thus extending his life as he will be required to show the King's men the location. The dreaded Spanish, god-fearing people; also seek the elixir, intending to destroy such things which unbalance their faith.

Some 40 minutes in and Ian arrives as the infamous pirate; a foreboding, formidable presence with bad teeth mixed with gold ones and an almighty sword, known as the Sword of Triton, that seems to encapsulate magical powers. His opening words are listened to by Jack and his fellow mutineers who are subdued by his powers. In a dark outfit topped off with a large tricorn hat, long beard and hair, the former is braided and took some time to be applied in the make-up room for the actor. Blackbeard's reputation precedes him and he is feared by all.

"Your words surround you like fog," he begins to Sparrow, with Ian delivering the dialogue written by Ted Elliot & Terry Rossio, as if it were some mellifluous poetry, "makes it hard to see." He

Photo: Author's Collection

threatens Jack with death if his quest for eternal youth is not met. At this stage, Penelope Cruz's character seems untrustworthy, as she dupes Jack into believing that she has convinced Blackbeard that she is his daughter. However, Blackbeard seems doubtful of it at times, too. Featuring lots of close-ups of Mr Depp & McShane, director Rob Marshall delivers a cracking adventure brimming with fun, however superficial.

Returning to the plot, Blackbeard orders Sparrow to find and return to him with two challis (metal goblets) although he has little trust in the fellow pirate either. Tears of a mermaid are required to help activate the healing powers by being placed in a chalice and Blackbeard tricks a young religious man (Sam Claflin) into helping him after they take a solo mermaid left behind after a trap.

Jack (Depp) does return and leads them on until Rush & his men confront them. As Barbossa, Rush, whose accent the author could not place, had previously assisted Sparrow in locating the goblets but is in cahoots with the zealous Spanish.

A confrontation begins and we watch as Blackbeard battles with Barbossa. During the mêlée, the pirate is stabbed with a poisonous blade and Angelica accidentally cuts herself with it. Sparrow fills one challis with the eternal water whilst the other is said to produce instant death. He offers them and Blackbeard sips from one but you will have it to discover the outcome.

Elsewhere Jack & Gibbs reconvene with their treasure and the adventures are set to continue (more sequels have since followed). Having claimed Blackbeard's dark, well-worn ship and crew as his own, new Pirate Captain Barbossa sail off, utilising the huge magical sword and a hat belonging to Blackbeard.

Based on the Disney film Pirates of the Caribbean, the characters were adapted with the film suggested by the novel by Tim Powers. Ian was third billed after Miss Cruz and Depp, who has his name before the titles, in another massive collaborative production with a larger budget than awarded to the previous trilogy. Look out for a small cameo by Ian's theatre co-star Judi Dench at the start of the film (but not featuring with him).

The Pirate franchise has been a popular cinema phenomenon with Depp fans loving the films and hungry for more. Merchandising was vast, including a soundtrack release, Lego association, its own Monopoly board game, books, toys, action figures and more. As well as featuring on the main cast theatrical poster, Ian also featured individually, in character, on 2 others. Filming his role took him to Hawaii, L.A. and London.

Released in the UK in 3D, on Tuesday 18 May after its Friday 7 May premiere in Disneyland, which Ian attended. Tides also had a premiere at the Westfield Centre, London on Wednesday 12 May, in which Mr McShane also appeared.

It then advanced to the more glamorous Cannes film festival which Ian again attended alongside the principal cast. Bizarrely, Muppet man Kermit the frog was at the Disneyland event and interviewed cast members and got a showbiz kiss from many, including Ian! Watch this, and your swash will be truly buckled!

In the following year, Snow White and The Huntsman (2012) featured lots of bloody battles, battlers on horseback in shining armour and a mesmerising Charlize Theron as the evil queen, Kristen Stewart in the title role, there is also some stunning imagery in this retelling of the Grimm's fairytale. Following her escape from years of imprisonment at the hands of the malevolent queen, Snowy is quickly recaptured by a drunken huntsman (the wooden Chris Hemsworth) forced into the role but fearing her fate, he is reluctant to return her. Unaware of her true identity, the mismatched couple flee, trudging their way through a treacherous forest whilst attempting to avoid its perils and capture by pursuers led by the queen's devoted brother, Finn (a superbly torn Sam Spruell).

Just before the hour mark, they face a new danger: dwarves. Attacked and swiftly strung upside down from a tree by a band of 8 they are led by a mini Ian McShane who spent many hours in make-up having prosthetics fitted.

Fending for themselves, the group lost everything when King Magnus was murdered by an evil new Queen. Disney might have had Snow White & her 7 dwarves but not here.

Ian is joined by Bob Hoskins, Muir, a sightless elder dwarf and seer and supported by Toby Jones, whose father Ian had acted with, Nick Frost & Brian Gleeson. The remainder were all actors either known to Ian or subsequently: Ray Winstone, Eddie Marsan and Johnny Harris (from Sexy Beast/ 44 Inch Chest, Ray Donovan and Jack the Giant Slayer & Jawbone, respectively. Snow is another of those expansive fantasy/ fairy tale retellings but to contrast the seriousness of the main story the real fun involves the marauding dwarves, or "kind of ninja dwarves," as Marsan termed them during an onset interview. A grotty group, with long curly hair and a heavy beard, Ian adopts a broad Scots accent as Beith, the leader, who knows of the Huntsman but was unaware of Snow White's true identity. With the queen's men nearby, the couple is released and the group flees.

This introduction proved itself to be quite intricate to shoot in that so many characters are onscreen, each had to be shot and melded together. In a film blending green screen work and actors being shrunken down, camera tricks and skewed perspectives, prosthetics, special FX, CGI and wide screen shots, the group also had doubles. This was because the little people were utilised to appear in functional moments alongside other characters to extenuate the size difference. Ian and his fellow actors also practised hard in getting their movements right and worked with a motion coach and their mini-me's to synchronise their walks. "I wanted to find tough guys with big hearts," remembered first-time director Rupert Sanders who convinced the cast to trust him in being capable of pulling things off. McShane's mini version was played by Jo Osbourne in a rousing piece whose screenplay was created by a trio of writers with a multitude of projects behind them for what became a multi-award winning production filmed in the UK often in cold conditions. "It's a mediaeval war film," proclaimed its director.

Advancing to a new environment alive with creatures, it is revealed as "Sanctuary: the home of the fairies." Snow White (Twilight star Ms Stewart) is entranced by the place. "She's destined," rasps Hoskins, "The question is huntsman, for what?" Filmed in such a way that makes the actors look smaller, a perfect example sees Beith (Ian) talking with Chris Hemsworth (the Huntsman of the title).

Come the morning and she is compelled to walk towards the most amazing sight: a white stag.

Watched on by the dwarves, they observe her being blessed by the white beast, symbolising nature, with Muir adding, "She is life itself....she is the one." This magical moment is violently interrupted by an arrow striking the side of the creature and the group running off before a battle occurs with the queen's men, including Finn (a superb Sam Spruell in the villain with a heart stereotypical role).

It looks like the Huntsman will be killed until a rapid piece of improvisation saves him and results in the death of his adversary. Elsewhere the queen agonises; ageing rapidly and with her life force zapped. William (Sam Claflin, who had recently acted alongside Ian in Pirates of the Caribbean: On Stranger Tides) is reunited with Snow White, a childhood friend who managed to flee during a past invasion of the castle and living with his father, the Duke (Vincent Regan). Having lost one of their team, Gort (Winstone) pledges the dedication of the dwarves to Snow White.

It is here where the group is heading and where an incredible scene follows featuring the deadly poisonous apple. At its conclusion we see Ian and Mr Winstone share a moment.

If you know the story, the following will not be unfamiliar; Snow White's body is brought to the Duke and something miraculous occurs: she rises to lead her followers back to her rightful home. As is the norm, a final great battle will come.

The dwarves are utilised to clandestinely enter the evil queen's castle via the tight sewers as a great horde on horseback, Snow White in amongst them, sprints on towards their magnificent but highly-protected destination. With the Duke demanding that they retreat, the portcullis opens to allow them entry watched over by Ravenna, keen to face her nemesis.

The dwarves are pretty mean fighters and use their diminutive heights to see-off many soldiers as the battle roars on.

As an aside, in one scene the group are seen wadding in the raw sewage which in actuality was lukewarm water. An ad-lib by Mr Winstone was kept in the film and its director acknowledged that he felt that he was a headmaster trying to control wayward children who were always playing pranks on each other! It was here that we see the little warriors demonstrating that unique waddle walking style which raises a smile.

Finally the confrontation between the ice-cold queen and Snow White occurs in a rousing closing scene. White is crowned queen with all her followers gathered in a church including the dwarves. "Hail to the queen!" proclaims Ian's character.

The film was premiered at the world-famous Odeon cinema, Leicester Square, London, on Monday 14 May, in readiness for its general release a couple of weeks later. Most of the cast were in attendance including Ray Winstone alongside a long-haired Mr McShane back at a well-known venue for him. Some cast members had still working on scenes only days before being introduced on stage by their director before the screening. Other premieres also occurred in Sydney & Los Angeles.

Briarcliff Insane Asylum in the 1960s was not a place that any right-minded person would want to visit let alone be a patient at. As multiple killer Leigh Emerson, Ian features across 2 consecutive episodes of the award-winning TV show American Horror Story. The second season comes under the banner "Asylum" and his first appearance is in Unholy Night. Shown on 5 December, it was episode 8 and The Coat Hanger followed the next week.

In Night, he is seen at the start of the story outside a department store berating a Father Christmas then after breaking into a family home where he meets little Susie (Tehya Scarth). She wonders why he has blood on his suit and how come the dishevelled Santa is visiting with more than a week until the big day. She soon finds out: as do her parents.

He is a sociopath who goes on a killing spree resulting in the deaths of 18 people with the above visit occurring before the opening titles. Co-created by Ryan Murphy and Brad Falchuk, the imagery presented in the titles alone is enough to deter us before we see Ian given a "Special Guest Star" accreditation.

An outstanding piece and multi-Emmy nominated, Asylum is a hellish watch. As the pitiful Emerson, Ian is constantly shackled whenever his killer is in the company of other patients but across his 2 episodes, we learn that he has suffered at the hands of pious zealot Sister Jude Martin (Jessica Lange in extraordinary form and who we have the pleasure of seeing her act with Ian). However, when the power changes, evil incumbent Sister Mary (Lily Rabe) comes to be in charge and astonishingly Sister Jude ends up as a patient herself.

It is Sister Mary who forces Leigh (Ian) to wear the Santa suit amongst the patients and further manipulates him following his attack on affable security man Frank (Fredric Lehne). Returned to his solitary cell, the serial killer is equally shocked and thrilled to watch her slash his throat.

Rocking the bedraggled look to perfection, Mr McShane is later able to confront former tormentor Sister Jude, who is betrayed by Dr. Arden (James Cromwell). Wearing his festive suit, he tells Jude how he is going to hurt her. The dark and shadowy hellhole that is Briarcliff had previously seen her inflict corporal punishment but now he has control and he gives her ten of the best lashes, as she had done to him, previously.

An asylum, the place is more like a living hell.

About to rape her, she stabs him in this stunning episode.

Making an immediate return, Emerson's horrific past is revealed and whilst remaining an unbearable character, the viewer gains a little insight into his psyche. Cunning and conniving, he manages to manipulate well-meaning Monsignor Howard (Joseph Fiennes) into believing that he has repented for his past sins. He joins Arden and others convincing and imploring the controllers that Sister Jude should live out the remainder of her life as a patient at the asylum (he lies and says she killed Frank).

Bringing Leigh before the secured former bride of Christ, we see flashbacks where the positions were reversed in the recent past. With his character seemingly having found faith, he tells the Monsignor that he has rehabilitated himself much to the satisfaction of the latter. However, Emerson is still kept in handcuffs and leg chains at this point.

Offering himself up to be baptized in a full-size font, he is immersed in the water by Monsignor Howard. "Thank you father, I feel like a new man," sighs Emerson before grabbing the holy man and attempting to drown him. In another busy storyline, other arcs are included such as the ongoing struggles of fellow patient Lana (Sarah Paulson). She worked with McShane on Deadwood.

Ian added his name to a sterling cast that included the considerable talents of Ewan McGregor, Eddie Marsan and Bill Nighy in support of young leads Nicholas Hoult & Eleanor Tomlinson in this retelling of the classic Jack & the Beanstalk.

In Jack the Giant Slayer (2013), as King Brahmwell, Mr McShane is first seen posing for a royal portrait whilst chatting with his daughter, Princess Isabelle (an appealing Ms Tomlinson), a young woman keen to experience life away from the confines of the kingdom of Cloisters. He looks hilarious in his favoured but faintly ridiculous oversized cape and gold-coloured armour which resembles a samurai design. He is naturally overprotective of her since his wife has passed away.

Coincidentally, as children both Isabelle and Jack (Hoult) adored hearing the tale of Jack & the Beanstalk and now in his late teens, Jack becomes part of a true-life adventure that takes a slightly different slant on the familiar fairytale.

He notices an attractive young woman enjoying a travelling production of the tale before her true regal identity is revealed, her protector, Elmont (McGregor having great fun and sounding like he should be in a World War II British film; at one stage he even says "Tally ho!), is assisted by Crawe (Marsan). The villainess Stanley Tucci is the duplicitous Lord Roderick to whom Isabelle is bequeathed. Circumstance brings her to the home of Jack and his uncle during a rainstorm and an adventure commences for the youngsters when the beans he was given earlier sprout forth a massive beanstalk. The edifice grows so violently it takes the house up into the air with the Princess and Jack within (until the latter falls away after losing his grip).

Knocked unconscious, when he awakens the diminutive King is above him and asks why he has a bracelet belonging to his daughter. Cloaked in the absurd body armour, cape and on a horse with its own elaborate outfit, the concerned Brahmwell seeks to find the missing Isabelle and agrees to Jack accompanying Elmont and his guards in scaling the beanstalk to return her.

And so begins the arduous climb to take them to the land of the giants where they will find great danger and eventually, the princess. Much double-crossing from Roderick and his assistant played by Ewen Bremner follow and not all will return alive.

Intended as a child-friendly film, there is a great deal to enjoy in Jack, with performances and a fun script guiding proceedings. Director Bryan Singer, not the original choice, made changes to the project and utilised a lot of digital effects.

Back to the story, with Isabelle captured by the giants, Jack is separated and proves to be the only hope for saving both the lives of the pretty princess and the valiant Elmont before they end up being served up as pigs in blankets or worse!

Elsewhere, the cunning Roderick (Tucci) obtains the ultimate power: a golden crown that makes the barbarians bow down to him in subservience. The others look on incredulously as he seizes power and denies their freedom. However, Jack managed to free them in time & the trio set off back to Cloisters after dealing with a sleepy giant blocking their exit.

Cataclysmically, his falling to the land below causes King Ian to decide to cut down the beanstalk as it has confirmed his belief the legend. "Forgive me, Isabelle," laments his royal highness, unaware that his daughter and Jack are on their way back.

A fatal scuffle occurs between Roderick & Elmont which only results in the power of the ring returning to the wretched General Fallon (voiced by Bill Nighy & John Kassir).

The beanstalk acts like a vortex between one land and another and so the ruthless Fallon leads an attack on the kingdom below.

Brahmwell and the others look on in horror as the beanstalk comes crashing down and we see Jack & Isabelle excitingly manage to save their own lives and reach the land below. The King looks crestfallen after thinking that his daughter must have perished as a result until his joy abounds upon seeing her alive. Updated about the events occurring above, King Brahmwell thanks Jack, "As a king, I can reward you with many things," he begins, handing the farm boy a bag of coins, "as a father, I can never reward you enough." Isabelle and Jack have fallen in love but the story is not yet over.

Those damn beans still play a part and the marauding giants appear and chase the King, who loses his crown, and his equine entourage, with Jack lagging, into the protection of the kingdom.

Inside the grounds, Ian and the others look on as the monastery bell crashes into a statue of the King and decapitates it.

Watching the film, Ian reminds the viewer of Bert Lahr from The Wizard of Oz, and he seems a bit miscast in a screenplay that saw a contribution from Usual Suspects writer Christopher McQuarrie.

With the King instructing his daughter and Jack to flee and warn other principalities of the attack, he remains with Elmont and his men to defend the land. Noble as that may be, the attackers soon reach the portcullis and destroy it swiftly to enter inside. They seem unstoppable now until something happens: in a repeat of an earlier gag, Elmont acknowledges that there is something behind him and turns to see Jack wearing the crown recently held by the two-headed Fallon as a ring on his finger. The order of power reinstated.

Massively entertaining viewing, even here the story is not completed; simply the film.

Shot in the UK, including Lovejoy country, Ian knew his director socially before making the film and seemed comfortable with his director, who had enjoyed an eclectic career, in wanting to give his own take on the classic English fairy tale.

Jack received a Hollywood premiere in February before its general release in the States on 1 March.

As Bruce Garrett, in Cuban Fury (2014) everyman actor Nick Frost is past child Salsa champion who abandoned his career following a bout of bullying back in the mid-1980s. We see his former mentor, Ron Parfitt aka Ian, in a throwback scene during the opening voice-over credits for a project that took 15 months to make from script to shooting. We know it's his name as he has "Ron" printed on the back of his garish, multi-coloured tracksuit! It is as loud as the one he wore previously in The Hot Rod. Wearing his hair in a ponytail and pulled back tight back in flashback scenes (there is an excellent poster ad featuring him in the get-up subtitled 'Lord of the Dance').

Advancing to 25 years later and Bruce is now an engineer with "douche" boss Chris O'Dowd constantly teasing him and the arrival of likeable new American boss Miss Rashida Jones taking both their fancy but in very different ways. We watch as the colleagues compete for her attention but it is Bruce (Frost) who discovers that she loves Salsa dancing and attends a local class. His supportive sister Sam, played by the always-lovely Olivia Coleman, encourages him to put himself out there again and dance his way into this woman's affections! Reigniting his love for dance, he glances over his old cuttings book showing his past triumphs and one clipping features him with Ron in an article headlined "The Salsa-ers' Apprentice". A national treasure, Ms. Coleman confessed that as a child, her family home was used for location shooting for an episode of Lovejoy. However, her mother failed to warm to the visiting Mr McShane; perhaps he was cogitating about the scene to be shot?

Back onscreen, tracing Ron to a grubby basement studio space under the El Corazon monocle, Bruce doesn't receive a warm welcome after discovering that Parfitt still holds his frustration from being dropped all those years ago on the eve of a big final event. A simple request for some 1-to-1 tuition to refresh his dance skills is coolly embraced and Bruce is told to return when the studio is open. Frost and McShane prove a smashing screen presence together via TV writer Jon Brown's screenplay developed from an original idea by the actor which Ian liked a lot. Director James Griffiths, like Brown, hailed from a TV background.

His return visit proves challenging but Bruce perceives she is keen to impress Julia (Ms Jones).

New friend Bejan (the hilarious Kayvan Novak) helps spruce him up a little and the odd couple pay a visit to dazzling Salsa club Koko. Found in Camden, London NW1, this former theatre/ cinema/ live venue first opened in 1900 and provided the location for Ian's first scene to be shot. Frost has said how he was overwhelmed at having such a star actor join in the fun, "You certainly know a silverback's on set when he rumbles into town," he joked on the DVD extras. The two reunited after being in Snow White and Nick had first muted the project to Ian at the première of that particular project.

Surprised to have seen his former protégé join the beginner's class previously, Ron dressed all in black and his long hair greased back, sees Bruce stumbling on the dance floor. He orders him to stop, demanding that he dances with heart rather than merely knowing the sequence of steps.

Infuriated, Bruce shows his passion before being deflated at the sight of seeing Julia with his nemesis (O'Dowd) nearby.

Just as Rocky or any other sports-related movie has its training montage, so too does Cuban Fury! After Bruce returns to the dance studio to talk with Ron, following a seemingly random game of Trivial Pursuit, the former dancer confesses that he quit because he was abused by fellow youngsters back in the day and it left him traumatized. It is thanks to Ron that he can express this and thereafter begins the training routines.

Touchingly, the mentor presents his former discovery with a pair of dancing shoes before Bruce tells him that he is entering a Salsa completion with Julia and wants him to come and watch them. Not even this moment is without comedy as he smells the shoes and is wisely advised to stop by Mr Parfitt in an onscreen moment enjoyed by cinema audiences.

Come the night of the competition and plans have not gone well; it is Sam who partners with her brother after a mix-up saw Bruce unable to ask Julia who he thinks is involved with the wretched Drew. In addition, Ron is nowhere to be seen as the contest commences and the siblings end up as runners-up. The former does arrive and kisses Bruce full on the lips after an uplifting groove sequence is enjoyed on the crowded dance floor.

Fury has lots of fun moments and was released in UK cinemas on Valentine's Day; the movie received a rainy, mid-week, West End première in Leicester Square on Thursday 6 February. Twickenham Film studios were also utilised and audiences would have seen Ian in the trailer as a Mr Miyagi-type character inspiring Nick Frost to believe in himself. The author feels that the film could equally have worked as a TV comedy-drama across say 6 episodes, slowly developing the characters as the film itself is not cinematic.

Tara Brady of the Irish Times interviewed the actor, "It was a funny character," McShane rumbles. "...it sounded fine and it was. Films don't always turn out as you'd expect. This did. It's very funny...down-to-earth. They're all hilarious..."

The prospect of watching any film with Dwayne 'The Rock' Johnson as its star offered no appeal but Hercules is an exciting epic that proved to be the exception.

In the dark days of folklore aimed at frightening the masses and intimidating foes, Hercules (Johnson), the greatest Greek hero admired by the Romans, leads a group of mercenaries but is a troubled man who has experienced great personal loss. One in his line-up is Amphiaraus, as portrayed by Ian; a grizzled warrior who has foreseen his death and throughout the film thinks it imminent but he always gets rescued instead! Outfitted in a kilt that reaches slightly beneath his knees, his battle-ravaged face looks the part.

McShane's old drama school pal & flatmate, John Hurt, is cast as the ailing Lord Cotys, whose daughter, Rebecca Ferguson, asks Hercules to help fend off deadly peer Cotys manipulates him into fighting an arch enemy who might not be so troublesome as defined.

The two are seen on screen and reunited some 50 years since making The Wild and the Willing in 1962. "It was great to see them together...they were excellent," conceded director Brett Ratner, "They grounded the movie and gave us the depth."

In Hercules, there is a lot of dialogue explaining the present situation and characters/ struggles being experienced which proves a little tiring but is common to films of this genre. As Hercules and his team agree to train the remaining men to be fit for battle but the task cannot be sorted immediately.

The army has been depleted and most of the remaining men are ordinary, unskilled fighters making them vulnerable.

Enmasse, the group move off but are startled to be confronted by a force already waiting for them.

Having walked into a trap, a bloody battle follows after the cunning Lord Cotys had suggested that they go on and confront the enemy, following a rallying cry from the likes of Amphiaraus (Ian McShane) and Hercules (Johnson).

Huge numbers from both sides are lost and we see Ian involved, slaying many men, in the first of such skirmishes seen in the film which were shot on location in Hungary and at Origo film studios in Budapest. They also utilised Pinewood, back in the UK but here, 7 sound stages and outside (for the battles) became home to the production.

However, looking likely to be over-run, Hercules and his trusted Amphiaraus jump onto horse-drawn chariots and succeed in swiftly wiping out many of their aggressors to save the day. All the actors involved with Hercules trained extensively for the film although Ian jokingly denied doing anything. An experienced horse rider off-screen, he did concede to doing some training and said the whole thing proved quite enjoyable. Also, he had narrated QED: Monty Roberts - a Real Horse Whisperer shown on BBC 1 back in July 1997.

As Cotys, the noble Lord feigns distress at the losses received whilst Hercules informs him that he needs more time to bring them up to standard and so begins a training montage.

Playing Hercules, Johnson is capable as a hero who has yet to confront his past, "Man cannot escape his fate," advises Amphiaraus. We learn later that the former has lost his wife and 3 children when they were slain on the orders of the wretched King Eurystheus, Joseph Fiennes from American Horror Story is on excellent form; a man willing to do whatever it takes to stay in power.

The curly-haired Ian tells Hercules that he has foreseen his own death which he believes is coming within the week and that he is prepared for it after a long and arduous life. And so a running gag flows throughout the remainder of the film.

Another battle follows on a massive scale, with the filmmakers utilising 1,200 Hungarian extras for filming during a scolding summer. Ian had been in the country a few years previously shooting another picture and empathised with the conditions for the supporting artists.

Rhesus (Tobias Santelmann) rides up to Lord Cotys (Hurt) and Hercules alongside his entourage to suggest that they surrender as they are massively outnumbered. The offer is declined. Hercules speaks to the men before the battle which is another case of kill or be killed and where strategy also plays its part. Observing the enormous numbers opposing, Amphiaraus thinks that perhaps today is to be his final day. Ian is a master at delivering humorous asides and here he makes the comment when a mass of burning arrows are seen above him and about to reign down. "Maybe not," he quips, opening his eyes as they crash down but fail to strike him.

Thankfully the battle is won and Rhesus is captured and returned back. It is now that Hercules realises that he has been used and that his foe is not the man responsible for the recent carnage and aggression.

Cotys, a frail John Hurt but still with a spark in his eye, pays Hercules and his team for their endeavours whilst the latter decides to leave. He is an honourable man, despondent by the deceit and the life that he has endured. The dedicated Amphiaraus and all but one of the team decide to continue.

Subsequently returning, they are imprisoned by Cotys as is his daughter, Ergenia, Miss Ferguson, whilst her young son is kept as the future heir. Here the despicable and ambitious King Eurystheus (Joseph Fiennes) takes great delight in informing a chained Hercules that he ordered the slaying of his family. Tension mounts when Ergenia is brought in to be beheaded, as the group watch on helpless to intervene as they are all caged.

It is here that Amphiaraus gives Hercules a rousing pep talk and the latter uses his superhuman strength to break free and save her.

The King flees whilst Cotys sets a trio of snarling wolves onto Hercules who, in turn, manages to fight them off. Ian's character says that it is all over now but the protagonist says that things have just started.

With an observation often voiced by McShane during the film, burning spearheads are shot directly toward him as the group attempt to escape. "Excuse me. That was my moment; my fate!" gasps the battle-worn Amphiaraus, as Hercules grabs hold of the thing and lobs it back from whence it came above.

Hercules pursues the King, kills him before it looks like he has met his fate when Sitacles (a brilliant Peter Mullan), is about to slay him. That is until Iolaus (Reece Ritchie) nephew of "the mighty Hercules" eliminated the threat.

Young Arius is found safe and they venture outside where the sight of Lord Cotys and hundreds of his men await.

The latter orders Hercules to bow to him or that the lad will be killed, decreeing that he is a mere mortal and not a demi-god to be feared. Hopelessly outnumbered, they are joined by a member that had left as a final confrontation is faced.

In a super show of strength, the hero pushes over a statue of Hera, Queen of the Greek gods, onto the aggressors below.

Cotys is killed as the soldiers bow down to Hercules.

Looking on as Ian's voiceover talks about the legend or mythology of Hercules being true, the viewer laughs as the camera pans across the group before his final line, "...what do I know? I'm supposed to be dead by now."

Second billed, Mr McShane, like the rest of the European cast, is given his moment in the spotlight via a screenplay from Ryan J. Condal & Evan Spiliotopoulos in their exciting epic, which contains lots of visual effects, directed by Brett Ratner. Intending to move away from the myth, the filmmakers appreciated Ian's involvement. "Ian brought such a great weight to his role, articulated former WWE wrestler Johnson, "and he grabbed this right by the throat."

Adapted from the graphic novel by Pauls D.Storrie, the film cast of Hercules attended a photocall in London's Trafalgar Square on Wednesday 2 July with Ian joining John Hurt and others to publicise their new project. It would be one of the numerous events that he attended to help sell the project. In the following month, he was in Berlin for the German premiere on Thursday 21st August after attending a Hollywood screening event on Wednesday 23 July at the legendary Chinese Theatre.

Focusing upon the Strait of Gibraltar; a small stretch of water that connects Europe with Africa via the Atlantic and the Mediterranean, El Niño follows a disparate group whose lives are entangled in the drugs trade that runs through it. A dangerous existence, people are regularly killed or imprisoned whilst attempting to profit from the transportation of the valuable cargo brought from neighbouring Morocco.

A gorgeous-looking film, Mr McShane is known only as "The Englishman" by undercover police pursued by the dogged Jesús (Luis Tosar) and Eva (Bárbara Lennie), intent on catching him and those above him responsible for the deadly trade.

As a Brit residing in Gibraltar, Ian reminds the viewer of The Man from Delmonte ads; white/ cream suit and hat, he is a go-between always about to instigate things on behalf of his powerful bosses. We first see him in a betting shop where a port worker is passed a slip containing code numbers. The police tail Ian and he is aware of them doing so, casually walking along the tourist-strewn streets near the rock. Intervening, the authorities view the code which transpires as being the number of a container stored at the busy port. With the Spanish police unable to arrest Ian's character as they are outside of British jurisdiction, something repeated throughout the film, drugs are not initially located.

The Britisher works for a heavy-duty criminal gang of Eastern Europeans who will stop at nothing to protect their profits. This means killing anybody viewed as a threat or weak link (which the un-named port worker discovers to his detriment when he is found decapitated; a newly-common warning to others that they mean business). Only in a surreptitiously recorded audio conversation is Ian's voice heard by the police and even then they do not have enough for an arrest.

Jesús is a wanted man by the criminals and so his boss recommends that he temporarily transfer back to his previous helicopter duties involving the pursuit of traffickers using the seas to collect and transfer drugs. It is here that he comes into contact with the bolshie Niño (a debuting Jesús Castro) who with his pal Compi (Jesús Carroza) and new criminal associate Halil (an excellent Saed Chatiby) become involved in the dangerous transfer from Morocco. Jesús is a dedicated police officer and he is soon watching the Englishman again. Returning at the hour mark, McShane is seen in a cable car taking visitors up to the famous WWII tunnels, followed by Jesús, but he is here to meet with a dangerous individual involved in the drug trade.

An engrossing and absorbing drama, El Niño shows the perils for all those involved and the varying motivations behind their participation (sometimes desperation).

Well into the story Ian finally meets Niño, picking him up in his white Porsche and offering him a job at a time when no others are prepared to risk using the trio after Jesús and his team are almost killed in an exchange on the water with him and Halil. All this is being recorded and towards the close of the film, Jesús also comes into direct contact with those he is pursuing. The authorities believe that the Englishman and his organisation are using the lads as a decoy, to throw them off and enable them to get through a valuable delivery in the confusion. Desperate to raise the money demanded by Halil's old boss and uncle, they need to risk doing one more job to help get Compi back from his vicious mitts.

In El Niño, no one can be trusted and it leads to an intense, absorbing finale which results in drugs being found and this particular job by the criminals being thwarted. This leads to a most gruesome fate for Ian's character, as he suffers the same demise as the port worker he spoke with at the start of the film.

On 28 August, Ian joined his fellow actors and director Daniel Monzón at a premiere of this Spanish-language film in Madrid.

This year the John Wick franchise was introduced to cinemagoers and continues to enthral and produce outstanding box office returns creeping up to a decade later.

Our first glimpse of Mr Wick, as played by the wooden Keanu Reeves for whom the genre suits, is of a bruised, bloodied and battered man, distraught at the loss of his beloved wife. Flashbacks show the couple enjoying moments together but we don't yet know what happened to her. He gets an unusual special delivery of a Beagle puppy accompanied by a note from her which moves him greatly. A now-retired assassin for an all-powerful organisation existing in the earthly world but adhering to its own rules, ironically, the little canine, Daisy, will bring more woes into his life than his wife could ever have anticipated.

A wealthy man living in a post-modern home and driving a snazzy sports car, the vehicle is noticed by some men at a gas station where Wick converses with the aggressive Iosef (an excellent Alfie Allen doing his best Russian) whose aggressive offer to purchase it is politely declined.

Later, a home invasion sees the men steal it, batter Wicks and murder his dog. We watch as he clears up blood and mess with fury cloaking his face.

When Iosef and his boys visit Aurelio (John Leguizamo who plays a very different role in The Hollow Point as the hired gun that batters Ian) at his chop shop, he declines to take the car as he knows who it belongs to and soon enough Mr Wick's arrives to see if it is there. They are both linked to the organisation. The viewer learns that the cocksure Iosef is the son of Viggo Tarasov (Michael Nyqvist, who sadly died in 2017), a major villain.

Iosef is chastised by his father as he knows Wick of old and realises what peril they are all in, "John is a man of focus," begins the tattooed elder, "Commitment, Sheer will…." We learn that Wick was given a near-impossible task to complete to allow him to leave the organisation and live a quiet life with his wife. Viggo tells his son that John Wick will come for him soon and that he will not be able to stop him. He calls him but after the line remains silent, the former organises a team to kill his old acquaintance before he does the same to his son. Elsewhere, Wick unearths weapons that he had buried in the basement and prepares for the task ahead including a stash of gold coins, the currency used by those in the know in exchange for goods and services. Later defined by Jerome Flynn in JW3, as being "a social contract….commerce of a relationship…." **203**

Sending men to the house, John kills 13 in all via his martial arts skills and precision use of weapons in a breathtaking initial show of strength by the man in black. A figure away from the scene for some 5 years, he still has connections, visited by a friendly police officer before a team led by Charlie the Cleaner (David Patrick Kelly) arrives to clear up and dispose of the dead.

Upon hearing of the failed attempt, Tarasov puts out a $2m contract on Wick; this figure rises exponentially throughout.

Some 40 minutes in and Wick travels into New York City to an exclusive hotel called The Continental, where the aforementioned gold coins are the familiar form of payment system. Using another to allow him entry into a hidden bar, who should be there but Mr McShane? "Jonathan!" greets the sharply-suited Winston (Ian), in another open-necked shirt and cravat accompaniment, bushy hair ala Code Name: Diamond Head, now absent. Familiar with each other, Winston warns Wick that he might become embroiled with the organisation again if he goes looking for Tarasov's entitled son.

Enjoying a cocktail and wearing reading glasses, Winston always greets Wick formally and the latter amusingly replies the same throughout the films.

Seen at the rainy funeral at the start of the film, Marcus (Willem Defoe) accepts the contract to terminate Wick.

Told where he can find the Russian, at an exclusive club/ spa complex, Wick tools up and heads there. Firstly, he as to get past the many bodyguards, some of which he knows. He kills many of them whilst getting closer to Iosef who is partying at the venue. The body count is astronomical as the carnage continues through the club, spilling onto the packed dance floor before the young hoodlum manages to flee. John is not a superman, getting beaten and shot and almost killed in the process as the film speeds past the hour.

As Winston, Ian does not feature greatly but his character is a telling presence.

Returning to the hotel all bloodied and shot, his appearance doesn't faze the concierge, Caron (Lance Reddick) who calls the hotel doctor. Exhausted and resting, Marcus (Defoe) is opposite the building armed with a telescopic rifle. Wick is not safe from fellow guests either; with Miss Perkins (Adrianne Palicki), an old colleague almost killing him before Marcus intervenes.

The clever Tarasov uses a church to keep his stash of money and valuable documents/ photos of incriminating evidence and it is here that Wick visits next.

More bloodshed occurs via a big gun battle and the only way the villains can subdue Mr Wick is to run him over (something that occurs numerous times in the films).

A man of few words, John Wick moves precisely and as and when required.

Awakening from being knockled down, Wick finds himself handcuffed to a chair and being spoken to by Tarasov; why he simply doesn't kill him is beyond the viewer but then every villain has to explain the plot/ reasoning to the hero, don't they. Articulating their similarities and the harm they have done to others around them, Wick warns his old work colleague to hand his son over for killing his dog, the last gift from his wife, or he will die too.

A hidden shot from Marcus enables Wick to try to free himself whilst Tarasov flees.

He is stopped by him before Tarasov reluctantly provides the safe house address for his son, warning that he is expected.

Checking out, Wick is surprised to be given a luxurious car, courtesy of Winston.

Meeting Marcus with I think the Brooklyn Bridge in the foreground, they are watched by Perkins.

The latter is subsequently taken to Tarasov, battered and murdered, aided by Perkins. Wick will discover the body of his old friend later.

Almost an hour and a half in and Ian returns as Winston. Overseeing the termination of Miss Perkins, he calls "Jonathan" to tell him that Tarasov is about to get a helicopter to escape.

Rushing to the port side, night time location, an awe-inspiring car battle ensues. We might be warned not to use mobile or 'cell' phones whilst driving but the info hasn't reached John Wick!

He drives at high speed and shoots his guns to kill those protecting the villain and eventually just the 2 men remain.

205

In a scene reminiscent of Blade Runner; there are many in the films including the rainy locations accentuating the night-time neon street signs, Tarasov demands that they fight like men, minus weapons. Even here, the former is not to be trusted, drawing a knife and stabbing Wick with it. They fight and spoiler alert or not, only one remains alive. And so the film ends, with Wick breaking into a vet to treat his wounds and gently removing a dog from one of the cages. The clever screenplay from Derek Kolstad was co-directed by Chad Stahelski and the unaccredited David Leitch. The former had been a stunt performer who had worked with Reeves before.

Running for 7 seasons across 8 years until surprisingly being cancelled by its U.S. network, the third 'season' Ray Donovan aired on Showtime on Wednesday 15 July 2015, with Ian appearing in the first 9 episodes all shown that year.

Like all good dramas, the key to success is to draw in the viewer despite there being little to like about the main character. Arguably, this is the case with the stoic Donovan (as played by Liev Schreiber). In a show created by Ann Biderman, season three is packed with storylines involving the main protagonist and his family; brothers Terry (Eddie Marsan, nailing the accent) & Bunchy (Dash Mihok), as well as his estranged family. Ray is a 'fixer' a man you call when you want something done, no matter what methods are used; these include violence, manipulation via blackmail, and more.

At the commencement of a new season there is always a lot to consider from before and here is no different. Into the fray come billionaire businessman Andrew Finney and his adult children Paige (a strident Katie Holmes) & Casey (Guy Burnet). A reluctant Donovan is summoned to a lavish Bell Air home to a meeting with Mr Finney, whose son has been kidnapped and a $5m ransom demanded. However, none of the family can be trusted, as he will discover, and doubts remain as to whether or not the whole thing is a rouse concocted by Casey. A gravely-voiced Ian tries to persuade a circumspect Donovan to find the son and seems genuinely concerned for his welfare. "My father was a criminal," begins the moneyed whisky-drinker, "and he ensured that I didn't have to be."

Tasked with negotiating with the kidnappers, Ray transports a briefcase full of cash to a disused warehouse where things go fatally wrong. Not for him but for those holding Casey. The go-between is not a man to be trifled with; having a powerful reputation and seeing his son term him a "thug".

Returning the young man home, Ray watches as the father hugs his son.

Episode two sees the hard-drinking fixer receiving a call from Paige, a married woman prone to infidelity but with good reason, as we discover later, struggling with a complex relationship with her father. A major manipulator, at this stage both utilize Ray's services but the viewer would unsure of either.

A threat to kill one of the American football stars at her club by the cuckold husband, a Navy Seals vet, sees Donovan used again as a facilitator. Duped just like the husband, he takes a major hammering from the man upon returning his promised hush money. Donovan has integrity but he is often at loggerheads with the corruption around him.

Meanwhile, his brother, as portrayed by Snow White & the Huntsman / Jack the Giant Slayer co-star Marsan is in the penitentiary and having a terrible time of things.

Come and Knock on Our Door finds Donovan rejecting the offer to work for Mr Finney. Meantime his estranged father, the wily Jon Voight, develops his criminal enterprises amidst a heavy-going storyline to follow.It seems that Ray circumnavigates a world where if someone has something over somebody else they will manipulate the situation into getting what they want from them. When all else fails, Donovan goes to Finney, looking stylish in blacks and beige, to help him free his brother from the joint and thus avoid being murdered by neo-Nazis therein.

With some 10 minutes of the storyline remaining, Ray calls at the mansion and before long the 2 are in Finney's chauffeur-driven car on their way to sort things. The actors share a terrific scene where neither looks at each other directly. Andrew is a major influencer and successfully manipulates a local politician into releasing Ray's brother. This he does but the price for Donovan is a heavy one: he has to now work for the Finney organization. It feels like he has sold his soul to the devil.

The other brother, Bunchy, runs the family-owned gym.

Continuing to be an entertaining watch Breakfast of Champions sees Paige & her father working on selling the film studio Imperial Pictures to a Chinese business consortium. Finney (Ian) hesitates in selling but she convinces him that the capital generated will be used to enable further developments to allow her football team to have a new stadium built in L.A. This is a particularly insightful episode as Ray is told by Finney that he works for him and not his daughter, whilst an underlining mutual attraction between the former and Paige is apparent.

"Ray's my guy," explains Andrew, with Ian looking tiny next to the 6' 3" Schreiber. Amusingly a stray dog adopted by Abby, Donovan's estranged wife, played by the brilliant Paula Malcomson, who had worked with Ian on Deadwood previously, also features in this episode.

Donovan is a formidable person and knows others that are equally good, something not going unnoticed. She is implicated in some dubious messages left on a cell phone which he is tasked with obtaining. This he does but things are complicated when he pays a late-night call at the Finney mansion to find the home-owner enjoying milk and cookies in his dressing gown. On the surface, father and daughter look like they get on but simmering under is a duo at loggerheads and Ray finds himself caught between them. However, his loyalty at this point remains firmly with his employer.

Mr McShane is absent from a couple of storylines across the dozen episodes in season three, looking somewhat portly in a dressing gown Anthony next informs Donovan that he needs to make certain that a rival bidder fails to arrive at a meeting attended by himself and the vendor. This is taken care of by Mr Fixer and an able team including Katherine Moennig as Lena Burnham, Ray's investigative assistant & Avi (Steven Bauer).

Even Paige is impressed by his capable nature and in an interesting and unexpected reveal, she discloses to him that her marriage to Varick (Jason Butler Harner) is a sham. He and her father have been in a relationship and their union is merely one of convenience.

We learn of this with the mention of a love letter given to her father from her husband! Both Finneys are great planners, strategists, and business people but on Election Day, the foregone result does not favour them and their development of the venture.

Invited to a dinner at the luxurious Century Plaza hotel, Donovan brings Abby and it is a joy to see the actress next to her Deadwood co-star. "The beast brings his beauty," grins Finney.

Implicated elsewhere, Donovan retrieves a cell phone which has personal stuff on it appertaining to Paige (Miss Holmes) in a strong entry in the series. However, he doesn't do this for free, with the two bartering for shares in the team being allocated to Donovan (which her father will discover later and be most annoyed with).

With his politician unexpectedly losing, a furious Finney rants at Donovan for not making it happen.

At the start of each episode, there is a brief recap for viewers but we hardly need to be reminded of the drama occurring. Expunged from both the business and family, with divorce papers filed by Paige, a despairing Varick manages to gain access to the mansion and confront a surprised Finney found cosied up by his fire. Threatening to expose "Finn" as an embezzler and for his closet homosexuality, things do not end well for the younger man. The callous Anthony denies any feelings for him and awkwardly kisses him to crudely prove the point. Not willing to allow any such revelations to be made public, Anthony (Ian), a moment later strikes him in the head with a poker found next to the fireplace.

This time it is Mr Finney who needs help and calls in Donovan to "repay the kindness" of earlier and clear up the whole mess on his behalf. Avi & Lena, involved in similar distasteful events previously, assist and initially, Finney is complicit in what Donovan orders.

Keen to retire, he tells his daughter that he will turn over his business affairs to her once the properties surrounding the proposed stadium build have been purchased and environmental concerns crudely quashed.

Former cop Hank Azaria enters the scene as an investigator known previously to Ray, who later joins Finney to frame him for the murder in this strong entry.

Ray sets up a back story to cover Finney's steps and frame Verick for embezzling $8m intended for the couple. However, the business mogul re-emerges and is frustrated at having to allow Donovan to control everything; he also wants the body returned.

Meanwhile Azaria, as Hank, delves into things & the disgraced former cop is pretty good at investigating and discovers the murder weapon secreted away. The episode ends with him tapping at Anthony's window, displaying the said poker but he too is in deeper than he could imagine. We notice how Ian speaks in a slow, considered drawl that reeks of dominance.

Interviewed by the L.A.P.D's Chief of Police, in Poker, Mr Finney (Ian) is soon utilizing his sway with others, explaining to Paige (Miss Holmes), "There's a mountain of favours owed to me in this town."

He asks her to support his story that Donovan is the killer but she is reluctant to lie in a storyline bringing tumultuous changes.

With the discovery of the body ever closer, Avi has the task of digging it up whilst Donovan speaks with the police. The canny fixer manages to dispose of the poker only seconds before officers find it in his apartment following Hank being shot and bound and revealing he had hidden it there.

Moments before being interviewed, Paige is spoken to by Ray who explains that he has the body, murder weapon, and Hank so there is little she can do to frame him. Afterwards, she pays a late-night visit to her father, who is seated outside by the swimming pool with another drink in hand. She thanks him for everything and is a little astonished; he thinks she is being sentimental. "We did the right thing," he comments hollowly. She leaves and a second or two after the trash skip in the yard outside ignites as sirens are heard wailing away and coming near: the body of his son-in-law and the murder weapon is contained within! Checkmate. Daniel Attias season two director on Deadwood worked on episodes here.

Bilal (2015) found Mr McShane lending his voice to the character of Umayyah in a stunning animation that looks almost life-like, such is its perfect crafting. Inspired by a true story, he is initially seen as a young man wielding much power who pays for a boy enslaved to assist him on his trading missions. That person is Bilal. Umayyah's son Safwan is seen bullying him also.

He endures tremendous brutality and grows up under the control of this unpleasant man with a fixed scowl and prominent eyebrows. "...the difference between us is I worship whatever empowers me," begins a now-older Umayyah, "You, worship something that will destroy you."

A stunning-looking film, rich in colours, an epic battle lasting some time forms the climax of the picture. A mass of soldiers and horses gather and we see an adult Bilal, now trained in combat, off to confront Umayyah on horseback.

Also rousing, this story of religious figure Bilal Ibn Rabah, a companion of the Islamic prophet Muhammad, is well-worth seeking out.

Ian's narration for the short One received a premiere in L.A. in February 2016 (and another in Paris). He also featured in a glossy ad alongside George Clooney for coffee brand Nespresso.

In any Sasha Baron Cohen movie, you are guaranteed a few things: grotesque comedy moments as well as some fantastically funny ones, often offensive and provocative at the same time. Released in March 2016, Grimsby was also amusingly known as The Brothers Grimsby. But this is no genteel Ealing comedy and although Ian is seen in the trailer, his role as an MI6 boss is purely rudimentary. We see him several times in the busy Comms room tracking the whereabouts and actions of elite special agent Sebastian Graves (a sturdy Mark Strong auditioning for James Bond but resembling Uncle Fester) and later, tracking him with long-lost idiot savant brother Nobby (Cohen at his crudest), who reunites with his younger sibling after many years apart.

Looking smart in a suit, Mr McShane sanctions the order to have Strong and his errant brother terminated after the former is mistakenly appearing to assassinate someone official. Terminator Cochran is given the task whilst at HQ pretty Jodie (Isla Fisher) is Graves' only alley able to help him clear his name.

In the meantime, Sebastian needs to hide out and so reluctantly agrees to return to Grimsby and the squalid locality known to Nobby.

Many of the characters seem underwritten but the action sequences are convincing and look terrific. Whilst Grimsby hardly merits a mention on Ian's CV after watching it the viewer feels the need to have a nice wash.

Following the popular success of Downton Abbey, its creator Julian Fellowes fashioned an ambitious small screen adaptation of the weighty Anthony Trollope novel Doctor Thorne.

One of 47 written by the author, his 1858 book was shaped into three parts (four for America) and shown on ITV in March.

Fellowes, a pal of Mr McShane's for many years, was optimistic that they could do justice to the novel and Ian was cast as the bumptious Sir Roger Scatcherd. Included on the DVD cover with the main cast, he looks the part in an oversized velvet top hat and Deadwood-style sideburns!

Over in the UK visiting family, he was offered the role after agreeing to another on Game of Thrones.

Partly shot in the tiny Wiltshire village of Lacock, now preserved and owned by the National Trust, its picturesque nature has seen it utilised for film and television projects.

Celebrating his birthday whilst on location, as Scatcherd, Ian is a self-made, plain-speaking man who has made his fortune from the railway. A true 'rough diamond', success has brought him wealth and a title and a dwelling at the luxurious Boxall Hill. However, now ailing from years of alcohol abuse his time is almost up but not yet before some astonishing moments.

A man with a past, Sir Roger served a decade in prison for the manslaughter of Henry Thorne (Tim Wallers) and we see all of this at the start of the opening episode, where we see him confront the cad who seduced his sister, Annie. The story begins in 1836 on a dark evening when who should come into view but Ian.

Resembling an older Oliver Twist, with the actor shown unflatteringly in flashback, they scuffle and the other man stumbles and is accidentally killed by the drunken Scatcherd.

Time jumps 20 years and we are invited to look in on the beautiful country lives of affluent gentlefolk. Vivacious ladies dress in lace and discuss weddings and suitable husbands whilst the gentlemen are seen in tall top hats and suits with waistcoats. But beyond the surface, there is much going on, with financial concerns seemingly ruling most decisions.

Young Doctor Thorne (Tom Hollander) is the personal physician to the now-poorly Sir Roger and visits him at Boxall where he finds him in bed. Lady Scatcherd, Janine Duvitski, initially comes over as a maid but she has a long connection to the main plotline which is revealed later. She and the Thorne plead with Sir Roger not to stand as the prospective MP for the area against the unctuous Moffatt.

Doubting his strength to manage such a task, the grouch still decides to run as it means he can upset the feisty Lady Arabella (Rebecca Front) by winning. They share a mutually antagonistic relationship, as the Lady does with many in the locality! She and the Countess De Courcy (Phoebe Nichols on excellent, stirring form) favour the uncouth Moffatt as he is from a moneyed family. Ian termed the show as a "Victorian soap opera" and also confessed that he never read the book which it is based.

Caught in between, Doctor Thorne, we never learn of his first name, terms Lady Arabella "a spiteful cat". He is the executor of Sir Roger's will and is spoken to bluntly by his patient, "What gives you the right to lecture me? What have you ever done that I should listen?" Wheezing and looking all his 70+ years, as Scatcherd Ian puts in another rounded performance.

Rightly terming his character a "gentle hero", Hollander is memorable in the lead role and manages to contain his anger/ distress or whatever else under his large top hat.

He loves his niece, Mary (the terrific Stefanie Martini) who is in love with Frank Gresham (Harry Richardson) despite him being arranged to marry the feisty and affluent American Miss Dunstable (a sparkling Alison Brie) who is not so desperate to accept.

Called to return to the house by Winterbones (Andy Linden) Thorne is puzzled until Sir Roger tells him of his new will and that he is the sole executor. Roused from his sickbed, he informs him that his family will be cared for and that his son, Louis, (as played by Ed Franklin) who will inherit much of his accumalated wealth. And what with his owning most of their Greshamsbury Park estate, the repercussions of the calling in mortgage debts could prove devastating for the family. If Louis should die before 30 then the fortune will transfer to an unknown person: the son or daughter of Sir Roger's late sister. Alarmingly, and unbeknownst to Scatcherd at this point, that person is Mary. She had been the result of an illicit encounter with her mother fleeing to start a new life in Australia and the younger Thorne (Hollander) raising her as his daughter.

Plot contrivances prove most entertaining and the whole thing is played out with such panache making this exceedingly well-made production a pleasure to watch.

The second episode sees Ian on the hustings and speaking to locals, charismatic but ailing, he takes a swig from a hip flask, unable to do without a drink. Carousing those gathered with humour and bravado when Moffatt attempts to speak, he flops badly and will go on to narrowly lose the election. Agitating the crowd, some throw eggs at the poor man until Sir Roger falls to the ground.

Returned to his bed-chamber, Scatcherd is cared for by Doctor Thorne, magnanimously accepting that the death of his brother was unintentional. He is surprised upon Mary's arrival in support of Lady Scatcherd. His concern is made apparent whilst the young woman helps care for the patient, who appreciates her support without either realising their connection. In his last moments, Sir Roger pleads with Thorne to let him know who his niece or nephew is and the good clinician reveals that it is the caring girl in front of him. Astonished, he articulates his thanks to her but does not disclose what he has learnt and around the hour mark Sir Roger dies in another screen death for Ian to act out in his impeccable style.

The doctor leads Lady Scratched to her husband before Mary offers her support at his passing.Having also arrived, the wretched

Louie offers no such thoughtfulness, informing Thorne that soon after the funeral he will return to London and for any money to be forwarded there. He also shows a strong attraction to Miss Thorne but will see his advances gently rebuffed. As is often the case, past events are revealed and much drama subsequently occurs as a consequence of Sir Roger's death and the entanglements of his will. Spurned by Mary, the immature, heavy-drinking Louie speeds off on his horse and hits his head on a wayward branch before dying in the same bed as his father.

Afterwards, Doctor Thorne tells the widow who the heir to the Scatcherd fortune now is. Mary will inherit 500k from the various accounts and after bowing to the unruly bullying of the punctilious Lady Arabella and Countess De Courcy she agrees to call off her marriage to the former's son, Frank. This is due to financial proclivities but after her uncle reveals the truth to her, she realises that the marriage can go on unhindered.

A divine watch, Doctor Thorne proves a joy.

Symbolism in the Western genre has always played its part and in The Hollow Point, it is also visible at times. None more so than in the final, post-credit scene between Sheriff Leland Kilbaught (Ian) and local car salesman Shep (a superb Jim Belushi playing against his usual comedic type).

At times the film tries to sound profound, with prosaic dialogue usually delivered by an on-point Mr McShane or lead Patrick Wilson. Whilst in other moments it is purely linear. "In the end," offers its Spanish director Gonzalo López-Gallego, about whom Ian was most complimentary. "It's all people trying to survive in a forsaken town; trying to escape their monsters."

A modern-day Western noir set in a dusty town on the U.S/Mexico border, many of the residents in Los Reyes County are not best pleased by the return of Wallace Skolin (Patrick Wilson, excited to have the opportunity to work with the Deadwood star) as their new sheriff. In fact, throughout this violent tale, many either inflict violence or fall victim to it in a screenplay from the mysterious Nils Lyew. He had been invited to visit the set during production but failed to accept the offer for a project that had been in development for 2 years with various cast changes along the way.

It was also originally titled The Man on Carrion Road.

Beatings, gunfights and death are prevalent throughout and delivered by a top-notch cast led by Mr McShane as a hardened, booze-loving local sheriff who floats between being on the side of upholding the law or maybe, ultimately, working in spite of it.

"It felt that the role was written for Ian McShane," reflected producer Andy Horwitz. And watching the Lancashire-born actor put in another fine performance, I agree.

Like all the main characters, as Leland, he gets bruised and battered; shot and almost beaten to death by cartel killer John Leguizamo. As Atticus, the latter is convincing as a hitman exasperated upon seeing that despite a pounding the veteran officer will not give in.

As Sheriff Kilbaught, Ian lives in a wooden house complete with stars & stripes flag out front. With a liking for wearing large cowboy hats, he looks rough throughout most of the film. Known to everyone locally, he seems able to function despite being a heavy drinker (we actually see him slugging away at the start of the film when he is involved in a fatality). That death sets off a chain of events that proves both profound and fatal for many. The officer beats off an attack by a young man involved in the widespread delivery of ammunition into Mexico by locals in the county. But Wallace knows that the criminals involved will not leave things as they are and that trouble is coming. Another man disappears, known to him and even his ex-wife is disgruntled.

The investigation takes a particularly gruesome turn when a scuffle with Atticus (a horrid John Leguizamo from the John Wick films) results in the younger lawman having his hand sliced off.

At home and in unflattering long johns and dressing gown, Kilbaught is shocked to discover a bloodied and distraught Wallace outside some hours after the fight. Revitalised, Sheriff McShane speaks with underachieving car salesman Shepard "Shep" Diaz (Belushi), a man known to him but

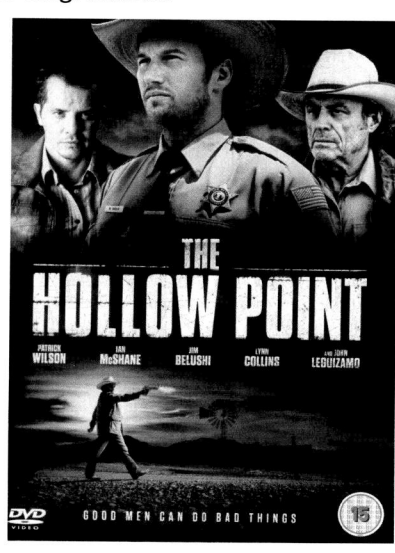

is shot; more soon follows for the bedraggled officer. Now a one-armed gunslinger, Wallace almost kills the wrong man (who looks very similar to the assassin) but his colleague encourages him to keep looking. "What a pair!" Kilbaught sighs after newbie Wallace (Wilson) begins delving deeper into the supply chain. Each taking pain killers, both are already exhausted but combine to sort the case out which sees lots of people implicated.

Returning together to locate Shep, a gunfight at a desolate trailer park ensues, with Belushi's debt-ridden salesman playing well in scenes with Ian.

Hospitalised, the latter visits Shep and is offered a deal to allow him to go free.

We wonder if he can be corrupted as he never rules it out.

Sheriff Kilbaught (Ian) recruits some seemingly formidable new men to combat the criminals and he engages in a horrifying fight with the younger Atticus after 2 of the new supporters are killed. The assassin demands that the battered officer takes him to the hospital where he visits his girlfriend (Karli Hall). A waitress, she plays a major part in proceedings. "You ain't gonna make it," sighs the lawman to the equally fatigued murderer. With 2 people on the list for him to erase, Leland pleads with him to let one of them go but his request is rejected, with Atticus demanding that he complete the task.

In a tension-filled climax, Wallace crashes into Leguizamo's car and it results in Atticus being hurt in the collision, giving him the chance to draw a gun on the ailing killer.

The wiser older officer tells him not to shoot in cold blood but moments later he lets off his gun multiple times.

Sheriff McShane orders him to go and he walks off as Ian sits down next to the body.

Wallace is seen along a deserted highway as the day begins and a little later a vehicle pulls up driven by Marla (Lily Collins) and they drive away in a beautifully photographed final piece. The title "The Hollow Point" is displayed on the screen before an additional scene occurs which is a must-see for Ian fans.

Dressed in a large black cowboy hat and matching coat, Kilbaught casually walks into a diner and takes a seat next to a surprised Shep. Outfitted in garish vacation-type clothes, he repeats his offer of a bribe whilst some cryptic dialogue is spouted by the visitor appertaining to disappearing and death. You will have to watch the film to see how it finally ends but suffice to say that Belushi & McShane are excellent.

McShane attended a premiere of The Hollow Point at the Cabos Film Festival to help promote the piece.

Displaying scant regard for recognising the preciousness to which fans hold their favourite shows, Ian McShane upset many when mentioning his involvement in Game of Thrones. Speaking with the Telegraph newspaper after spending a week on location in Northern Ireland to shoot his involvement, he thoughtlessly gave away some indication concerning the fate of one of the main characters. Accepting the one-off role at the behest of his grandchildren, who enjoyed the show, the fan base was furious and so perhaps in hindsight, Ian should have known better? After all, he would come to realize the pleasure that his television shows Deadwood & American Gods gave. But he simply dismissed the disappointment here by aptly describing Thrones as being "only tits and dragons."

As for his involvement in The Broken Man, episode 7 in season 6, he plays Brother Ray; a former arsonist/ thief and murderer now turned pacifist and leading a small community. After never seeing an episode of Thrones previously, the author was aware of the phenomenal popularity of the show.

A smashing entry in the series; forces are seen gathering in anticipation of the battles to come including John Wick cast members Jerome Flynn & Alfie Allen. Neither feature in scenes with Ian in a story shown on Monday 6 June 2016. Coarse language is heard throughout and a bit of gratuitous female nudity is also thrown in.

Brother Ray is immediately seen supervising the work being carried out by his community by erecting a wooden-framed construction in a lovely, rural location. One of them, an outsider called Sandor (Rory McCann) had been rescued from near-death by the Septon, previously.

Ian, as a man with a past, now leads the mixed community called Seventh Saviour.

Visited by three men on horseback led by Lem Lemoncloak (Jóhannes Haukur Jóhannesson), asks the convivial leader what they have in their possession. Ray tells them that they have nothing of

value and little food but that they are welcome to join them. Scoffing somewhat, Lem and the others leave but voices an ominous warning, "Stay safe. The night is dark and full of terrors."

Afterwards, Sandor speaks of his concern and worry for the group's safety whilst Brother Ray ponders what he thinks they should do, "Violence is a disease. You don't cure a disease by spreading it to more people."

Incidentally, one of the menacing horseman is Ian Davies, seen previously as a policeman in Grimsby. The battle-scarred Sandor gathers wood to combat the cold night ahead but upon his return, he is greeted by a most heinous sight. Every single person has been slain, including Ian's character: who has been hanged. The discovery proves a gruesome end to an otherwise entertaining watch across its running time of just under an hour.

Abram Tarasov, brother to the late Viggo, steps into the throng in John Wick: Chapter 2 (2017) which takes up where the original finished. Wick (Keanu Reeves) wants his speedy sports car returned so he can drive along at night in the rainy metropolis and look all arty. If you love high-speed car chases in neon lighting this is the franchise for you. Throw in martial arts and lots of killing and bob's your uncle. Wick also a new dog.

He gets his vehicle returned but it is smashed to a buckled mess, to the exasperation of mechanic Aurelio (John Leguizamo) who calls at his luxurious property. The Mustang has sentimental value to it for John, as it reminds him of better times spent with his late wife.

Past associate Santino D'Antonio (Riccardo Scamarcio) is not a man that you want around, as Wick discovers to his detriment; demanding that he return to assassinate his sister, Gianna (Claudia Gerini) who is seeking to be a part of The High Table within the criminal universe. A menacing force, he departs with Wick declining to get back involved, only to destroy the house by burning it down!

Having lost everything, a desolate John walks to the Continental hotel where he speaks with Winston (McShane). At almost a half-hour in, they chat outside in a stunning location (the Rockefeller Plaza building) with the gorgeous St. Patrick's Cathedral in the background. Ian again looks dapper in his usual get-up of dark suit and cravat ensemble. As the mellow Winston, he recommends that he do the job and then kills Santino afterwards, should he be so inclined. Staying at the hotel, Wick brings his dog with no name too.

Off to Roma, at the Continental over there, he meets Winston clone Julius (Franco Nero) and sets off to find Gianna who is in the capital. Getting through her security, as the reticent Wick, Reeves' performance is weaker than in the other films, he finds her but things get very dark when she cuts her wrists before he eventually shoots her. Shot at repeatedly, here his bulletproof suit protects him against many attempts to kill him. The death toll makes for exhausting but rousing viewing whilst the stunts and fighting are astounding.

Duped by the Italian, Santino makes it public that he will avenge his sister's death and a $7m bounty is put out on John's life. Once again there is danger all around, with globally interested parties keen to pick up the money for rubbing him out.

Shot in Manhattan, onscreen a visiting Winston, contemptuous of D'Antonio, calls on him to inform him that Wick's completed the task and that his friend will retaliate if he survives to do so. An absurdist piece of dialogue convincingly delivered by the actor follow but the audience has to stifle a giggle, "You stabbed the devil in the back and forced him back into the life he had just left," begins Winston, "You incinerated the priest's temple. Burnt it to the ground. Now he's free of the marker...what do you think he'll do?"

Wick unwisely steps out and is stabbed again whilst fighting for his life on the Metro system. With the contract activated, to locate D'Antonio, the help of the influential Bowery King (Laurence Fishburne) is sought out but not even he will go against the wishes of the clandestine society. After all, no one is above the order of The High Table.

A showdown in an art exhibition space proves the highlight before Wick returns to the Continental, where no murdering is allowed to be committed by the many assassins that gather there to make deals/ exchanges.

Returning alone to visit Winston at the hotel HQ, D'Antonio complains about Wick but the former is having none of it, John returns to the lounge, and defying house rules that no "business" be conducted on the premises, Wick is unable to control himself and shoots the younger man dead. The ballroom of the Jane Hotel in Greenwich Village, New York was used.

After collecting his dog, back at the charred remains of his home, he finds the necklace that he had given his wife in amongst the rubble.

A dutiful Caron (Lance Reddick) requests that he accompanies him to a meeting with Winston. Throughout JW2, Keanu's face is blood-stained and tellingly the fatality count is higher than in the first film. Ian aptly termed the sequel as being "A wild ride".

The final moments of Chapter 2 are brilliant.

Taken to the stunning Fountain and Bethesda Terrace in Central Park, with the Angel of the Waters in the background, an elegant-looking Mr McShane is dressed in black all apart from a burgundy scarf on what looks like a cold day on filming. Wondering why he hasn't been killed, Winston cuts in, "Because I deemed it not to be." A man of immense power, we watch as the people milling about the popular tourist landmark suddenly stop and turn to look at the two men once Winston has commanded them. He then gives a nod and they continue about their day in a moment reminiscent of a scene in one of the Paranormal Activity films for its creepiness.

Giving Wick a chance to survive, he presents him with an apparatus to help him flee but before he departs, he declares to Winston that he will kill anyone who comes after him. The camera provides a close-up of the two actors and Ian's character replies, "Of course you will," then smiles before adding, "Jonathan." Setting off swiftly, a rightly worried Wick glances at those in the public park as the clock is ticking before the contract is made available for his life following Winston's call to activate it.

Chapter 2 received its U.S. premiere on Monday 30 January at the Premiere Arclight complex in Hollywood, L.A. And after he completed work on the project Ian went straight on to shoot Pottersville in January 2017.

From the glamour of a big Hollywood film, McShane rejoined Ray Winstone for first-time director Thomas Napper's Jawbone (2017), a slight tale focussing on the struggles of former youth boxing champ Jimmy McCabe (Johnny Harris, one of the dwarves from Snow White and the Huntsman). Also written by him, he gives a heartfelt performance as a desperate man close to the edge, homeless and reliant upon alcohol. Both Messrs Winstone and Harris come from a boxing background as youngsters, so it's a semi-autobiographical story, partly a tribute to the men behind the boxing clubs, resonated with the Sexy Beast star. Ian also had Scoop producer Mike Elliott on board.

Alas, Jawbone does not feature Ian with Ray directly but it still proves a worthwhile watch. "...McShane again....he turns up everywhere.....he keeps following me about," joked Winstone at the small-scale premiere held at the BFI in London on Monday 8 May (and released theatrically the coming Friday).

Involved for the first 3 days, filming had commenced in the capital back in February with Ian coming over from the States.

Following the passing of his mother some 12 months previously, Harris as Jimmy, is lost and alone but begins to frequent his old haunt; a boxing club run by Bill (Winstone on fine form). Noticed by the initially frosty proprietor, it seems that the two have a history that is not yet spoken of. To gauge his level, Bill suggests a little sparring in which rusty Jimmy fares poorly.

In need of money, a meet with Joe, a promoter of unlicensed boxing bouts, as portrayed by a convivial Ian McShane is arranged. An offer of a 2.5k purse, with more if he manages to go the full distance with a younger and stronger fighter, is snapped up by Jimmy. Desperate, he asks Joe not to visit the gym owned by Bill, as the latter wants nothing to do with such contests as competitors can get badly hurt.

Creeping back into the gym every night, one evening Jimmy finds Bill there and the two talk. Bill reveals that he has a terminal illness and only his trusty side-kick Eddie (the always-reliable Michael Smiley, who like Ian is an avid Man United fan) knows. The former has heard about the fight and tells him that Eddie will help train him during the 2 weeks before the event.

And so begins an extensive fitness regime only interrupted when Jimmy falls out with Eddie and continues alone.

The two reconcile once the news of Bill's sudden death is revealed and despite previous protestations, Eddie accompanies Jimmy to the event as his cornerman.

A grubby hall sees the baying crowd keen for blood and Jimmy takes quite a hammering whilst Eddie instructs him to stop trying to fight and start boxing instead. Naturally, things turn around and his artfulness sees him through. In a final scene, at the graveside, we see Jimmy standing next to Eddie and Bill's family with Ian's character alongside the boxer. This is the only other moment that McShane features in Jawbone, a "beautiful, simple story" that was BAFTA-nominated. Ian termed it an "....an emotional hour & half."

Mr McShane had been cast to play 'Vengeance' alongside Sam Rockwell and Michael K Williams, each representing parts of the brain of music man Dr Dre in his semi-autobiographical work Vital Signs (intended to be 2017). Intended to be a 6 part series made for Beats TV, a company owned by Apple TV, it was to be quite a contrast to finish work on Jawbone over in the UK and to act in this. It seems the show was axed before it went into production due to its content concerns.

Apple CEO Tim Cook shelved the project due to its graphic depictions of gun culture, violence, sex and drug use and told The Wall Street Journal that the company would not wish to be associated with such a series.

Written in the late-1990s, American Gods by Neil Gaiman was published in 2001 with the first season of the TV adaptation by Michael Green & Bryan Fuller airing from Monday 1 May. Green was the creator and sometime-writer of the ill-fated Kings; a series that gave Ian the lead and shown in 2009.

Too difficult to squash into a film, running across 8 episodes, the small screen Gods received a London premiere on Thursday 6 April, ahead of its official launch and Ian attended a Los Angeles event two weeks later.

McShane loved the book and felt certain that fans would enjoy the show so long as it returned to its core source. Promoting it in the UK on This Morning, he termed it "a surreal tribute to the heart of America, in a sense..."

Shot in Toronto, he had worked with Gaiman on Coraline, previously, and attending a Comic-Con event, the actor acknowledged the author as being a hugely popular guest there. Ian first saw American Gods whilst a guest at the annual SXSW festival in Austin, Texas.

What rich source material the book is! From the opening episode, he receives a special credit as "Mr Wednesday" a confessed thief, liar and possessor of supernatural powers who seek out Shadow Moon (fellow actor Brit Ricky Whittle) to seemingly offer him a job as the driver of his black Cadillac.

Transporting him Stateside to recruit others opposed to the "New Gods", these are represented by Media (the ravishing Gillian Anderson, an actor who can do no wrong); the disturbing Mr World (eccentric actor Crispin Glover) and the irritating Technical Boy (Bruce Langley) collectively fighting against the old guard represented by Wednesday and others.

Shadow is released after serving 3 years in prison only to discover that his wife, Laura (the superb Emily Browning) has been killed in a car crash. His pal was also in the vehicle and it is also revealed that they had been engaged in a sexual relationship whilst he was incarcerated.

Ian and Shadow first meet at an airport where the latter is on his way back home to attend the funerals.

Wednesday (Ian) seems to know a lot about the younger man and delivers a great deal of snappy dialogue in his role as an incessant chatterbox. Indeed, throughout the opening season, McShane is tasked with voicing many tongue-twisting lines which he does with aplomb. Seeing him manipulate others, Shadow needs to go home.

Renting a car after the flight is cancelled; Shadow is irritated to see the re-emergence of the mysterious Mr Wednesday, "You're a little creepy," barks the young fella, "And you're forward. And familiar...I don't like you..." But he does wonder who he is as things develop between them. Also introduced is the bizarre Matt Sweeney (Pablo Schreiber) aka "The tallest leprechaun in the World," who revels in violence. Clad in a Columbo-type Mac, McShane looks tiny next to Whittle & Schreiber and sees his character having a glass eye which is a nod to his mythological heritage. Ian met co-star Whittle on the first day of shooting and they hit it off immediately: brought up in Manchester and Ricky in Oldham, 8 miles apart, both being ardent Man United fans this was a spur to their friendship.

Tech Boy wants to know what Wednesday is up to and almost kills Shadow in the process in scenes of intense imagery and graphic detailing which some viewers will find shocking. There is also nudity, other violence and much more disturbing visions in each episode.

Utilising snippets from the book outlining people's struggles to reach America, Wednesday and Shadow drive across the country (no highways being a pre-requisite) and the old god they meet is the rather unpleasant Czernobog (Peter Stormare), someone with a long shared history with Mr Wednesday. He lives with 'seer' Zorya (Cloris Leachman, who like Ian, provided a voice for The Simpsons) and her sisters. Another is Vulcan, as played by Corbin Bernsen, one of his oldest acquaintances but someone who is slain by Wednesday in a horrible moment towards the close of episode 6, with the show entering the realms of absurdity as it advances.

Shadow is constantly challenged by what he sees and by the stunningly-photographed images in his mind and he asks Wednesday what is real or not, "What a beautiful, beautiful thing to be able to dream when you're not asleep," comes the response. Is the odd Mr Wednesday a figment of his imagination? Later we learn the truth but for now we have to be content with many cryptic quotes, "If I told you," begins Ian when asked by Shadow who he really is, "you wouldn't believe in me."

Pursued by a dead wife, psychopath, Salim (Omid Abtahi) and another, the author wonders how the show was pitched to Amazon.

Guided by raven spies, Wednesday is alerted to the presence of Shadow's recently-returned, deceased partner before the duo is arrested for the bank robbery arranged in a previous episode.

Following a visit from Mr World, Tech Boy and the chameleon-like Media, Wednesday had attempted to explain the story to a bemused detective but it sounds so ridiculous that little wonder it sounded preposterous.

Absent from a couple of background episodes, in the season finale Ian shines brightly after finally revealing himself to Shadow as being Odin, one of the principal gods in Norse mythology, via an awe-inspiring speech. Assisted by Easter (Kristin Chenoweth), a fellow god that initially resists helping Wednesday, they succeed in fending off the New Gods or at least until the start of the next season. We also learn that he sacrificed Laura (Ms Browning) as they needed Shadow.

The story closes with Wednesday asking if the young man believes and he replies that he does: in all of it.

The opening season is a mad delight and American Gods is like nothing that had come before to the small screen (or at least not since Twin Peaks). The viewer's mind is continually blown by further moments of precocity, terror, humour and nonsense all mixed into an unforgettable television experience. However, I would say that 8 episodes were ample for the first trip into this world/ realm.

Travelling worldwide for work, Ian received a special name check on the opening titles of Pottersville, a gorgeous-looking film photographed by Damian Horan with director Seth Henrikson & writer Daniel Meyer working on their debut picture together. The former was also a Cinematographer and it shows.

Pottersville is another small-town America struggling to keep afloat when its major economical source, its local mill, closes. And with many shops closed, only Greiger's general store manages to struggle on despite the downturn. Run by Maynard (Michael Shannon) and ably assisted by the pleasing Parker (Judy Greer) one of the regulars is Bart (a bearded Mr McShane), a hunter who brings in various meats for him. Enjoying a perpetual drink of his home-brewed moonshine, he advises the shopkeeper to be aware of time passing and to embrace it whilst he can.

Heading home early to make a surprise meal for his wife, Connie (Christina Hendricks), he discovers her fooling around with local sheriff Jack (Ron Perlman) and indulging in their shared 'furry' fetish.

Drunk and abandoned, Maynard improvises by dressing up in some gear sold at the store in a vain attempt to appeal to his want-away wife but he only manages to cause a stir within the town. When it seems that a bigfoot-type creature has been seen around the locality, as reported by the local television station, this leads to a surge in visitors due to the subsequent publicity.

As Bart, Ian watches on in amusement as phoney Australian investigative reporter Masterson (Thomas Lennon) arrives; keen to exploit the sightings for his benefit, regardless of their authenticity. Bart, who drives a beat-up truck and lives in a wood-made cabin, offers his services to track the Sasquatch which is accepted by the Monster Finder host who is accompanied by Sherriff Jack.

On the snowbound trail, the visitor is terrified upon thinking that the sounds emitted by a hidden Maynard are genuinely that of a yeti and the latter is caught. Things are further complicated by Parker realising Grieger's involvement in the whole thing.

Bart realises the truth but after a deflating public revelation to the locals, this is revealed whilst a groggy Maynard awakens.

After only Parker and Bart remain supportive of him, many of the townsfolk turn against the affable shopkeeper, disappointed that they have been deceived. That is until Parker makes them realise that he was well-meaning and that he helped many of them out financially when they couldn't pay for groceries at one time or another.

Ian commenced work on the film after finishing John Wick 2 and advancing to shoot in Central New York locations in early 2016, Pottersville proves a gentle watch but the viewer does wonder who the film might be aimed at; it has the feel of being a kids feature. The poster's bye-line of "It's a Magical Life", offers a clue but such a comparison proves ill-judged.

Pottersville received a premiere at Hamilton Movie Theatre (one of the actual locations used for the film) in November 2017.

By 2018 Mr McShane would combine a trio of vastly different projects: animated fun in A Wizard's Tale, the genteel Age of Sail and small-screen oddness via American Gods.

"Let's put an end to happiness!" chortles doom-monger wizard The Grump (as voiced by Ian McShane) in the colourful animated delight A Wizard's Tale. Released on 11 May, he was top-billed in this Mexican-produced piece based on the 1960s TV series called Here Comes the Grump wherein Rip Taylor voiced Mr McShane's character of The Grump. Originally utilising this same title, it subsequently saw a name change.

Once known as "The Grin", sadly, life has made him into the aforementioned Grump. With a huge nose, sprawling moustache and tufts of long hair sprouting out of his cap, Ian offers lots of cackling to accompany casting his "spell of gloom" on the inhabitants of Groovingham. A bright, barmy tale written by Jim Hecht, we follow The Grump on his dragon, Dingo, in pursuit of Princess Daisy (voiced by Lily Collins from The Hollow Point) and young Terry (Toby Kebbell) a reluctant hero on a quest to find the key to happiness.

Lots of things happen to them and throughout the principal characters burst into song and of course, there is redemption for the villain in the end when it is revealed that Terry is the grandson of Mary, The Grump's long-lost love.

"The story that he wrote was lovely. It's about an old guy (William Avery) who lost his faith in the world. Lost his faith in everything..." summarised Ian whilst laying down the vocals for this gorgeous tale. Running at less than 13 minutes, Age of Sail is a short that unusually utilises a Virtual Reality experience that resembles a simple animation. Lovely to look at, the project was built around the voice of the actor by past Academy Award winner, writer/ director John Kahrs who grew up around sailing boats built by his father.

His story saw him joined by Jonathan Igla & Blaise Hemingway as writers for this Google Spotlight Stories project.

As the grizzled seaman, he resembles a silver-haired Captain Haddock from Tin Tin, with Ian's character off on his final voyage, feeling useless in the world until a feisty young girl falls from a huge steamer and is rescued by him in his little sailboat.

She wants to rejoin the ship and pushes him to realise that he is not alone now and that they need to catch up with it in a tale set in 1900. "He's absolutely fabulous," commented co-star Cathy Lang as Lara Conrad, "He fits this character perfectly. He brings this amazing sailor to life."

Begrudgingly agreeing, in their pursuit, Avery accidentally gets thrown overboard into the ocean before Lara returns; but the little boat sinks and they are both in danger of perishing. Something that the old sea dog accepts, it looks like he has drowned until he pops up and they are rescued. The Emmy-winning Age of Sail was also Oscar-nominated and selected for the Venice Film Festival. It was produced by Chromosphere/ Evil Eye Pictures and can be viewed via YouTube.

McShane's involvement in Hellboy (2019), the third live-action, gothic interpretation of graphic novels created by Mike Mignola came after his old mate John Hurt had previously played the same role in a 2004 version (with Ron Perlman from Pottersville in the lead). However, Ian was keen to stress that this was a complete reboot and very different from previous screen outings.

Released in the UK on 12 April, the trailer is a hilarious forerunner of what audiences could expect. Over in Bulgaria and shooting his involvement across 3 weeks, it was cheaper to do it there with tax breaks to encourage filmmakers. He told the Reiss sports show "It's very violent...very profane...."

It is Ian's voice that we heard at the start of the film, relaying the mythical story of Merlin (also repeated in other works that he has featured in). And later, a group will return to ask for help and make the revelation that Hellboy is the son of Arthur.

Whist a mainly perfunctory role his relationship with his adopted son and its origins prove most heartening. However, as the story progresses things become more and more absurd with many jaw-dropping moments that make Hellboy a ridiculous and at times, quite absurd, watch. Its violence proves unpleasant viewing and the film rightly received multi-nominations at the "Razzies"; an alternate awards platform, including one for most gratuitous amounts of needless deaths.

His adopted son is a hulking great, red-skinned devil with a tail, peculiar club arm and horns which he regularly files down. Enjoying an endearingly antagonistic relationship with his father, Hellboy is a sensitive creature troubled by his past and surprisingly vulnerable.

Returning to base, Hellboy (David Harbour) is visited by Professor Broom (Ian; although in the comics he is named Bruttenholm), the head of the Bureau for Paranormal Research & Defence group for which he works. Regarded as providing "...the land in the sand", by his father, Hellboy struggles with being a hired killer. Indeed, around his father, he plays the petulant teenage-like son with low self-esteem and personality issues. In their first onscreen moments, Hellboy is seen filing down his horns whilst his pater encourages positive self-esteem.

In charge at B.P.R.D. Broom tells Hellboy that an occult society has requested their help. Ian's character knows them well and had been a part of their Nazi-hunting team tasked with eliminating creatures created via their fascination with the occult. Begrudgingly agreeing, the red-hued investigator subsequently makes a startling discovery, "So I'm devil's spawned and a Nazi? Thanks, dad!" Shockingly, Broom had been tasked with killing him as a baby but saw the good in him and was inspired to raise him as his son.

Elsewhere, Nimue (played via an extraordinary performance from Milla Jovovich) has been raised from the dead to reap her revenge. Ably assisted by pug monster servant Grugach, as voiced by Pirates of the Caribbean actor Stephen Graham, he delivers many a witticism via Andrew Crosby's screenplay.

Confronted by her on several occasions, the 'Blood Queen' wants Hellboy to join with her. He is quite affected by her allure and this is noticed by his father back in the London bunker H.Q. Amusingly entered via a terribly British Fish & Chips shop, the city is ravished by a plague created by Nimue.

Hellboy, young Alice (Sasha Lane) and others return only to find it wrecked and with no sign of Prof. Broom.

A final confrontation between opposing parties takes place in St Paul's Cathedral where Hellboy faces the might of a now super-sized Grugach revelling in facing the "red-faced twat." Almost defeated, the plumy-voiced Daimo (Daniel Dae Kim) morphs into a leopard-like creature, much to the surprise of psychic side-kick Alice, and combines with Hellboy to fight off the swine. When the Queen arrives, she shrinks and vanquishes her servant and repeats her request to join forces.

With the Excalibur sword exposed in the mayhem, Nimue encourages him to pull it from the stone. At first, he resists, fearful of the repercussions, until the serenely malevolent Queen brings out a battered Professor. On his knees, she kills him. In a gob-smacking moment that would not be out of place in American Gods, Hellboy draws the sword and morphs into a most astonishing sight: his horns matured and with burning headgear, he is seen holding Excalibur aloft. The Blood Queen is elated and says he is the true incarnate of evil. Meanwhile, Alice is overtaken once more; spewing forth another serpent-like manifestation only now with Ian's head upon it! The moment is beyond trippy and proves to be a superb climax to the film.

Hellboy decapitates Nimue and she is furious after suffering the same indignity centuries ago. Broom gives a heartfelt speech to his son in this final onscreen moment, "Being your father was the best decision I ever made..." The visual effects are simply astounding and the author imagines that the film would have been quite the shared experience when watched at a cinema. Hellboy has cult film written all over its blood-splattered marrow and is recommended viewing.

Returning for a second season, American Gods immediately picks up from where it ended; with Mr Wednesday (McShane) and Shadow (Ricky Whittle) joined in "Bettie" the Caddy by Laura (Emily Browning) and Mad Sweeney (Pablo Schreiber). As the battle against the New Gods rages on, the return of the intense Mr World (Crispin Glover auditioning for a Batman villain role or at the least, stepping straight off the Twin Peaks set) and a now more threatening Tech Boy (Bruce Langley) is ensuing. Some changes amongst the cast have occurred including New Media (Kayhun Kim) being introduced whilst the astonishing Yetide Badaki continues to mesmerise.

The return was heralded via a premiere at the Theatre at Ace Hotel, in Los Angeles on Tuesday 5 March with author Neil Gaiman co-scripting the opening episode broadcast the following Sunday. Cleverly, details are revealed that relate to the opening storylines and help us gain a better understanding of the characters and their motivations (or as near as we can).

Now made by cable and network company Starz, the cast had commenced filming in April 2018, seeing Ian's character slowly morphing into Lt. Columbo and the first episode proved a hallucinogenic delight.

Soaked in special FXs, the old Gods meet up and conclude with an astonishing close after a dream-like Carousel sequence.

Following Shadow's battering by John Wick actor Dean Winters, the second season is good in that it sees different characters spending time together e.g. Wednesday with a resentful Laura and a gravelly-voiced Ian with the foul-mouthed Mr Nancy (Orlando Jones having a ball). Once more producing astounding visuals Gods 2 is also uncomfortable viewing with episode three particularly.

Wednesday shows his coarse side via the unique way that he propagates a tree sapling and continues to drive his beloved car, often wearing a dainty 'Miss Daisy' hat.

For fans, episode 6: Donar the Great has to be a favourite. With echoes of his role in Young Charlie Chaplin, it opens and closes with a song from the actor seen wearing a straw hat, dickey bow tie and suit in a flashback story which introduces his son, played by Derek Theler, as Doner; a young god with a differing opinion of things to his father. The genetic link between Wednesday and Shadow is made apparent in the next season and the continued request to repair a Gungir spear belonging to Odin (McShane) runs through the episodes. It is here that it is broken during a confrontation between them. Later he offers, "What was broken can and must be repaired...for the sake of the future."

At the episode close, a melancholy Ian gets to sing the Bing Crosby classic "Brother Can you Spare a Dime?" on an empty stage and with great poignancy (perhaps that difficult second album could still come for Mr McShane?).

Deadwood's Billy Sanderson, another actor with a distinctive speaking voice, features in episode 4 where Crispin Glover returns at its close.

By the time of its penultimate story, and with the threat of the oncoming confrontation between the gods, Mad Sweeney is still beholden to Wednesday, whom the former describes as being a "horny Musclehead" when remembering their initial meeting. Many sights seen in American Gods are somewhat gruesome and here is no exception: with one sequence seeing Ian's severed head held aloft in busy story arcs. Sweeney joins him and the others before the battle, always being seen as coming soon, nears. He insists that he has now paid his dues to Wednesday and wants his spear but Shadow intervenes.

In a gory confrontation, the huge Leprechaun is impaled upon it. Even at the moment of death Sweeney still tries to tell Shadow that Wednesday is using him just as he does with the others: a thread running through the third season also. Sneaking away at the start of the final story, Odin/ Mr Wednesday will return towards the close of the episode, seated in an empty restaurant, alone. He, Shadow and Salim (Omid Abtahi) are shown on local television as wanted suspects but none are apprehended so American Gods can continue.

Musician and billionaire hotel magnate Dan Pritzker directed and co-scripted Bolden alongside David Rothschild highlighting the bandleader and cornetist credited as pioneering the jazz sound: Charles 'Buddy' Bolden. Termed "the first king of New Orleans music" by Louis Armstrong in a 1931 radio broadcast little else is known about him. As a child, 'Satchmo' remembered seeing and hearing Bolden and his band play in the rag-tag community dancehalls. A man destroyed by fragile mental health, Buddy died in the Louisiana State mental institution that same year. He was 54.

Not a linear biography, much is imagined and Pritzker saw his project progress following a few blips and false starts, settling upon the right cast, and shooting across 6 weeks in Atlanta. Reconvening for a further week of exteriors and establishing shots including the numerous asylum-set scenes, Bolden saw a theatrical release across North America on 3 May.

Arriving onscreen at around 20 minutes, a bearded Ian voices elongated sentences in a Southern twang in remembered moments by the incarcerated music man.

The whiskery McShane can be glimpsed in the trailer saying "This is America, Bolden; how far you think you gonna get?" Cast as the well-dressed and affluent Leander A. Perry, Chief Judge of the Orleans Parish, he plays a key part in Bolden's life as in the film we see him gleefully sign the order of admittance to an asylum for the troubled soul. Onscreen the Judge decrees that he will not allow the continuation of Bolden's music incitement toward his perceived "god-less" crowds. However, according to James Gill writing for theadvocate.com, "racist Judge Leander A. Perry, who, though his name was presumably inspired by the old Plaquemine Parish segregationist boss Judge Leander Perez, is an entire fiction..." Also shown on screen is Perry holding onto a cylinder phonograph said to have contained a primitive recording of Bolden's band.

To this day it has never been recovered.

Just how much longer can the John Wick franchise continue? Well, parts 4 & 5 have been announced since JW3: Parabellum (meaning "Prepare for war") was released in America on Friday 17 May after a very busy week for Ian and the cast promoting the project. He was back in Brooklyn on Thursday before, where location filming had occurred, for a promotional event at the gorgeous 1 Hanson Place. Whilst the day before a handful of cast members joined Keanu Reeves and Ian in front of the world-famous Chinese Theatre in Hollywood for the star's hand and footprints ceremony. The same venue also held the première for JW3 after a similar event in New York 6 days earlier (Ian attended both). A guest on the Rich Eisen Show, Ian described Reeves as "a top man".

Parabellum came after Ian's other movie, Hellboy, had been released in cinemas.

Now with a $14m bounty on his head, Wick (Mr Reeves) is seen immediately on screen, entering the Continental hotel run by Winston (McShane) as the story picks up straight after Part 2. Now less than an hour before his contract goes live, he rushes through the wet metropolis with his dog by his side before the 6 pm activation time.

Confronted by a giant man at the New York Public Library, the two engage in a squirm-inducing fight that ends in a most grotesque death. JW3 shows itself as the most graphically violent and brutal of the films and unpleasantly so.

"And away we go!" sighs Winston, as poor Mr Wick begins his many scuffles with various adversaries keen to pocket his termination fee. Knives are more commonly used but the martial arts remain a breath-taking constant.

A killing machine, Wick takes to riding a horse, motorbikes and still fights off opponents!

Cruelly, anybody known to have aided and abetted his escape is dealt with by representatives of The High Table, which "stands above all else," as Anjelica Huston reiterates in a brief but memorable cameo. She aptly defined it as being a "fealty". Represented by The Adjudicator, Asia Kate Dillon, resembling a **233** malevolent pixie, Winston and Bowery King (Laurence Fishburne) are given 7 days to vacate their involvement with the organisation and for the former, after giving 40 years of service.

Stabbed, shot, beaten and run over, Wick manages to survive it all and venture to Casablanca to reacquaint himself with Sofia (Halle Berry who would be photographed with Ian at the premiere but they do not appear together on screen). A fellow dog lover, she reluctantly agrees to assist after he shows her the marker and reminds her how he helped her previously. The two fight their way out before visiting the sinister Berrada (English actor Jerome Flynn of Game of Thrones fame) in search of contacting the Elder, Saïd Taghmaoui, the head of the organisation. However, once he locates him, the given options are daunting: die or continue working for them. Wishing to honour his wife's legacy, he chooses the latter but is shocked to learn that his first task is to kill Winston.

The third picture is the most exhausting watch; so much fighting, so many deaths and Wick receiving his fair share of hammerings with the running gag of stopping to reload his various weapons remaining.

Almost killed, he makes it back to the Continental to speak to Winston. The latter wonders if he is there to kill him but Wick says he is not.

This infuriates The Adjudicator and the hotel is deconsecrated, meaning that it makes it open to attack from operatives globally.

Winston secretes himself away into a vault, casually relaxing and enjoying a cocktail as Wick is joined by concierge Caron and others to defend the place.

When an impasse is reached, the Adjudicator speaks with Winston on the rooftop location seen previously and a deal is struck to allow things to continue.

Having fought off bald guy/ fanboy Zero (Mark Dacascos), John hears his friend proclaim a renewed loyalty to serving The High Chair but is shocked when Winston shoots him multiple times. This sees him fall heavily from the roof and eventually crash onto the road in an alleyway behind the hotel.

Leaving, The Adjudicator takes a look to check in the area and is astonished to discover the body has vanished. Winston pleads disbelief when she informs him but knows better than to believe that he is dead. If Wick is alive, the after-effects will cause a great deal of grief for all opposing him.

Having been scooped up by one of Bowery's men, Fishburne is unhappy at his treatment by the organisation and asks if John feels the same: barely moving, he manages to muster all his strength to voice his agreement. And so it continues.

JW4 was announced on social media but personally, the author found three outings to be ample. However, because the franchise had proven to be a money-maker, and as long as the creative team behind it can keep devising exhilarating scenarios, the films will continue to be made.

Aside from the movies, Ian leant his voice to the John Wick Chronicles virtual reality game and at the time of writing, there is a Payday 2 John Wick Heists video game, also. John Wick Hex (also 2019) features a digital likeness of Ian and his voice as Winston in a flat graphic look & Lance did his voice, too.

A poster reading 'Welcome the F@@k back' (cleverly camouflaged by a man with a gun) announced Deadwood: the movie in 2019. Premiered at the ArcLight Hollywood on Tuesday 14 May, it aired on HBO on Friday 31 May at 8 pm. Running for almost 2 hours, director Daniel Minahan had previously helmed 4 episodes of the show, whilst the movie return follows the same residents a decade later when Deadwood is now part of the state of Montana. Nominated for 8 Emmys including Outstanding Television Movie, as Swearengen, "whore master" as series creator David Milch termed him, his place in the annals of American television was set. "It's weird," Ian giggled telling Tara Brady of the Irish Times, "People would suddenly come up to me and say: 'Would you swear at me? Will you insult me?' You remain very polite and you keep walking."

Now established on American Gods, the cast there had a month off just before the Christmas holidays and so this was when Ian rejoined his old Deadwood team to shoot the film. Spending 5 months in Canada working on the project, as a viewer, seeing the cast reunited is a pleasure.

Advanced a decade to 1889 with Ian as Al still looking the same; everyone else seems a lot older, a little greyer.

However, by now, Swearengen's liver is shot and he is not quite the force he used to be. Farnum, Billy Sanderson, is in amongst the likes of Trixie, Bullock and others. Amusingly, he revealed that Mr McShane tended to veer off-script, something which initially threw his colleague until he embraced it too.

Written by Milch with Bryan Law, the railway encroaches on Deadwood and the telephone arrives, too, at the former camp. The past is brought up as if it has never gone away, especially with the unwelcome return of Hearst (Gerald McRayne, in a role as horrible as ever). By now a Senator wanting to develop locally by facilitating the installation of the aforementioned communications system, he soon engages in behaviours that ultimately sees people killed.

Al, short for Albert, has taken the lives of many people admits his feelings for Trixie and his reluctant murder of a girl in season three, to protect her, is mentioned again. She introduces her new baby daughter to him, fathered by Sol (John Hawkes). Offering to leave her his bar, Trixie (Paula Malcomson) is getting married and he makes a point of attending as he gives her away.

Elsewhere, following the death of a much-loved local, the townsfolk batter Hearst prior to Sherriff Bullock (Timothy Olyphant in the lesser-revered role) intervening.

Languishing in bed and tended to by Trixie & Jewel (Geri Jewell), the latter sings Waltzing Matilda. He joins in (in a clumsy unsynchronised moment) as the film comes to a close.

Illustration by Suki-Michelle

236

Realising the seriousness of his condition, Trixie begins to recite The Lord's Prayer before Al atypical offers a colourful repose.

U.S. TV never does anything by half and so NBC ordered 20 episodes of Law & Order: Special Victims Unit which made it the first show to go into its 21st season.

Ian's involvement opened the new season on Tuesday 10 December and what a vile character Sir Tobias Moore is. A brave part to play, he uses a broad northern accent as the British head of a studio/ streaming service who abuses aspiring actor Pilar (Carmen Berkeley) before the opening credits.

Able to cover his tracks, the wretched Moore is subsequently shown as being a serial predator with a liking for young women.

The dreaded 'casting couch' is referenced by him once Olivia Benson (Mariska Hargitay) and her team start to investigate.

He is revealed to have a long history of paying-off victims and of all Mr. McShane's roles, this has to be the most uncomfortable one to view.

Sir Tobias has major political connections and hides behind a veil of protection. Wealthy, married, and well-dressed he may be but his sense of entitlement is abhorrent. "Guys like this," summarises Benson, "they rule by fear. Nobody likes them."

Needing to gather evidence, specialist undercover officer 'Kat' Tamin (Jamie Gray Hyder) is brought in to attend one of Moore's auditions; where he records the reading and uses the same contrived patter before pouncing. The Special Victims Unit is in an adjacent room and finally, an arrest comes after several false starts.

Showing the complex machinations of those in power, Olivia and her colleagues arrive in court and upon entering the building are astonished at what they see. Many are there holding up placards **237** acknowledging their assaults by Moore in a deeply affecting moment in a most uncomfortable but necessary storyline brought by writers Warren Leight & Peter Blauner.

Now extended to 10 episodes, the anticipation for the third season of American Gods had seen many fans disappointed at a perceived anti-climax at the close of the second in 2019. Beginning its run on Monday 11 January 2021, the father-son status between Wednesday & Shadow is confirmed.

And what an exhilarating pre-credits sequence to its opening story A Winter's Tale which wonderfully sees Ian crowd surfing at a gig by Johan (played by barmy musician Marilyn Manson).

As Wednesday, McShane returns to find Shadow (Ricky Whittle) striving to lead a new life well away from his father and all that follows him. But he is never too far away and after helping an elderly lady down the street, poor Shadow gets a shock when she suddenly turns quite different and finally Ian's voice transmits from her dainty frame. Looking somewhat haggard in his customary Hawaiian shirt, grey-flecked beard, straggly hair and sheepskin coat, Wednesday wants his son to help him against the new Gods. Temporarily driving a clunky motorhome, later Wednesday and Shadow approach a police roadblock but in a majestic piece of driving and urged on by his father, they manage to circumvent capture and enter into a wood via a static home! Gods 3 continues to push the kaleidoscope of imagery and violence still lingers around the colourful characters.

A hectic opening storyline introduces Cordelia (Ashley Reyes) as Wednesday's driver. Also responsible for all his online communications and oblivious to his true identity, she forms an immediate bond with the hunky Shadow. He declines to travel with them but despite his best efforts, he is led to the same town as Wednesday had suggested.

As Bilquis, Yetide Badaki is not someone that you want to come into contact with as she proves a lethal mate. Old gods return to remember Zorya (Cloris Leachman) at a wake held in Chicago where Wednesday (McShane) and Czernobog (Peter Stormare) gleefully engage in some sort of wrestling ritual, egged on by the friendly crowd of mourners. Antagonism comes in the form of Salim (Omid Abtahi), distraught that Wednesday has vanquished his friend and lover, The Jinn.

Now smartened up, Wednesday reconnects with his estranged wife and fellow god, Demeter (a super Blythe Danner). She just happens to be ensconced in a mental institution and is seemingly content there until his arrival when she slaps his face upon seeing him. His need to get her out sees him stage a rouse to get himself admitted into the same facility: after a heavy night's drinking with the psychotic Johan (Manson), he dashes into traffic and flashes at the drivers! Reunited with his love, the two have a long history and some regrets from their shared past. They make a wager that he will not last a week within the place. Shadow visits Wednesday and takes him for a walk in his wheelchair, with Ian looking splendid in a bobble hat.

In a tender moment, Wednesday puts on and narrates a shadow play for Demeter and the others, revealing a painful moment from the past which ultimately pushed them apart. An old friend and now foe, Tyr (Dennis O'Hare) returns after integrating himself into normal life as a dentist. However, the two both love Demeter and despite 250 years passing, the animosity remains. Sadly, she will not be reunited with Odin (McShane) after all, as by the close of Sister Rising her essence vanishes into the sky in a beautifully-shot moment.

Elsewhere, Laura and Salim meet Mr World (now in the guise of Danny Trejo) who wants to work with them in eliminating Mr Wednesday.

Driving along, a corpse falls from the sky and in front of the Caddy and here Wednesday tells Cordelia, his protégé, the truth about himself after which she chooses to remain with him as life can hardly be the same for her now. Mr McShane was one of many Executive Producers on the show which seems to be in its final outing at the time of writing.

Gods 3 is well-worth a binge-viewing as it draws the viewer in despite gruesome mortuary shots of bodies being spliced open thanks to Mr Ibis (Demore Barnes).

Shadow comes into things more so in the third season and wants to lead others despite his father's failings and the final episodes convey a deep sense of foreboding.

Particularly so when Ty coerces that Shadow into thinking Wednesday needs to see him.

Wednesday, illustrated on page 236 by Suki Michelle (see the thanks pages for contact details) arrives to confront him and demands that they sort out their issues the old way: via a sword fight. Transported to a desolate location, the two battle it out, Ian looking striking in Odin's full-body armour as blows are exchanged.

Shadow intervenes when it looks like he is beaten by his powerful opponent only for Ty to make the fatal mistake of turning his back on his opponent. About to kill Shadow, a sword is thrust through his chest from behind by Odin after which Ian tells his screen son that he is now no longer obligated to him.

Forever scheming and anticipating things, Odin knows that Laura has his mighty spear and that she will soon kill him with it.

A pessimistic Wednesday/ Odin tries to convince Czernobog that he wants peace with the new gods but fails, "You know, I'm sensing a pattern," offers Cordelia, " we drop in on old friends of yours; they hate your guts and freak out…."

Met by "Savile Row psycho" Mr World (Crispin Glover), his ideas are hastily quashed by the combative visitor who tells him he can simply have his life if he goes away and does not interfere with their developments in the future. And if he does, he and many others will be killed.

Foreseeing his death, we watch as Odin is slain by the diminutive Laura and his spear.

For the final episode, Ian only features at the end. Shadow refuses to avenge his death by killing his murderer: his wife, preferring to strive to make things better for all.

On a desolate homestead, Shadow sacrifices himself in a stunning scene via a bizarre ceremony that sees him enveloped in the branches and roots of a giant tree, the world tree, which is part of Norse mythology. Gaiman's fascination with it was the inspiration for the original novel.

Mr McShane reappears when his son awakens on a plane and opposite him is his father. They talk briefly before Wednesday opens the door and leaps from the aircraft and on into martyrdom.

Back on the ground, a bemused Czernobog asks,

"Is this the death of the old gods?"

To which Ibis replies, "Or something much worse?"

Created by Matt Groening, animated gem The Simpsons became a pop culture phenomenon soon after its launch in mid-December 1989. But who knew it is still being made? It is, and Ian leant his honeyed tones to The Last Barfighter; episode 22 of the season 32 finale shown on Sunday 23 May 2021.

Seasoned bar keep Mo serves regulars like Homer Simpson and his buddies but after work, frequents The Confidential; a hidden society and "The one bar where they listen to the listeners".

Serving there is Artemis, resembling a retired magician with his speckled goatee and cravat, who is voiced by none other than our Mr Ian McShane.

Mo (as voiced by Ray Donovan's Hank Azaria) is bemused by Homer and the other barfly deadbeats that consider him a friend and after a night of boozing together he returns to the bar only to be chastised by Artemis for not keeping secrets.

An obvious parody of Winston from John Wick, unlike Mo, the latter proves an "honest drunk" who had spilt all their confidentialities and spoken lots of home truths to the shocked group. Mo is ordered to surrender his membership of The Confidential and in addition, his friends will be "cut off"; no longer able to enjoy a drink, with accompanying side effects!

Wife Madge and the children are initially pleased and after some adjustment, the others all seem content with their healthy new lifestyles. As a group, the fellas say even though they can never drink again they still want Mo to be their barman. But when Artemis calls into the bar and is initially impressed, he opens up a suitcase full of antidote to allow them to enjoy a tipple again.

242

Naturally, they seize upon it, all apart from Homer. He heads home but Artemis keys in a request to "Rebooze Homer Simpson" and the episode closes with the yellow man being chased by barmen with syringes!

references & thanks

Some dates/ information might be incorrect in the text but due to the nature of time passing, this sometimes happens. Corrections will be made for any revised editions.

Up in the Clouds, Gentleman Please, John Mills, Orion, 2001.

My books (Gary Wharton): Hayley Mills: IN PROFILE, 2021 & Rita Tushingham: IN PROFILE, Lushington Publishing, 2019 for info email me: vetchbook@yahoo.co.uk

John Hurt, David Nathan, W.H. Allen, 1986.
https://catacombs.space1999.net
movieweb.com (Hot Rod snippets)
The Dark is Rising DVD: cast interviews
Cuban Fury: Tara Brady interview, irishtimes.com
Nerdist podcast no. 843, https://nerdist.libsyn.com
Various film locations: atlasofwonders.com
ITC Press release for Sewers of Gold, 1979.
cathoderaytube.co.uk (interview with actor Anneke Wills re: The Pleasure Girls film)
L.A. Times: interview with Roger Mann (25 August 1982)
mckellen.com: The Promise play
trollopesociety.org
rafbf.org
matrixtheatre.com reviews and for the kind use of their Inadmissable Evidence publicity photos
joeorton.org
Thanks to Monica for enabling me to view The Lives of Jenny Dolan. Visit her tribute site found at stephenboydblog.wordpress.com
Love to Sharman Towers & a big thank you to Alan Leventhall for reading the manuscript.
National Centre for Early Music for allowing me to use their York Mystery photos. Visit them at ncem.co.uk
Angela Beadle for her Lovejoy illustration. See her work at notonthehighstreet.com/angiebealdesigns
Suki for her American Gods illustration. Find her at: https://fineartamerica.com/profiles/suki-michelle
Cherry Red Records for their And This is Me cd cover.

selected index

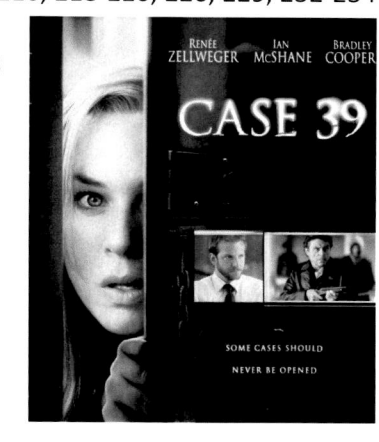

Television appearances continued

Will Shakespeare 12, 60-61

Disraeli: Portrait of a Romantic 12, 27, 55, 60-63, 81, 84, 161

The Pirate 63-64

Armchair Thriller: High Tide 75-78, 125, 132, 146

Magnum: Skin Deep episode & Black on White episodes 79-84

The Letter 81, 83

The Quest 81, 83-84

Marco Polo 81, 84, 109, 131

Grace Kelly 85

Bare Essence 86-87

Evergreen 62, 95-96

A.D. 44, 56, 96, 109

Braker 96-97

American Playhouse: Rocket to the Moon 34, 97

Lovejoy 12, 14, 26, 31, 38, 47-50, 64, 83, 84, 96, 98-101, 112, 116, 124-125, 128-131-133, 149, 153, 161, 176, 195

CBS Summer Playhouse: Barrington 101

Miami Vice episodes: Knock...Knock & Freefall - 96, 102-104, 123-124, 146

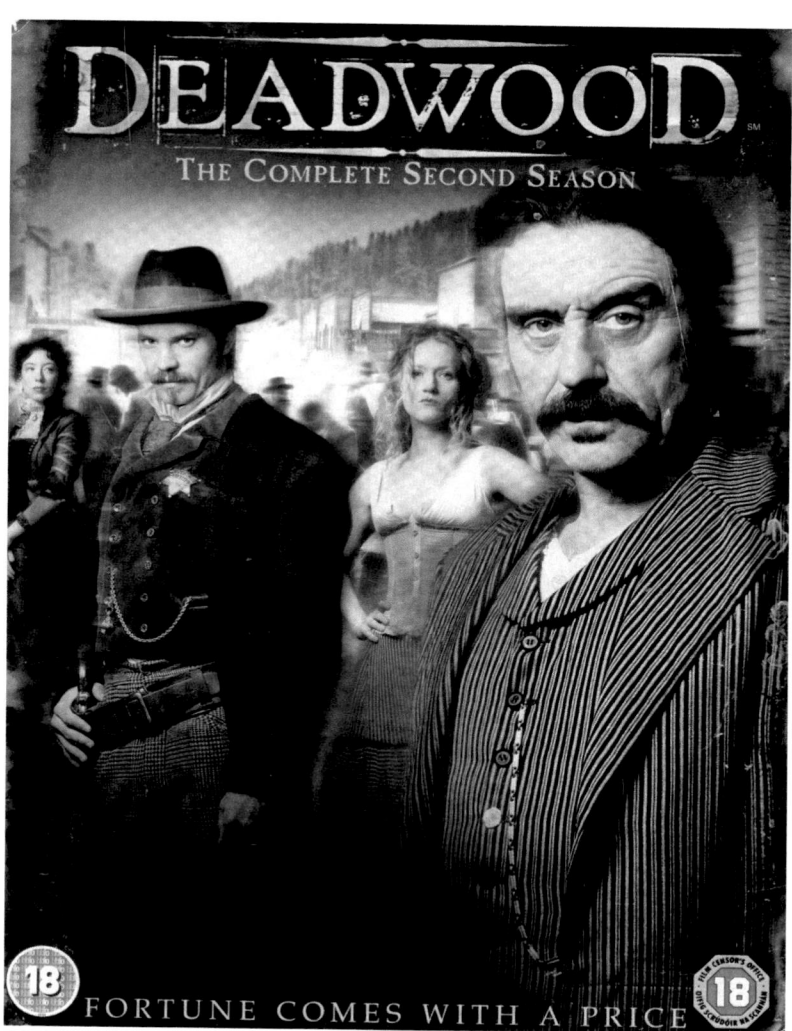

Photo: Author's Collection

249

Television appearances continued
American Gods 171, 172, 216, 230-231,
237-241
Deadwood: The TV Movie 234-236
Law & Order: Special Victims Unit 236-237
The Simpsons 241-242

AMERICAN

GODS

BELIEVE.

18

COMPLETE SEASON ONE

4 DISC SET

IRISH FILM CLASSIFICAT
18
OIFIG ÁNOITHE SCANNÁN

EMANTLEMEDIA

STUDIOCAN

Theatre work (in order)

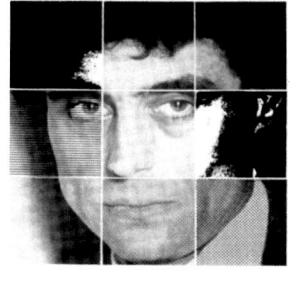

251

Photos from Inadmissable Evidence.
Courtesy of the Matrix Theatre

Audio work (see main text also)

People & Places: select A to Z

254

Richard Burton 34-37

David Butler 62-63, 84

Kim Carnes 89-90

Agatha Christie 86, 87

Cinerama Dome 160

Sam Claflin 187, 189

Warren Clarke 63, 125

Dick Clement 34, 125, 128, 132

James Coburn 43, 45, 69-74

Olivia Coleman 195

Jackie Collins 67-73, 226

Lily Collins 216

Sean Connery 44-45

Bernie Cooper 37, 64

Pictured above:
The Connaught Theatre, Worthing, back in 1950, some while before Ian played there in How Are You, Johnnie? See page 10.
Photo courtesy of the theatre.

James Cosmo 27, 164

Brian Cox 161

Penelope Cruz (as seen above with Ian in Pirates of the Caribbean) 185

Tim Curry 60-61

Sinead Cusack 31, 33

Cyrano De Bergerac 4

Dame Edna Treatment 129

Blythe Danner 236

Desmond Davis 876-88

Eric Deacon 131

Judi Dench 24, 187

Johnny Depp 185-187

Barry Devlin 133

Neil Dickinson 96, 98

Alan Dobie 10-11

Clive Donner 16

Brad Dourif (opposite with Ian in Deadwood) 156

Hamilton Dyce 19, 22-23

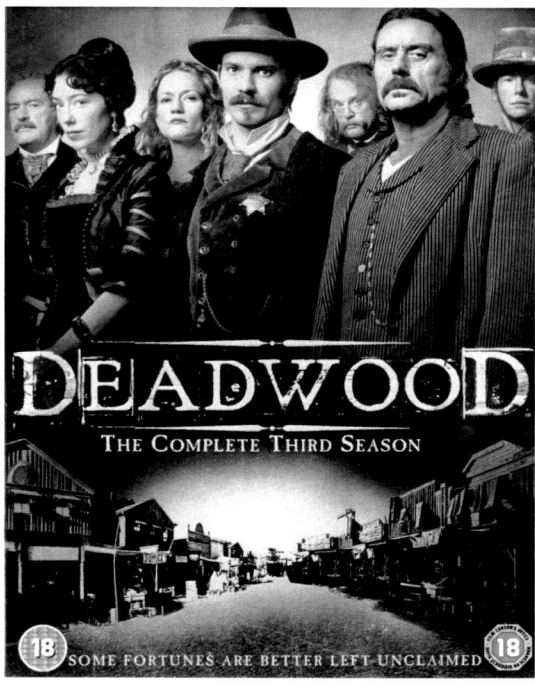

Pictured below: Golders Green Hippodrome 15, 17: where Ian played in Loot & The Glass Menagerie. Nowadays sadly no longer in use as a working theatre.

258

Dwayne 'The Rock' Johnson 197-200, 258

Freddie Jones 40, 130

Grace Jones 89, 96

Shirley Jones 53-55

Chris Jury 100, 130, 132

Ken Kercheval 130

Denis King 96, 123

Klaus Kinski 16, 83

Nastassja Kinski 16, 85

Don Knight 56

Sylvia Kristel 66-67

Sam Kydd 69-74

Alan Lake 38, 68, 70

VAUDEVILLE THEATRE

STRAND, W.C.2

Telephone: TEMple Bar 4871

By arrangement with J. A. GATTI

HAROLD FIELDING

presents

How are you, Johnnie?

by

PHILIP KING

IAN McSHANE

NIGEL STOCK

DEREK FOWLDS

HILDA FENEMORE

with

LUCINDA CURTIS   **PHILIP NEWMAN**

Directed by GUY VAESEN

If you liked this book, then you might well enjoy these other titles also written by Gary Wharton.

For full details please email:
vetchbook@yahoo.co.uk